The Lost Art of
COMPASSION

The Lost Art of
COMPASSION

Discovering the Practice of Happiness

in the Meeting of

Buddhism and Psychology

LORNE LADNER, PH.D.

HarperSanFrancisco
A Division of HarperCollins*Publishers*

HarperCollins books may be purchased for educational, business, or sales promotional use. For information please write: Special Markets Department, HarperCollins Publishers, Inc., 10 East 53rd Street, New York, NY 10022.

HarperCollins Web site: http://www.harpercollins.com
HarperCollins®, 🏭®, and HarperSanFrancisco™ are
trademarks of HarperCollins Publishers, Inc.

FIRST EDITION
Designed by Joseph Rutt

Library of Congress Cataloging-in-Publication Data is available upon request.
ISBN 0–06–053685–3 (cloth)
04 05 06 07 08 RRD(H) 10 9 8 7 6 5 4 3 2 1

For my grandparents
David & Lillian
who showed me the abiding joy
that comes from loving wholeheartedly

CONTENTS

FOREWORD

The English word compassion is used to translate the Sanskrit *karuna,* which is etymologized as "suspending happiness." To feel compassion, you must turn away slightly from your own focus on superficial happiness to sense the true condition of others, honestly facing their pains. This turn is considered the key to expanding awareness from its habitual imprisonment in self-centered states of mind, by nature always unsatisfactory, and to connecting with the feelings of others, through which real satisfaction becomes possible. It is thus an open-hearted empathy for the suffering of others and the wish to free them from it. It is the twin of another powerful emotion, "love," Sanskrit *maitri,* which means the wish for the beloved others to be happy. To succeed in making others happy, it was long ago discovered, you must develop the kind of deeper happiness within yourself that only increases when you share it.

The West has long upheld the example of Jesus and many other saintly rabbis, priests, sufis, and mystics. Yet in modern times, with the advent of scientific materialism, these ancient ecstatics have come to seem unreal, mere legends, at the very least unrealistic. People who live for others, who thrive on compassion and love, are made to seem foolish and misguided, and we are taught to feel that our own natural feelings of love and compassion will lead us to disaster. We associate callousness, anger, and violence with power and success, and sensitivity, compassion, and gentleness with weakness and failure. So we seek fulfillment by being as hard as possible and righteously selfish, and, while we may have some moments of elation, we doom ourselves to a life of interminable dissatisfaction. Our scientific psychologies most often consider our imperfect experience to be a sign of realism, and try to help us intellectually or pharmacologically resign ourselves to our fate. As Freud said, he could only help his patients overcome neurotic suffering so they could learn to live with ordinary suffering.

For thousands of years in many different societies, the Buddhists have been strongly in tune with the ancient spiritual adepts of the West, finding that it is entirely possible to achieve a higher happiness in life by living in the light of love and the energy of compassion. Further, from day one they began a long, systematic, cumulative, and scientific work of psychology to develop more and more effective methods and arts of not only *feeling,* but *cultivating* compassion, *developing* love, *empowering* the humanly natural altruistic outlook and habits that are the real key to the greater life energy of real happiness and joy. This multi-millennial, tried and true tradition of spiritual psychology is called "Inner Science," considered the Queen Empress of all the sciences, and upheld as the most precious jewel of the Buddha's legacy, beautifully polished for millennia in all Asian spiritual institutions, especially in India and Tibet.

Now is the time when adepts, teachers, and scholars of that ancient spiritual and scientific tradition are beginning the individual—and world-transforming work of sharing this psychology of compassion, love, and happiness with the "modern" world. Dr. Lorne Ladner's *Lost Art of Compassion* is a major step forward in this monumental task. He is himself an experienced meditator, a deep explorer of the self. He is a keen scholar of both Western psychology and Tibetan Buddhist psychology. And he is a skillful practitioner of compassion in action in the most intimate healing setting of all, as a therapist and spiritual friend (*kalyanamitra*) of intelligent contemporary people who are suffering from the kind of confusions and stresses of the modern psyche and society that we can recognize all too well. I am utterly delighted to present to you his wonderful, beautiful, and useful book. Just reading through it has already given me great relief by helping me turn my attention a bit more away from my stressful preoccupations and habitual distractions toward the more meaningful ways of being alive I know are there within my reach. I am confident that if I work with it more frequently, day by day, "baby step" by "baby step," it will continue to help me practice better what I am always preaching. So I invite you too, to open the door of this fine book and slowly but surely, and ever more joyfully, develop your own art of compassion!

Robert A. F. Thurman
Jey Tsong Khapa Professor of Indo-Tibetan Buddhist Studies
Columbia University;
President, Tibet House US

New York City, October 28, 2003

INTRODUCTION

The dialogue between Western psychology and Buddhism is continually deepening and having an ever greater impact on our understanding of our minds and emotions. This book is the first to focus primarily on bringing Western psychology into dialogue with the Tibetan Buddhist traditions for cultivating compassion. Most of the helpful and meaningful insights to come out of this cross-cultural dialogue thus far have been derived from the Buddhist practices of mindfulness and Zen meditation. As these Tibetan traditions for cultivating compassion focus on understanding and transforming our emotions, I believe they are particularly well suited for helping Westerners. The purpose of this book is to integrate ideas from Western psychology with a number of practical methods from the Tibetan Buddhist tradition so that readers can use them to cultivate positive emotions like affection, joy, love, and especially compassion.

Years ago, when I was studying at a Buddhist monastery in Nepal, one of my teachers noted that it seemed strange that one could go through many years of Western education without learning how to develop positive emotions. These qualities are essential to our own happiness, to healthy relationships, and to the well-being of society, but learning to cultivate them is not seriously addressed in our culture, educational systems, or traditions of psychology. Friends who have been through medical school have told me that empathy or compassion for patients is actively discouraged in their training. There is a fear that such feelings might make doctors less objective or might slow the process of treatment delivery by causing them to spend more time than necessary with individual patients. Even in the field of psychology, feelings of compassion are often discouraged. Freud once wrote that psychoanalysts should "model themselves during psychoanalytic treatment on the surgeon, who puts aside all his feelings, even his human sympathy." Heinz Kohut, the founder of Self Psychology, who is famous for his insights on the role of empathy in human development and psychotherapy, advises that one should empathize with patients to accurately understand their inner experiences, but he warns that empathy shouldn't be confused with "such fuzzily related meanings as kindness, compassion, and sympathy."

When I teach graduate students in psychology or counseling, I often ask them whether their education has included training in developing their compassion, empathy, and patience. It's naturally important for therapists to be good at empathizing with unfamiliar mental states and at having patience and compassion, particularly when working with difficult people. The students always say no. They're taught to identify and work with psychopathology, but they aren't taught how to cultivate positive qualities in themselves or others.

Over the past few years the American Psychological Association has begun recognizing this deficit. In an issue of *American Psychologist* dedicated to "positive psychology," a journal article coauthored by Martin Seligman, former president of the APA, says, "The exclusive focus on pathology that has dominated so much of our discipline results in a model of the human being lacking the positive features that make life worth living." Historically, this focus on pathology grew out of the medical, disease model of looking at human beings, in which one strives to repair damage rather than promote health or optimal functioning. Most of the best thinkers in Western psychology from Freud's time on have developed their ideas by identifying a specific pathological condition or developing a new method for treating one.

Freud's insights came largely from treating people with hysteria and other neuroses; other thinkers have focused on treating depression, anxiety, obsessions, psychoses, relationship problems, personality disorders, and the like.

The Buddhist tradition of psychology is quite different, since for over two millennia it has emphasized the study of positive emotions and mental states. Among all the positive emotions we humans experience, Buddhism views compassion as the most important for living a happy, healthy, meaningful life. Early on in my training as a psychologist, I was struck by the fact that, among positive emotions, Western psychology has neglected in particular the study of compassion. Having reviewed the literature, I think it's no understatement to assert that our Western traditions of psychology, psychiatry, and counseling don't offer even one clear, practical, well-researched method for people to use to develop compassion. A number of thinkers have traced our cultural tendency to discount compassion back to our scientific and economic traditions, which value only those things that can be measured easily. For example, William Kittredge explains that over the past seven centuries our traditions of mathematics, science, and capitalism have placed more and more emphasis on those things that can be counted, weighed, measured, and given specific economic value. He says, "Europeans taught themselves to believe anything that cannot be priced is without worth. Values like compassion and empathy, unquantifiable and therefore impossible to commodify, began to seem archaic, maybe unreal."

To paraphrase Dr. Andrew Lewin, although compassion is not easily weighed or measured, it counts; although it cannot be assigned some specific price, it is valuable. The longer I work and live, the more clearly I see what our cultural devaluation of compassion has cost us as individuals and as a society. Without any means for developing the qualities that give life meaning and that bring genuine peace and joy, we are left to follow the advice of advertisers, purchasing things and seeking entertainment to find the happiness for which we hope. The more psychologically minded of us are left to seek pills to bring happiness through changes in brain chemistry, or we're left to think endlessly about our childhoods, our self-esteem, our boundaries, and our coping skills for getting as many of our desires met as is humanly possible. Without any real emphasis on sincere love, compassion, contentment, and joy, we are left with a terribly limited approach to psychology, which is useful in curing certain pathological conditions but offers us almost nothing when it comes to living good lives or teaching our children to do so. In brief, we are left poor of heart.

On a cultural level, when our negative emotions such as hatred, greed, jealousy, and rage are not addressed and counterbalanced by strong positive values and emotions, this can result in many destructive events. In recent decades politicians, researchers, and psychologists have begun considering the idea of prevention—preventing domestic violence, child abuse, suicide, school violence, drug abuse, racial discrimination, terrorism, corporate scandals, and the like. Too often, our prevention begins at the line of last defense. In homes already filled with tension and anger, we strive to prevent aggression; in schools filled with alienation, despair, and rage, we strive to prevent violence; and in corporations filled with greed, we strive to prevent scandals. To the extent that we feel caring and connected with each other in our homes, schools, and corporations, we naturally refrain from harmful behaviors. Empathy and compassion are foundational for natural ethics and for positive social relationships. Of course, a fear of punishment can stop people from engaging in behaviors that harm others, but empathy and compassion are much more powerful and effective means of prevention. When we empathize with and feel compassion toward others' suffering, this stops us from doing things that would have a negative effect on them. When we feel others' suffering as our own, we cannot bring ourselves to harm them.

Our traditions of psychology, education, and economics must take some of the responsibility for the various social ills that we face. If each of us doesn't take on the responsibility to develop positive qualities like compassion in ourself and to model these qualities and teach them to others, then things will not improve over the long run, for us individually or for our society as a whole.

Given our culture's lack of research or thought on the psychology of compassion, it's practical and natural to use the ideas and methods so freely offered by the Mahayana Buddhist traditions of Central Asia. In the West, psychology is a relatively small branch of science that has been developed over roughly a hundred years. In Tibet alone, the inner science of overcoming negative mental states and cultivating positive ones has been a central focus for over twelve hundred years. There were many great monastic universities throughout Tibet, some with thousands of monk-scholars in residence. For centuries, many of the best minds of each generation from Tibet, Mongolia, Bhutan, Nepal, and China came to these universities to study, analyze, debate, and experiment with a huge curriculum focused on inner development. So they naturally came to possess a vast body of practical research, thought, and methodology for cultivating positive emotions.

These traditions offer a complete inner technology skillfully designed to allow us to use our bodies, thoughts, memories, and imaginations in complex and integrated ways to overcome negative emotions and to cultivate our finest capacities. Of all the topics that Tibet's inner scientists studied, His Holiness the Dalai Lama notes that the most important subject has been "altruism based on love and compassion." The reason altruism was the focus of their studies and practice is psychological and practical. Perhaps the most significant finding from all the centuries of research is this: cultivating compassion is the single most effective way to make oneself psychologically healthy, happy, and joyful. The Buddhist tradition of inner technology preserved in Central Asia is among the great treasures of our shared human heritage. Failing to use the developments offered by this tradition would be tantamount to Tibetan monks, wanting to take an international flight, trying to reinvent the jet engine and the science of aerodynamics.

I began practicing Buddhist meditation long before I became a psychologist, and over the years I've had the opportunity to study with some of the best teachers who escaped from Tibet after the Communist Chinese invasion in 1959. People sometimes debate whether Buddhism is a philosophy, a religion, or a psychology (a science of mind). It seems that Buddhism contains elements of all three. However, the Buddhist ideas and techniques that I refer to in this book derive neither from the religious nor the philosophical aspects of Buddhism. They come mainly from two lineages or traditions of Buddhism that were brought to Tibet from India by the great teacher Atisha and are called the "stages of the path" and the "mind-training" teachings. These methods have been studied and practiced for centuries by Buddhist scholars, who have found them to be extremely powerful, practical ways of helping people make the most of their lives by cultivating contentment, peace, compassion, and expansive joy in their hearts.

People often associate Buddhism with sitting cross-legged on the floor, meditating. In Tibetan Buddhism, *meditation* actually means developing an understanding of your own mind in order to decrease your negative mental states (such as hatred, craving, and jealousy) and increase positive ones (such as patience, contentment, and love). If one uses this definition, then the methods presented in this book are meditations, but one need not sit cross-legged to use them. As you'll see, they are ideal for using in the midst of your busy life—while driving, doing your job, relating with your spouse, or walking around the mall. They are not something different or new to do; instead, they help you find a new, more satisfying way of doing the things you already do.

Many of the meditation techniques from which I derive these methods actively use your intellect, emotions, and imagination. People often think that meditation always involves relaxation or clearing and focusing the mind. In fact, the Buddhist tradition says that there are eighty-four thousand different methods for transforming the mind, and many of them involve a good deal of thought, analysis, and creativity. The methods in this book offer a flexible and open approach to working with your mind—analyzing your own experience as you actively experiment with thinking and feeling in new ways.

I also want to emphasize that the methods presented in this book are not uniquely Buddhist, and one certainly doesn't need to be Buddhist to use them. When I present methods derived from the Buddhist tradition, I focus on elements that are psychological in nature. In many cases I emphasize ideas and techniques from Western psychology, integrating them with Buddhist approaches to offer a method that Western readers can use easily. For those who are interested in reading about the methods as they are applied in the traditional Buddhist context, a number of good books are listed in the Resources at the end of this book. My intention here is to offer practical, psychological methods that anyone can use to become happier and more compassionate. Compassion is not about holding to any dogma; it is the human quality that allows us to reach out across differences in race, ethnicity, religion, or nationality, connecting with each other. Compassion is a direct antidote to prejudice and aggression, promoting peace in ourselves and in the world.

This book is part of a new, deeper level of dialogue between Buddhism and psychotherapy that began in the 1930s when C. G. Jung wrote forewords to a few of the first books published on Zen and Tibetan Buddhism. From Jung's time on, Western psychotherapists have been interested in Buddhism as a source of new ideas and techniques that could be used as part of therapy or more generally to promote well-being. During the past few decades in particular, Buddhist ideas and practices have had a pervasive impact on Western psychological research and practice. While many books and workshops for therapists are available that bring together meditation and psychotherapy, most therapists are not even aware that many techniques commonly used for treating anxiety, decreasing the impacts of stress, helping children work through conflicts, treating some personality disorders, managing anger, and increasing emotional intelligence were influenced by Buddhism. For example, Dr. Herbert Benson's remarkable research on the relaxation response was influenced by his studies of meditators, and many leading scientific researchers in the field today have been affected by their formal dialogues with the Dalai Lama and other Buddhist scholars. When I recently subscribed to a scholarly journal on emotions, I was surprised that one of the first articles I came across began with a quote from the eleventh-century Tibetan Buddhist doctor and yogi, Gampopa, in which he noted that anger is "like a poisonous arrow piercing your heart." The university researchers who wrote the article went on to show that Gampopa's assertion "holds up to the scrutiny of empirical investigation" by showing that when people become angry, they simultaneously manifest changes in coronary function that are associated with "serious and/or fatal coronary outcomes."

However, most of the techniques that have been taken up by Western therapists come from the Buddhist traditions of mindfulness, meditation, and Zen practice. Since Jung's early reflections on the archetypal symbolism of Tibetan mandalas and deities, little of Tibet's vast psychological literature and methodology has been analyzed seriously by Western psychology. In particular, the core practices of Tibet's practical, inner technology for transforming the heart, the practices for cultivating compassion, have barely been explored for their practical abilities to heal suffering and promote health. In this book I look at just those practices for developing compassion in order to provide Western readers for the first time with methods for developing compassion that are purely psychological in nature, presented outside of any formal, religious context.

Part one of this book provides a context for understanding compassion by differentiating it from other seemingly similar states of mind. It explains why compassion is so important to psychological health and happiness, also discussing some common obstacles to developing genuine compassion. Part two is the heart of the book; it provides methods for cultivating compassion in daily life. I combine Buddhist and Western approaches to these methods, using stories and metaphors to help readers not only gain an intellectual understanding of the ideas presented but also to begin understanding them emotionally. When sharing stories related to therapy patients, I have changed names and identifying details to protect confidentiality.

Many hundreds of psychological methods and ideas in the Buddhist tradition are yet to be explored by Western psychologists. I believe that this deep, ongoing dialogue provides an opportunity for Buddhist psychological ideas and methods to create a true renaissance in our approach to understanding and working with the human psyche. I hope that this book contributes to this important, ongoing dialogue between traditions and, especially, to a joyful increase of compassion in the hearts of readers.

The Lost Art of

COMPASSION

PART ONE

COMPASSIONATE VISION

The common eye sees only the outside of things, and judges by that, but the seeing eye pierces through and reads the heart and soul, finding there capacities which the outside didn't indicate or promise, and which the other kind couldn't detect.

—MARK TWAIN

ONE

LIVING DELIBERATELY

Buddhist masters always have emphasized that each moment of life is precious. In any given moment, we can allow life to pass us by or we can be mindful of what's most essential, living with genuine purpose, energy, and joy. Too often we find ourselves hurrying to grab our coffee, commute to work, and get to a meeting, rarely pausing to take a deep breath and seriously consider how we spend the limited number of precious moments that we have. When we're aware and awake in a given moment, we have the capacity to make that moment extraordinary.

So many of us come home from tiring days at work or school and automatically turn on a television or radio. We spend our evenings freely on such distractions, as though we had an endless supply. Once, my closest Buddhist teacher, Kyabje Lama Zopa Rinpoche, came to stay at our home for a few days. Rinpoche is particularly famous for using each moment of life with great awareness and compassionate purpose. After a busy day we had dinner together, and Rinpoche then retired to his room to meditate. So my wife and I cleaned up a bit and then sat down, as was our habit at the time, to watch a late-night talk show. After some time Rinpoche came out and sat down by us. He said, "Oh, is he the one who makes fun of people?" It struck me that Rinpoche looked at his own life and our lives as an anthropologist might look at the rituals of a tribe in some remote forest, with a mind always open and fresh, wondering what the purpose of these actions might be. As the talk-show interview about some recent scandal continued, I too began wondering what the purpose was.

We spend so much of our time doing things automatically that it is important to assess whether our habits bring us real joy. Whenever we think that how we spend a given day or even a given hour is unimportant, and whenever we think we need to rush through what we're doing so that later we can get to something more relaxing, meaningful, or important, we are cheating ourselves. In fact, we never know for certain that we'll be around for the future that we imagine. What is certain is that any of us can pause in this moment to consider what's most essential and then live this moment in a deliberate, meaningful, beautiful way.

WHOLLY IN THE MOMENT

Although each of us has only a limited number of evenings, thoughts, and breaths left in our lives, we rarely take the time to consider how they are spent. Such questions usually come up strongly during adolescence and early adulthood, when we challenge the values of our parents and our society and try to decide what in the world to do with our lives. These issues also may come up when we are faced with significant losses or transitions; a divorce, getting laid off, the death of a loved one, or the onset of an illness often cause people to reflect more deeply.

As a psychotherapist and teacher, I often ask people what they believe is most essential to living a happy and meaningful life. Many people say that although there is no question more important than this, they haven't thought about it in years. We become so busy and so engrossed in the small tasks of our lives that we find it difficult to step back and ask ourselves what matters most. If we haven't thought much about such issues and don't have a clear, personal answer, we probably will lack an overall sense of direction in life. It then becomes difficult to tell if we're making progress or going in circles. If we want to have a genuinely happy life, it's important to contemplate this question of what brings us joy and meaning throughout our lives. The more we consider what is most essential, the better our experiences can help us discover deeper answers.

When we ask what makes a happy and meaningful life, one problem that can arise is the tendency to respond with an answer that doesn't really come from the heart. At such times the conscious mind has one answer and the unconscious has another, so we become conflicted. An easy way to tell if you suffer from such an inner conflict is to see how well your daily activities match up with your beliefs. If you say that family is important but somehow don't find much quality time with yours each week; if you say that spirituality is important but spend only a few hours a week actively engaged in spiritual practice; if you say that helping others is important but you can't think easily of recent examples of your doing so, then there's probably a significant gap between the beliefs you hold consciously and the unconscious ones that are running your life.

Tibetans don't talk about unconscious beliefs, but they have a saying that's relevant. They say that a soup won't taste good if some of the vegetables just float around on the surface and don't get cooked. First we need to find our own deepest beliefs about what makes a meaningful and happy life. Then those ideas need to sink down and be cooked, flavoring our whole lives. One simple method taught in the Tibetan tradition to help facilitate this process is to begin each morning by thinking about how lucky you are to have another day of human life. You recall that no one is ever promised another day; you could have died last night, and this very day might be your last. An accident, a heart attack, or a murderer could take your life easily today. Then, you plan your day with this in mind. Considering our deepest beliefs daily in the context of impermanence can help give us energy for integrating those beliefs into the fabric of our daily lives.

Learning to live wholly from our deepest values takes time. For example, we may set out to be loving, but when someone annoys us we become angry and only later realize that we no longer feel loving. This awareness is an essential part of the process of integrating our beliefs into our lives. Recognizing such gaps between our beliefs and our actual feeling provides an opportunity to work on ourselves. As we continue working with our own minds, we gradually become more capable of facing difficulties while remaining loving. The more fully our deep values take their rightful place at the center of our personalities, the more we discover a sense of integration, wholeness, and contentment in the passing moments of our daily lives.

All of the methods presented in this book are intended to bring the conscious and unconscious aspects of the psyche into alignment with our deepest values so that we can live them in a genuine and spontaneous way. These methods engage your intellect, memories, imagination, relationships, and emotions in order not only to strengthen your conscious resolve, but also to transform the content of your unconscious. If you spend time and energy practicing these methods, you'll find sincere, joyful love and compassion coming spontaneously into your heart as you go about the activities in your life. For example, someone may be giving you a hard time, and rather than tensing up, you may find your heart unexpectedly opening in sincere compassion. There's a famous story of an Indian Buddhist master who went to a cave to meditate on love. After years of ascetic effort, he saw no obvious results, and so he gave up. On his way into town he came across a dog with a deep wound infested with maggots; suddenly he had an overwhelming and utterly transformative experience of enlightened love. His years of effort had set powerful forces in motion that his conscious mind could not see. A moment of deep compassion for the suffering of a dog caused this breakthrough of loving awareness, and its volcanic eruption radically transformed the landscape of his life and heart. Each time we practice methods like those presented in this book, though the results may not be apparent immediately, we too are setting in motion positive psychological forces that inevitably will bring about positive results.

CHANGING YOUR MIND

Just what do we mean when we say "mind"? The Sanskrit word *chitta* (*sem* in Tibetan) is ordinarily translated into English as "mind." The Buddhist concept of mind includes not only our cognitive thoughts but also our emotions. It includes what we're consciously aware of and also mental events that occur below the threshold of consciousness. Subtle levels of awareness such as those that occur during sleep and during deep meditation are included also in the Buddhist concept of mind. The most subtle level of mind is even said to continue after the death of the body. So what Buddhists are referring to when they speak of *chitta* is much broader than the typical associations with the English word *mind,* encompassing what we might call the heart, the psyche, and the spirit as well. Over the course of this book, I use the words *mind, heart, psyche,* and *spirit* to refer to various aspects of the broad, Buddhist concept of mind.

Throughout the book I also refer to both Western psychology and Buddhist psychology. I use the term *psychology* in the broadest sense, referring to the study of the psyche, which encompasses the mind and the heart. A long tradition of Buddhist psychology is devoted to helping people become more aware of the true nature of their inner experiences. Buddhist literature analyzes how we receive and process sensory input, describing how the mind organizes information, creates mental images of and judgments about objects, and then reacts to those

mental images with various impulses and emotions. Buddhist psychological literature also categorizes various emotions, thoughts, and other
inner experiences, describing the psychological mechanisms that cause
different positive and negative states of mind to arise, to become
stronger, to become weaker, and to cease. By studying this sort of literature, we grow in our ability to understand and control our own attention, thoughts, and emotions. Buddhist psychology also contains
detailed descriptions of the various levels of consciousness that arise
during sleep and meditation, providing ways of using these states of
consciousness for our own benefit. This tradition of mind-study is now
over twenty-five hundred years old and itself developed out of earlier,
Vedic traditions that already existed in India at the time of the Buddha's birth. One of the most essential insights, forming a basis for all of
Buddhist psychology, is that happiness and suffering are mental events
and that therefore their causes must also be primarily mental. The
main purpose of Buddhist psychology is to help people understand
which types of mental phenomena lead to happiness and which lead to
suffering and to provide them with methods for eliminating those that
lead to suffering while increasing those that lead to happiness.

This brings me back to the earlier question of what constitutes a
good, happy, meaningful life. When you ask Westerners this question,
some answer based on external accomplishments, such as gaining a certain amount of wealth, popularity, sensory pleasure, comfort, and social
standing. Others answer on a more deeply interpersonal level, focusing
on their relationships with family and friends and on making some significant contribution to the world. It's extremely rare for anyone—even
Western psychotherapists—to answer this question *psychologically*. The
Buddhist response to this question is deeply psychological: Buddhism
asserts that a good, happy life is determined not by anything external
but rather by the quality of our minds and hearts in each moment of
life. Regardless of what we do or don't do externally, a life spent cultivating wisdom and compassion is a good life.

C. G. Jung noted on numerous occasions that Western society is not yet psychological enough; for our own good we need more and deeper psychological understanding. We need to focus less on the external world and more on developing the best capacities of our own hearts. Happiness, contentment, joy, and a sense of meaning are all psychological in nature; they exist in the mind or the psyche.

Buddhist psychology observes that the main cause of any given thing (that out of which it arises) must have a similar nature to the thing itself. For example, an acorn is of a similar substance as a tree and serves as the primary cause for a tree's growth. Sunlight and water serve as conditions for the acorn becoming a tree, but by themselves they can never lead to the arising of a tree. In the case of happiness, which is a positive state of mind, only a positive state of mind can serve as its primary cause. External things like a house, a good meal, or time with one's family can serve as conditions supporting the development of happiness or contentment, but they can never serve as its primary cause. As a psychotherapist in the suburbs of a big city, I frequently see people who have achieved the outer conditions that nearly everyone else on the planet craves and still find themselves terribly unhappy. For example, if the members of a family are angry with each other, then spending time together even in a beautiful house with a gourmet meal designed to celebrate a holiday, birthday, or graduation will be an occasion for suffering. This is because the feeling of anger arises out of mental agitation and serves as a cause for further mental agitation and suffering. Even an abundance of water and sunlight cannot turn poison ivy into an oak tree.

By contrast, when our minds are filled with affection, compassion, or other positive emotions, even simple or rough circumstances can be enjoyable. When you think back to the happiest, most meaningful times in your life, you may associate them with certain places and people. However, if you analyze carefully, you'll probably find that you spent other times with those same people that were less happy and meaningful. And if you returned to those places, you likely would not find your old happiness there as an inherent quality of that place. As you think back, you'll discover that those outer circumstances served as conditions for deeply positive emotions to arise. Perhaps you fell in love, or you felt sincere affection and intimacy for your family, or you were curious and energetic about learning new things, or you felt calm and connected with others and with the natural world around you. Whatever the outer circumstances, your inner thoughts and emotions were the main causes of your joy or happiness.

We experience many different positive emotional states. A few examples are confidence, self-respect, affection, energetic curiosity, contentment, nonclinging, peacefulness, and patience. Buddhist literature names a greater variety of healthy emotions than does the English language, allowing for finer distinctions between different positive psychological states. For example, while we have one word for compassion, Buddhist literature describes many different kinds and levels of compassion. However, the most common Tibetan word for compassion is *nying-je*. *Nying* means heart, and *je* means the foremost or most exalted. So compassion is the most exalted of all states of the heart or mind. The implication is that among all the positive emotions that people can generate, compassion is the very best. If we want to be happy, compassion is the mental state that most effectively grants us our wish.

So if one were to give a psychological answer to the question of what constitutes a good, happy, meaningful life, the response would be: a life spent cultivating compassion. As a state of mind or heart, compassion serves as a direct psychological cause for contentment, happiness, and joy. Many of the things we usually associate with a good life—contributing something to the world, being close with family members, having deep friendships, inner peace, and peace between people—actually result from living compassionately.

Like most things of value, compassion does not come easily or quickly. All of the exercises in this book are designed to help us in this process of living a happy, compassionate life. Before getting to the exercises themselves, I address some common obstacles that can block us from developing contentment and compassion or can make our efforts to develop them much less effective.

OVERCOMING OBSTACLES

Works of love are always works of joy.
—Mother Teresa

Some years ago I was working full-time at a residential treatment program for autistic and schizophrenic clients while also taking a full course load at school and working on a book about a Tibetan Buddhist meditation ritual for developing compassion. Around this time I came across a quote from Lama Zopa Rinpoche that said, "Real happiness starts when you begin to cherish others."

Somehow, I felt a bit upset when I read this. I thought, *All right, I'm doing all this compassionate stuff for others, so why am I so tired and stressed out? Where's the happiness?*

The problem was partly that my schedule was too hectic for me. However, I also wondered if there might be a different, more openhearted and joyful way of being as I went about doing things in my daily life. I realized that I needed to learn more about compassion, to understand it more clearly, differentiate it from other states of mind or heart that might look similar from the outside, and also discover how it might lead to "real happiness." I began checking out my own experiences and the experiences of other people around me to see whether or not the Buddhist assertion that happiness comes from compassion is true and how this might work psychologically.

Early on in this inquiry I realized that I didn't even understand clearly what compassion, love, or altruism really are. Good definitions of these terms don't exist in Western psychology. Western researchers rarely use the term *compassion,* since they find it difficult to study something that is not easily measured or quantified. Rather, they speak of altruism, defining it according to a person's behavior: if one is helping another person, one is behaving altruistically. This is the definition of *compassion* I was relying on when I thought about how I was working, studying, and writing to help others but wasn't feeling real happiness or contentment. I was focusing on my behaviors rather than on what was in my heart.

Emerson said eloquently that real compassion cannot be defined by external actions:

> We have no pleasure in thinking of a benevolence that is only measured by its works. . . . We know who is benevolent, by quite other means than the amount of subscription to soup-societies. It is only low merits that can be enumerated.

True benevolence is felt directly by the heart; it transcends any egoistic accounting of our apparently good actions. Because compassion is a state of mind or of heart, it cannot be measured by a person's outward behaviors. It is not the behavior but the state of mind motivating the behavior that determines the presence or abscence of compassion. As a psychologist, I see people who exhaust themselves doing things for others out of a desire to be liked or out of a fear that others will get angry at them if they don't do so. I see burned-out social workers and teachers who go through the motions of their jobs wishing that they were someplace else. I see wealthy businesspeople who give money to charities in order to gain status in the community and build new business connections. In all of these instances, people's outward behaviors may appear benevolent, but the motivations are self-centered desire, fear, or habit rather than a genuine feeling of compassion in their hearts.

So a valuable definition of *compassion* must begin by recognizing that it is a state of mind or heart. Buddhism defines *compassion* as mental state of wishing that others may be free from suffering. Compassion is closely related to love, which Buddhism defines as cherishing others—feeling a sense of closeness with and affection for them—and also as the state of mind wishing that others may be happy. I use *state of mind* rather than *emotion* here because Tibetan Buddhism doesn't have a word corresponding to *emotion*. Buddhism does not distinguish strongly between thoughts and emotions. The Buddhist view is that our thoughts give rise to and underlie our emotions, so emotions might be described as thoughts combined with a strong component of affect or feeling. Whether we're aware of it or not, thoughts, beliefs, or cognitions always do underlie our emotional experiences. For example, when we feel angry we believe that others are inherently unpleasant and are causing our unhappiness, and when we feel loving we believe that others are precious and are deserving of happiness. From a Western psychological perspective, compassion is an emotion, but here I define it primarily as a state of mind to avoid the dualistic, Western assumption that as an emotion it is somehow opposed to reason. In fact, from a Buddhist perspective, healthy emotions like compassion are grounded in valid and reasonable thoughts about ourselves and others, while unhealthy emotions like hate or anxiety are grounded in mistaken, inaccurate thoughts. This is why Buddhism views wisdom and compassion as closely related; as we develop the sort of wisdom that correctly understands reality, we naturally become more compassionate, and as we become more compassionate, we naturally become wiser and more reasonable in our approach to life.

The purpose of defining different mental states in Buddhist psychology is to provide aids for introspection, to help people assess the contents of their own hearts and know themselves better. As most of us are not accustomed to differentiating carefully between the qualities of different mental states, a more elaborate definition of *compassion* is useful here. I define *compassion* as a state of mind that's peaceful or calm but also energetic, in which one feels a sense of confidence and also feels closeness with or affection for others and wishes that they may be free from suffering. This is real, healthy compassion. Such compassion can be directed toward one person or any number of living beings.

Using this definition, I can look back and see why I wasn't contented or really happy. First, I was assessing my benevolence on the basis of my behaviors rather than the state of my heart. Second, as I became busier and more stressed, I began feeling more distant from others, focusing on what I felt I needed to get done. So I wasn't feeling the closeness and affection that are so essential to compassion. And when my schedule got me overly tired, my sense of confidence and energy waned. As these difficulties compounded, I found myself focusing on the wish that I, rather than others, might be free from the suffering of my own stressed-out body and mind. Although I believed that I was quite busy doing things for others, I wasn't really feeling much love or compassion. When you're stressed out or overwhelmed, you can't generate healthy compassion.

Stress, grounded as it is in the inner conflicts negotiated by the ego, runs counter to developing positive emotions in general and compassion in particular. Freud and Jung did a great job of describing how we get stressed. Our days are filled with so many desires. Our ego continually struggles with reality, trying to get self-centered desires met. Freud emphasized that the ego is quite small while the outer world is large, unpredictable, and obviously not designed to easily or consistently fulfill our wishes. As we try to plan and control things to get our desires met, we must deal with countless others whose desires may not coincide with our own, and we must also face natural, social, and economic forces that are much bigger than we are. Jung emphasized that the inner world of unconscious forces is also much bigger than the ego, which he likened to an island in an ocean of powerful instinctual and archetypal forces that sometimes threaten to wash away parts of the island or flood it entirely. As we try to maintain our emotional equilibrium, we may experience dreams, moods, compulsive desires, worries, obsessions, bursts of energy, fantasies, romantic longings, sleepless nights, and a wide array of other psychological experiences that come from outside of the ego's control. According to Freud, the ego's main task is to find compromises between the self-centered demands of our inner worlds and the limited resources of outer reality. When the ego succeeds in finding a compromise, then we attain a sense of inner balance, but this is always temporary. Changes in our outer or inner circumstances can arise at any point to disrupt it. When the balance is disrupted, we feel stressed. When we're stressed, it means that our ego's regular coping mechanisms aren't working well. So we don't know what to do, and a sense of pressure, frustration, and fatigue builds up from within. Unable to find an inner balance, we may pull away from others or become moody, gruff, and demanding. We may feel agitated, frustrated, angry, or exhausted. Object relations analysts who came after Freud and built upon his theories say that deep down near the core of the ego is the tendency to retreat from the frustrating and frightening forces of reality into a psychologically cut-off, schizoid, paranoid, and constricted inner world. The unconscious essence of our stress is a heart closed off from others in a claustrophobic inner world of agitated, fearful thoughts and feelings. Buddhist masters assert that simply having such a desire-driven ego is inherently in the nature of suffering. Most of us become aware of the suffering nature of the ego only when our desires are frustrated, our fragile equilibrium is disrupted, or our defenses are overwhelmed.

From this discussion you can see that feeling stressed or overwhelmed blocks a person from developing genuine compassion. When we're stressed out, we aren't calm or peaceful, we feel insecure, we lack a capacity for joyful effort, and we distance ourselves from others.

In my work with people in psychotherapy, and also when teaching meditation, I find that it's easy for people to fall into patterns that get them stressed out, keeping them from genuine compassion. By unconsciously and repeatedly engaging in ego-based coping strategies that we developed in childhood, we keep ourselves trapped, missing out on the opportunity for real happiness. In this chapter I present solutions to a few of the obstacles that often block us from finding healthy compassion and joy. Each of these obstacles is easy to mistake for genuine compassion but leads to stress rather than to happiness. One simple rule is that if you're stressed out, overwhelmed, or just not really happy, then you haven't been feeling healthy compassion.

WANTING TO BE LIKED

One common obstacle to compassion is the compulsive desire to be liked and accepted by others. Clearly, we all find it more pleasant to be liked and accepted than to be disliked, put down, ignored, or rejected. In everyday life this can be a positive force, leading people to be polite, flexible, and friendly with each other. However, as a psychotherapist I often meet nice, intelligent, caring people for whom this desire has gone too far and become destructive. As each of us strives to cultivate compassion, we should be wary of confusing genuine compassion with nice behavior motivated by the wish to be liked.

The compulsive desire to be liked and accepted by others is an ego-driven coping mechanism aimed at getting others to treat us well and also at compensating for underlying feelings of insecurity and low self-esteem. When we don't feel sufficient, confident, and calm within ourselves, we may begin working for others' praise and approval in the hopes that this will make us feel better about ourselves. We may even suppress aspects of our own personalities, including our wishes, opinions, and strengths, in order to be and do what we believe others want. If we use this coping mechanism often, we may become acutely sensitive to others' wishes and expectations, striving to mold ourselves to fit them. Many of us unconsciously have taken on certain interpersonal roles that we notice evoke positive responses from others. We may push ourselves to be the saintly and empathic adviser, the comedian always up for a good time, the caretaker who's always got it together, or the ideal employee ready to take on any task. There are countless variations, but the underlying similarity is that we suppress aspects of ourselves and step into limited, confined roles in order to seek acceptance, friendship, or love from someone else.

At first glance, we may appear terribly compassionate when playing such roles. We may even appear saintly or perfect. The role was unconsciously created precisely to appear this way. It's an idealized image, not a real, whole person. Out of an underlying insecurity, we fear that showing our imperfections and flaws will lead to rejection. By presenting a perfect image, we strive to avoid rejection.

Clearly, this isn't compassion as I defined it earlier. Compassion is about liking rather than being liked; it's about accepting, not being accepted. In compassion, we let go of the fearful, tight qualities of the ego. Unlike the desire to liked and accepted by others, compassion is not grounded in the constricted inner world of the ego. In those moments when we give rise to genuine compassion, we naturally let go of the compulsive desires and fears that lie at the heart of the ego. This gives us the confidence to open up to others in a genuine, affectionate way. In any given moment, compassion can free us from the suffering of the desire-driven ego.

Although our idealized roles may appear similar to compassion, they are actually a trap. Psychological research suggests that relating to others in this way makes already low self-esteem worse. We initiate this approach hoping to receive the praise and acceptance that we want so much. When we don't get this desired response, it's terribly frustrating. And, tragically, even when we do get the response we're looking for, it doesn't help. Deep down, we feel that whatever positive feedback, acceptance, or praise we do receive isn't directed at who we really are; we feel it's just directed at the role we've been playing. This is one reason that poor self-esteem can continue existing in our minds despite many external achievements and a good deal of praise from others. When we play an idealized role, we cannot win. If we don't get positive feedback, it's frustrating, and if we do, it never sinks in.

Low self-esteem is but one of the negative results of following the desire to be liked. Spending time with people we like should be fun and energizing, but when we're stuck in this pattern, just the opposite is true. Suppressing our real feelings and opinions while trying to live up to an idealized, perfect image is exhausting. When we strive to relate to others by way of an idealized image, then spending time with them leaves us feeling stressed out, tired, unappreciated, and out of balance. We have to pull away from others to relax and get in touch with our genuine feelings. Over time, this can lead to isolation, loneliness, and even depression.

Relating through an idealized image in order to be liked also winds up harming those who get into close relationships with us. In the beginning, things may seem great. We may feel pleased with ourselves for having received such a positive response, and the other person may feel that they've met their perfect match—someone incredibly kind, generous, fun, and easy to be with. However, before too long our own suppressed needs begin reasserting themselves. We begin feeling depleted by the relationship and resenting the other person for not meeting our deep needs and for not really knowing who we are. We feel that they don't appreciate or reciprocate our great generosity. Of course, we ourselves unconsciously set it up so that they couldn't possibly really know us or meet our needs; we presented ourselves as though we had no needs to be met. All of this inevitably leaves the other person feeling confused, dismayed, or even betrayed.

A patient of mine named Julia developed relationships based largely on her desire to be liked. From the beginning of her relationship with her fiancé, Mark, she consistently avoided asserting her own wishes and went along with his plans. She spent a good deal of time empathizing with him about his problems at work but rarely talked about challenges that she was facing. On the surface she seemed too good to be true. When they moved in together, Julia immediately took almost all of the household chores on herself, doing the laundry, cooking, and cleaning. Insecure and desperate for Mark's acceptance, she almost never asked him to do anything for her or to empathize with her. Over time, she gradually became tired and resentful. Afraid of making overt demands, she'd push Mark away, get moody and irritable with him, and question his love for her. When he sensed that something was wrong and asked her about it, she still didn't open up about her real needs and feelings. Their relationship was in jeopardy when I finally convinced her to share her real feelings with him. She confessed her imperfections, exhaustion, resentments, and doubts. Mark responded that he was relieved to finally know what was wrong. He reminded her of times when he'd offered to do more and she'd rejected his offers, continuing to do everything herself. He said, "Look, Julia, I'd be thrilled if you'd let me do more for you. You don't need to be perfect. I think that helping each other is what a marriage should be about."

Julia's efforts to play an idealized role had exhausted her. Her reluctance to admit her own needs and limitations to Mark had kept him from supporting her, leading to frustration on both of their parts. The gap between how Julia presented herself and who she really was blocked them from developing mutual understanding and deep intimacy as a couple. Julia's relationship with Mark also illustrates another disadvantage of this approach that's particularly important from a Buddhist perspective. If someone is playing an idealized role, the refusal to admit to suffering or to accept help blocks his or her partner from being compassionate in response. If giving compassion to others is a primary cause of happiness, then this holding back in fact keeps the other person from finding happiness. Accepting love and compassion from others is actually a form of kindness and generosity. By admitting our vulnerabilities and accepting another's compassion, we give that person the opportunity to find the joy that comes from heartfelt giving.

As each of us strives to become more compassionate, we must guard against the tendency to play a role of some idealized, compassionate saint rather than being ourselves and letting compassion fill our hearts and express itself naturally.

There are a few things each of us can to do counteract such tendencies. We can go out of our way to admit our faults and vulnerabilities to others. When we feel frustrated or upset with someone close to us, we can tell that person how we feel and talk it through. When we want or need support or help from those close to us, we can take the risk of telling them. When others offer kindness, we can accept it humbly. If there are gaps between how we feel and behave alone and how we are when with others, then we need to tell those close to us and find ways to close those gaps.

We can strive also to base our self-esteem on our inner qualities rather than on fleeting feedback from others. Self-esteem that is based on external rewards or praise from others is inherently unstable, like a leaf blown by the wind. But if we base our self-esteem on positive inner qualities like love and compassion, then it will grow steadily as we make efforts to develop these qualities. When we can judge ourselves through honest introspection, the fleeting opinions and actions of others will be like wind blowing against a foundation of stone. Building your confidence and self-esteem on your deepest values is a powerful and abiding antidote to feelings of insecurity and to the trap of enacting idealized roles in order to be liked by others.

NOT TAKING CARE OF YOURSELF

Another common obstacle to compassion is not taking care of yourself. This often appears in people who have become accustomed to leading busy lives and feel that they can't take time away to relax, reflect, and introspect. In our fast-paced society, it's easy to see being incredibly busy with no time to yourself as a normal way of life.

As a psychotherapist, I often work with people who have been so busy for so long that when I first suggest they take some time for themselves, they aren't sure what to do. We can lose touch with ourselves so much that we grow uncomfortable simply being with ourselves and looking at the contents of our hearts. I was surprised when I first began working with people who told me they could not fall asleep without the radio or television on. These were adults and teenagers who kept themselves busy or distracted day and night because they were afraid of being alone with their own thoughts and feelings.

It is particularly troubling to see families who are so busy that they rarely spend time simply being together. I often work with families whose members have lived together for years without really knowing or understanding each other. The great psychoanalyst Wilfred Bion says that parents spending time with their children in a state of relaxed, loving reverie is as important to the child's emotional well-being as milk is to the child's physical well-being. In our busy society, there are many emotionally malnourished children.

As adults, we also need to spend time in a state of relaxed, loving reverie with ourselves. This is the attitude necessary for introspection, and without introspection we will not know ourselves or be able to work with our minds. Introspection is essential to our psychological well-being.

When I ask people why they don't take time just to be present with others or with themselves, they often say they don't have time and that it seems selfish, irresponsible, or lazy. In reality, making time in our schedules to take care of ourselves, to practice introspection, and to be present with others in a loving way is very responsible. We all find time to eat and sleep regularly because we know that doing so is essential to our physical health. Too often we don't do the things that are just as essential to our psychological health, and the negative effects of this on our own happiness, on our families, and on our lives is profound.

For some people, the tendency toward guilt underlies a lack of self-care. We may assume that being compassionate means that if someone else in the world is hungry then we cannot enjoy eating, if someone else is poor we cannot enjoy wealth, if someone else is sad we cannot be happy. We may feel that we cannot relax because there is so much to be done. We may feel that if others are stressed out and miserable then we cannot in good conscience be happy and take care of ourselves. This is simply incorrect. It's an approach based on guilt rather than love. Our being unhappy doesn't benefit anyone. Buddhist teachings note that our practice of patience is perfected not when all difficult people are eliminated from the world but when all anger is eliminated from our minds. Our practice of generosity is perfected not when all poverty is eliminated from the world but when all grasping at "I" and "mine" is eliminated from our hearts. The ideal of compassion is not feeling bad for what we cannot do; it is joyfully and energetically doing all that we can for others in any given moment. Genuine compassion for others never harms and only benefits us.

A drawing by the humorous and sometimes irreverent Zen master Hakuin addresses the role of self-care in the practice of compassion.

He depicts Kannon, the enlightened bodhisattva of compassion, resting in serene contemplation in the midst of a garden of lotus blossoms. A bodhisattva is a Buddhist practitioner who has vowed compassionately to attain full enlightenment in order to benefit all sentient beings, freeing them from suffering. Next to his drawing of Kannon, Hakuin wrote, "She enjoys her spare moments when there is no connection with human beings. Who says her vow to awaken beings is deep?" Hakuin in fact was deeply devoted to Kannon. In this drawing he was poking fun at people who believe that compassion looks like not taking care of ourselves, being unhappy, and compulsively running around trying to solve others' problems according to plans devised by our own egos. That approach is driven not by compassion but rather by the ego's desire for omnipotent control. We don't find the time to take care of ourselves because our egos keep us too busy trying to manage everything in the world around us. Buddhist teachings note that even a Buddha is not omnipotent. Anyone who strives to control everything is sure to suffer great frustration. The Buddhist teachings on compassion assert that our task is not to stress ourselves out trying to control the world around us but rather to cultivate love, compassion, and wisdom in our hearts and then to express these qualities naturally and joyfully in our lives.

The ideal of the bodhisattva shows how taking care of yourself and taking care of others are interdependent. A bodhisattva gives rise to incredibly powerful compassion for all living beings everywhere and then takes on what the Dalai Lama refers to as the commitment of universal responsibility. Bodhisattvas take on a personal sense of responsibility for freeing every sentient being everywhere from every kind of suffering, and they vow to remain in the universe going anywhere necessary throughout oceans of time to fulfill their commitment to others. Upon making this vow, of course the bodhisattva begins working for the welfare of others. Her main task in the beginning, though, is to attain her own liberation from suffering and her own full enlightenment.

This may sound odd at first, but upon making a compassionate vow to spend all of eternity working for the welfare of others, the bodhisattva's first, main task is to attain a state of enlightenment that brings her total freedom from suffering as well as limitless bliss, intelligence, skill, joy, and wisdom. The reason for this is purely pragmatic. You cannot give others what you don't have yourself.

Kannon's serenity amid the lotuses symbolizes the inner realizations of liberation, contentment, and bliss that she herself has attained and to which she leads others. Even in the midst of difficult circumstances, the heart of the enlightened bodhisattva emanates a peaceful joy that reminds others of their own potential for freedom. This is a heart that has transcended the stress and constriction of the ego's manner of being in the world.

Sometimes people look at the examples of great saints and notice that they don't seem to be concerned about themselves, that they sacrifice themselves for the welfare of others. So people assume that if they too want to be compassionate, taking care of themselves or striving to improve themselves is not important. This is a misunderstanding. As you move into a deeper, psychological understanding of how compassion works, it will be clear that as you get to more advanced levels of compassion, what appears as self-sacrifice is actually an advanced form of taking care of yourself. When you get to that level, sacrificing yourself to take care of others becomes naturally a way of achieving your own highest welfare at the same time. Once a practitioner understands not just intellectually but also experientially how compassion leads to happiness, new challenges are viewed spontaneously as ways of developing greater compassion, which in turn will lead to greater happiness for themselves as well as others. Sacrifices become ways of breaking through old, confining habits of the ego to gain greater freedom and joy. For someone who regards freedom as the result of overcoming old habits of the desire-driven ego and who sees happiness as coming from compassion, opportunities for compassionate sacrifice bring enthusiasm and joy.

Each of us has to start where we are. I sometimes liken the process of developing compassion to physical exercise. For example, when you start weight training, you begin by figuring out how much you can lift safely, and then, as your strength increases, you slowly increase the amount of weight with which you work. Trying suddenly to lift twice what you're able to clearly leads to injuries and slows your progress.

People often make these sorts of mistakes when it comes to compassion. We focus too little time on developing our actual feelings of compassion, as the serene Kannon was doing in the lotus garden. Instead, we get extremely busy running from one activity to another. We may run between work, soccer games, carpools, volunteer activities, caring for ill or elderly relatives, and even meditation, spiritual groups, or church activities without pausing to realize that we're feeling stressed or depleted. We may fantasize about contributing something to society or to the world without noticing that we're not being patient and loving to those closest to us.

We must approach the task of inner development in a practical way, beginning by assessing how much we can do for others without feeling stressed out, overwhelmed, or depleted. Then we gradually build up our inner strength from there. In this way we are able to see clear, gradual progress. If we do things in fits and starts, we may find ourselves feeling discouraged after some time.

Both as a psychotherapist and as a Buddhist, I've found that understanding and working skillfully with my own mind is the single biggest factor in determining how effective I am at helping others. Learning how to help ourselves and others is a long, gradual, and often challenging process. Each step of the way, it's important to apply to ourselves whatever insights we've gained before we share them with others. We must take care of ourselves primarily by understanding and taking care of our own minds. Preaching something to others that we are not striving sincerely to practice ourselves is a sad sort of hypocrisy.

I mentioned earlier that you cannot give others something you don't have. This is very true emotionally. If you're feeling upset and anxious, striving to help someone close to you may only get that person anxious as well. This is true because we unconsciously communicate our emotional states through our facial expressions, body postures, and even our breathing. Other people can't help unconsciously picking up on these things. Like all mammals, we naturally resonate with the emotional states of those who are close to us. The same process holds true for positive emotions. If you're feeling peaceful and happy, then people close to you naturally will pick up on those feelings. So wisely taking care of ourselves naturally becomes a way of taking care of others.

HARMING YOURSELF

If it's true that how we treat ourselves eventually expresses itself in how we treat others, then any tendency toward harming yourself works directly against compassion. When Tibetan lamas first began teaching in the West, their new students sometimes asked them how to deal with self-hatred and self-destructive tendencies. The lamas at first replied that there was no such thing as self-hatred; they'd apparently never come across it in their culture. As they spent more time with Western students, these lamas became much more familiar with this phenomenon.

If we go deeply into this subject, we can find many different ways in which people unconsciously harm themselves. Some of them I address in detail in later chapters. Here I want to talk briefly about self-hatred or anger directed at yourself. As a psychotherapist, I've been surprised to see how common it is for people to direct anger or hate at themselves. Anger at oneself has both a cognitive and an emotional component. Cognitively, it usually includes the tendency to think negatively about yourself, to focus on your faults, and to expect negative things in your future. Emotionally, it usually includes the tendency to get stuck in negative emotional states, focusing on them in a way that might be described as psychological self-torment.

When people are caught up in self-hatred, they usually don't recognize how they are tormenting themselves. Usually they have been repeating silently a series of negative thoughts about themselves for so long they no longer even realize they're thinking them. These thoughts become like inner background noise. Here are some typical examples of habitual, negative thoughts: "I'm ugly and fat, so no one will ever be attracted to me or love me"; "I'm a loser who never has accomplished and never will accomplish anything good"; "I'm a real screw-up who isn't capable of having a loving relationship"; "I'm so dumb that I have nothing of value to offer"; or "I've done so many stupid, bad things in my life that there's really no hope for me."

People who engage in this kind of thinking are often quite nice to people they don't know well. They direct their anger, hatred, and other negative emotions primarily at themselves. To begin getting at these patterns, I advise writing down the worst, most negative things you ever think about yourself. Spend some time trying to recall your harshest negative thoughts. If you have a hard time bringing your negative thoughts to your conscious mind, then think about behavioral patterns that tend to undermine your happiness—things like ruining your relationships, smoking, overeating, exhausting yourself, or isolating yourself. Then contemplate what thoughts or beliefs about yourself might underlie those behaviors, and write out those thoughts. Next, look over the thoughts you've written down and imagine that you'd said those things to someone else.

If it strikes you that it would have been mean or cruel to say those things to someone else, it means that you've been cruel to yourself. Remember that being unnecessarily cruel to anyone, including yourself, is wrong. Also remember that if you continue saying cruel things to yourself, this cruelty will be expressed eventually to people close to you. Unconsciously, inevitably, this cruelty will be directed toward lovers, spouses, and especially your own children.

Along with the tendency to unconsciously repeat negative statements about the self, self-hatred often expresses itself emotionally through dwelling in negative emotional states. For example, it's normal to regret doing something foolish or wrong. Although such regret isn't pleasant, if it leads us to change our behavior in the future, then it's useful. People with the pattern I'm discussing, though, don't use the energy of regret to make practical changes. Instead, they dwell in it so that it becomes guilt. There is no word for guilt in Tibetan. It's really a kind of regret gone wrong. With guilt, we get stuck in regret so that it becomes a form of self-torment.

Anxiety is similar. I remember trying to describe anxiety to one of my Tibetan teachers, and he asked, "Don't you mean fear?" Fear is a normal response to danger. If it helps us to move away from a poisonous snake or get out of the water when we see a shark's fin, then it's a positive response. Psychologically speaking, anxiety is a state of dwelling in fear without using it for any positive purpose. When we're anxious, fear is pointlessly controlling and tormenting us.

For example, Mike, a patient of mine, had been working as an electrical engineer for almost fifteen years. Each morning anxious thoughts such as "I'm not good enough; I'm sure to mess up today; I'm a loser" raced through his mind, and his stomach tied up in knots as he drove to work. He was afraid that he would make some catastrophic error at work, that others would show him up as incompetent, that his boss would tell him off or fire him, that he wouldn't be able to support his family, and so on. As we explored his chronic anxiety, he told me that most of these fears had been with him for over a decade. I asked what he'd done about them in that time, and he replied, "I've worried about them almost all the time." Rather than leading to some specific action such as seeking extra training, asking for feedback from his boss, or deciding to change careers, Mike's fears had become a form of chronic self-torment. They distracted him so much that they kept him from doing his best work, made him feel terrible about himself, and literally made him feel sick almost every day. Through introspection, Mike became able to see that his anxiety caused him much suffering and brought him no benefits at all. He began addressing his anxiety by doing relaxation exercises to counter his physical symptoms and also by using cognitive strategies to challenge his distorted, negative thinking. As we worked on some of the issues from his childhood that had predisposed him to intense anxiety, he began developing a realistic sense of his strengths as well as his weaknesses. This new self-understanding eventually led him to change careers and become a math teacher, which brought him more satisfaction than he'd been able to find as an engineer. He later described overcoming his chronic anxiety as feeling like being released from a prison.

We can torment ourselves in many ways through dwelling in negative emotions. The point here is that whether we engage in negative self-talk or dwell in certain negative emotional states like guilt or anxiety, the pattern is one of cruelty. When such tendencies are extremely strong, as in cases of anxiety disorders, depressive disorders, and the like, then psychotherapy may be the most helpful intervention. In all cases of self-cruelty, though, we should not tolerate it any more than we should tolerate cruelty to others. Recognizing that cruelty is simply destructive and unhealthy, we should oppose it directly. Often this entails directly opposing our negative self-talk each time it returns, replacing it with more realistic and positive statements. And if we dwell in negative feelings, we need to make strenuous efforts not to let them control our behaviors, to move beyond them, and to cultivate positive emotions that serve as antidotes. The exercises for developing compassion that appear in the next section of this book can be used as antidotes to dwelling in destructive emotions.

In general, overcoming obstacles to compassion entails being honest with ourselves and with others. We must recognize and be direct about our unhealthy patterns and our limitations. Dealing with such issues through denial or by keeping them secret keeps us from working through them. As we acknowledge our limitations, we can begin dealing with them consciously, setting appropriate boundaries so we do not exceed our capacities, and asking others for assistance when we need it.

THREE

SEEING WITH THE
EYES OF COMPASSION

B oundaries play an interesting and sometimes complicated role in developing compassion. They are like the stake and wires that are used to help keep young trees rooted and growing straight. Early on in our practice or when we're faced with difficult, new challenges, a lack of healthy boundaries can lead to our compassion being blown away before it's had a chance to take root. As we develop, though, boundaries held too tightly can stifle our compassion and keep it from reaching maturity. In the process of developing compassion, we need to become skillful at knowing when to apply boundaries and when to relax or release them.

Setting healthy boundaries involves saying no, refusing to do something, or refusing to interact in a certain way when not refusing likely would lead us to feel stressed out, hurt, disrespected, resentful, or angry. Things that stress one person out might be enjoyable to another, so exactly where we set our personal boundaries is an individual decision. I remember once working with a teenager who had been abused. We were talking about how he could decide where to set his boundaries in various relationships. People who have been abused have had their boundaries violated, and so they sometimes have a difficult time knowing what it feels like to set up healthy boundaries. Tragically, this sometimes makes those who have been hurt in the past particularly vulnerable to revictimization. At first, this young guy couldn't quite understand what I meant as I tried to explain the concept of healthy boundaries. As we talked in detail about how he'd felt when he'd been abused, he suddenly looked up and said, "Oh, something is wrong when it hurts your heart. That's when there should be a boundary." His was a good, clear definition.

Setting healthy boundaries works directly against the negative patterns discussed in the last chapter, such as the compulsive desire to be liked, the tendency not to take care of ourselves, and the tendency to be cruel to ourselves. Setting boundaries involves being honest and direct with others even if they don't want to hear what we have to say. Setting boundaries also involves protecting and taking care of ourselves.

Each of us needs to know ourselves well enough to judge whether a particular action or interaction is likely to "hurt our heart"—to lead us to feeling frustrated, hurt, overwhelmed, or angry. While Buddhist literature doesn't use the word *boundaries,* it also addresses this issue. For example, Buddhism praises the value of generosity but warns that you shouldn't give something away if you're likely to be upset later and regret giving it away. Similarly, although it's good to help others, we shouldn't agree to do something for another person if it will likely lead us to feel exhausted, resentful, and angry at the other person. Each of us has to judge our own capacities and set our boundaries accordingly.

Healthy boundaries can be important for maintaining our sense of self-respect. Sometimes out of insecurity, fear, or a wish to avoid getting angry, we don't stand up for ourselves when others treat us badly or put us down. Setting a boundary can be a way of standing up for yourself without having to get angry. A story of Martin Luther King Sr., the father of the famous civil rights leader, who was also a pastor, shows clearly how to use boundaries in this way. Driving down a street in segregated Atlanta with his young son beside him in the front seat, the elder Reverend King accidentally drove past a stop sign. A white police officer pulled up to him and said, "All right, boy, pull over and let me see your license."

Without any hesitation, the Reverend King replied, "Let me make it clear to you that you aren't talking to a boy. If you persist in referring to me as a boy, I will be forced to act as if I don't hear a word you are saying." Setting boundaries often requires some bravery. Given the place and time, the Reverend King ran the risk of a violent reaction. Brief moments in which we act with bravery and self-respect can have surprising effects on our own character and on those around us. The Reverend King acted without violence to protect his own and his son's dignity. Who can say what effect this interaction had on the future of the young boy sitting beside him? The officer was so surprised that he silently wrote a ticket and drove away as quickly as he could.

This is precisely the way to go about setting healthy boundaries. You begin by correcting the person, telling the other how you wish to be treated, or stating what you are or are not willing to do. If this hasn't worked in the past or if you have reason to suspect someone won't readily comply with your wishes, then you also state the result—what will happen if the other person doesn't respect your boundary. Particularly when you're dealing with people who are not very empathic, who are quite self-centered, or who don't have good boundaries themselves, it's important for this second part of the process to be clear and firm without being aggressive. Sometimes you may have to say that if the person won't accept your boundary then you will decrease contact, will refuse to give that person something he or she wants from you, or will end the relationship entirely. It can be difficult in the short run to set a clear boundary with someone you care about, but not doing so often leads to many more difficulties over a much longer period of time.

Getting good at setting healthy boundaries is also effective for preventing and decreasing our anger. Anger is an agitated and aggressive state of mind that develops out of feelings of unhappiness and frustrated desires. Because the mind is agitated and wishes to harm others when angry, anger directly opposes the development of compassion. Considerable evidence from research also shows that anger is bad for our physical health, bad for our relationships, and bad for our inner sense of contentment and well-being. What often happens is that someone else doesn't do something we want or does something that bothers us. Either we don't tell the person how we feel or we don't set a clear boundary, so the behavior continues. Our feelings of annoyance and frustration build up until we can't stand it anymore. Then we blame the other person for our bad feelings and get angry.

A solution to anger is to be aware of and deal with our feeling of annoyance or frustration early on. Once we're aware of our feeling, we can make a conscious decision about how we want to handle it. If we decide to let the matter go, then later on we cannot blame the other person for continuing to behave in a way that bothers us. It was our own choice not to raise the issue, and we need to take the responsibility for that choice. Or we may choose to set a boundary about the issue. By setting a boundary, we either succeed in getting the other person to stop doing what bothers us, or we implement a consequence or a response that protects us from that behavior as much as possible. Of course, it's most pleasant when the other person does respect our boundary. However, my experience with many different people has been that facing someone who doesn't respect your boundaries and holding your ground in a firm but nonaggressive way, although it's challenging, winds up being an invigorating and empowering experience. Doing this often leads to an increase in self-confidence and self-respect.

OUTGROWING OLD BOUNDARIES

By this point, I hope it's clear why being able to set healthy boundaries is important. In my work as a therapist and in my personal life, I often find that people don't set clear boundaries and then wind up feeling resentful or angry. Often, setting healthy boundaries brings clear benefit not only to the person setting the boundary but also to the other. Relationships improve quickly in this way. And yet, as someone who values compassion, I still sometimes feel uncomfortable as I suggest to people that they do less for others or say no more often.

If this sort of boundary setting is practical and useful, it is also essentially self-centered. The inner process that we go through in setting boundaries usually involves being honest with ourselves about the extent of our own selfishness and then being honest with others about this, dealing with it in an open and straightforward way. When people fail to set healthy boundaries, it's often because they don't want to admit the extent of their selfishness to themselves or to others. They're mimicking compassion, which is very different from feeling it and which often leads to negative results. When we set a boundary, essentially we're admitting that our self-interest leads us to dislike a situation, and we therefore want to change the situation to suit ourselves better. Honest introspection usually reveals that deep down we're quite selfish, so it is important to be honest about our needs and limitations, setting boundaries accordingly.

Psychologically speaking, healthy interpersonal boundaries are positive coping mechanisms derived from the ego. If the purpose of the ego, as Freud said, is mainly to negotiate between our instinctual, essentially self-centered desires and the realities of the external world, then setting boundaries is a way of keeping the ego from getting overwhelmed. Boundaries are a means of satisfying our own needs as much as possible while still maintaining honesty and respect for ourselves and others. If we really want to develop powerful compassion and to learn gradually how to live our daily lives with our hearts full of compassion, then boundaries are important, but they also eventually become an obstacle. While they protect the ego from getting overwhelmed, they also protect the ego's self-centered core. As psychological walls, they keep out certain frustrations, but they also keep us separated from others.

We've all experienced moments in which we let our boundaries and defenses down. This usually comes about when we feel a powerful sense of love, compassion, or altruistic inspiration. People experience this when they first fall in love and feel that they'd do anything for their beloved. Parents often feel this way toward their young children. Some people have this feeling when they see their pet or another animal suffering; they would do anything to help. We also may feel this way when a loved one is suffering from a serious or terminal illness. Young people sometimes get such a feeling when they're first inspired by the great, altruistic deeds of saints and heroes from the past. Feeling love or compassion without any boundaries is a powerful, peak experience. As we go deeply into it, feeling so connected with others, we discover the naturally transcendent aspect of compassion.

After having such experiences, some people get so attached to their pleasure that they stop setting healthy boundaries in the hopes of returning directly to that level of openness and love. This is often a mistake. People who try it usually create lots of problems in their interpersonal relationships and wind up feeling resentful and exhausted. The main way to return to that experience and to learn how to sustain it, making it an inherent part of your being in the world, is to take a disciplined and steady approach, using methods like those presented in this book for developing compassion in your mind. In that way you can expand your boundaries gradually outward until you reach the culmination of compassion—a point at which instinctually you recognize your self-interest as inseparable from the interests of all other beings. At that point, all self-centered boundaries can be discarded genuinely.

A THOUSAND EYES OF COMPASSION

A famous story in the Tibetan tradition illustrates this point. It involves Avalokitesvara, who is referred to sometimes as the bodhisattva of compassion and at other times as the embodiment of the compassion of all the Buddhas who ever existed or ever will exist. Tibetans view the Dalai Lamas as incarnations of Avalokitesvara, whose mantra, *Om Mani Padme Hung,* is recited almost continually by many Tibetan Buddhists and appears on prayer wheels, prayer flags, and carved *"mani* stones" all over central Asia. This mantra is said to have many different meanings, but the most commonly taught one says that *Om* stands for the practitioner's body, speech, and mind; *Mani* means "jewel" in Sanskrit and stands for compassionate method; *Padme* means "lotus" in Sanskrit and stands for wisdom; and *Hung* signifies indivisibility. Therefore, the overall meaning is that our ordinary body, speech, and mind can be transformed into a Buddha's enlightened body, speech, and mind by way of a path of indivisible compassion and wisdom.

According to the story, long ago Avalokitesvara developed a vast sense of empathy and connection with all sentient beings. Clearly he'd had the kind of experience in which egoistic boundaries fade away and one feels the transcendental inspiration of a heart flooded by compassion. In such a state of mind, he went to his main spiritual teacher, Buddha Amitabha. Speaking from his compassionate inspiration, in the presence of his teacher, he made a solemn vow that from that moment on he would never be separated from compassion and would work unceasingly to liberate all other beings from suffering. So deep was his vow that he declared that if he ever again had a selfish thought, "may my head be cracked into ten pieces . . . and may my body be split into a thousand pieces."

After making this inspired vow, he worked for a long while at benefiting others. He traveled to many different places, teaching people and striving to free them from their suffering. He spent time meditating to develop his compassion further, and when he looked out at the suffering of the world he sometimes wept with compassion. After many years of sincere effort, he felt "exhausted by his efforts," and so he paused and "entered the meditation on restoration." I think that his exhaustion indicates that he'd reached a personal limit. So you might say that he set a boundary and took a break.

During his break, still feeling exhausted, he looked around and surveyed the situation. He found that although he had helped many beings, countless others still experienced almost unimaginable forms of suffering. As he looked at the infinite mass of all that suffering, he found it unbearable.

Looking at this story psychologically, I'd say that up to this point Avalokitesvara was feeling sincere compassion, but some self-interest still lodged deep in his heart. This could be likened to the situation in which most of us find ourselves. We may feel some inspiration for compassion, but self-centered concern still forms the core of our egos. We feel sincere compassion for others, but deep down our instinctual, self-centered concerns are still the determining factors in how we experience the world. So when we make strong efforts at compassion, our ego's defenses and coping mechanisms get pushed to their limits, and the self-centered feelings at the ego's core threaten to break out in full force.

Looking at all that suffering broke Avalokitesvara's heart. Feeling that all his efforts were insufficient, he cried out in anguish, "What is the use? I can do nothing for them. It is better for me to be happy and peaceful myself."

Through the force of his previous declaration, his head split into ten pieces, and his body broke into a thousand bits. Psychologically, I'd say that at this point the momentum and inner force of his long practice of compassion came into conflict with the remaining self-centered core of his ego. All of his old boundaries and limits split open; his compassion tore his old ego apart.

At this point in our story, his teacher, Amitabha, appears. He reassures Avalokitesvara and heals him. He transforms the ten pieces of his former head into ten new faces that look out in all directions. As a symbol of how pleased he is with him, Amitabha gives him a radiant, eleventh head, a replica of Amitabha's own. Amitabha transforms the thousand pieces of Avalokitesvara's body into a new body with a thousand arms. Each of his thousand hands has an eye in its palm. Where once there was an ego with a self-centered core, now there is expansive awareness centered in compassion.

In the moment when we push up against our limits and stretch our coping mechanisms to their breaking point, we have a choice. We can set a boundary, or we can choose to push beyond our former limits. We must be very careful in choosing when to push beyond old limitations. If we're not ready, pushing beyond old boundaries can be quite harmful. In such cases, spiritual or compassionate efforts lead to the ego's falling apart, but the self-centered energy at the core of the ego is still much more powerful than the inner force of our compassion. I've known many people like this, who pushed themselves too far too soon either in their meditation practice, in other spiritual exercises, or in their work to help others. After getting overwhelmed and having an intensely negative experience of falling apart, they gave up on their previous inspiration. Out of a fear of repeating this negative experience, they chose a much more conservative and limited approach.

Avalokitesvara was never the same again after his experience of falling apart, though in a very different way. He was not impulsive or premature in pushing beyond his limits. Since he had spent such long efforts in the inner work of developing compassion, the force of his genuine compassion carried him beyond himself. Also, you'll recall that he was practicing under the guidance of a teacher, Amitabha. When we reach the point of going beyond our previous boundaries, it is important to have external supports available to help us through difficulties. A good teacher who has been through the process and also good friends who are working in a similar way can be very important.

When we reach a limit and don't yet have the inner resources or outer supports to transcend that limit, it's important to set a boundary and wait until we're ready to reach beyond it. The forces at the core of the ego are powerful, and we must be prepared to meet them. Once we are ready, though, coming up against our old limits provides a powerful opportunity for positive transformation. The ego's view of reality is like the view of the universe that was popular before Copernicus. We imagine and feel that we're the center of everything. In those moments when we allow compassion to carry us beyond the boundaries ego sets, we let go of this perspective.

The perspective we gain is what Avalokitesvara's new body symbolizes. When we stop fixating on our own perspective, we can see things from many points of view. Our approach becomes flexible and fluid rather than rigid. Avalokitesvara's ten faces are sometimes said to symbolize his ability to view compassionately all the suffering in every direction without getting overwhelmed. His eleventh face symbolizes the enlightened mind that encompasses all of this empathy with wisdom. His thousand eyes indicate compassion's capacity for vast awareness. When we don't limit our approach to our own perspective, we become able to see things from others' perspectives. His many hands symbolize the vast ability to help others extensively in whatever way is necessary. His thousand eyes appearing in the palms of his hands suggest that this helping is inseparable from or arises spontaneously out of his compassionate vision.

This story also can be viewed as symbolizing what happens each time we compassionately push beyond an old boundary. Every time we get tired, stressed out, frustrated, exhausted, or overwhelmed, we can pause in that very moment and realize that we have a choice. We can allow ourselves to contract, pulling back inside the narrow world of the ego, which involves distancing ourselves from others and allowing negative emotions such as anger, despair, neediness, or self-pity to take over. Or, in that very moment, we can make the psychological decision to choose compassion. We can choose to keep our hearts open and to continue empathizing with others. As the story indicates, making that choice doesn't mean that suddenly things will become easy. We may still fall apart. But then falling apart itself becomes a way of progressing in seeing others and the world through eyes of compassion.

EMOTIONS AS WAYS OF KNOWING

The story of Avalokitesvara brings up another point that will be important to understand as we proceed. Our emotions are not just feelings; they are also ways of knowing. If you analyze your own experience, it's easy to see the truth of this.

When a man is madly in love with a woman, everything about her appears perfectly lovable, marvelous, almost divine. When he's lustful, everything about her appears sexual, gorgeous, alluring. But if he gets really angry at her, suddenly it's hard to see any positive quality—everything appears negative, polluted, annoying.

This is simply the nature of our experience. We always know the world and each other from a particular perspective. Any given emotion colors the mind in a certain way and determines how we'll view others and the world around us.

The strange thing is that most of us totally believe whichever emotional perspective we happen to be experiencing right now. When we're very angry, we think, "Oh, he's just horrible. Why didn't I see it before this? I must have been blind! How did I ever put up with him before? He's a total nightmare." Later, if we've made up and we're again feeling affectionate, we may think, "Oh, I totally overreacted before. It was just a misunderstanding. He's actually so sweet and kind. He's great. I just adore him."

Sometimes, when I'm working as a therapist with someone who's in a bitter fight with a spouse or lover, I ask him how he saw her when they were first getting together. The earlier view seems so different from his current one that he almost wonders if he was crazy back then. He may feel that his lover previously hid her true colors. But, if we analyze things carefully, we usually find that the same traits he now finds so annoying were present back then as well. It's just that back then he was viewing them from a different emotional perspective.

It's important to understand this truth about emotions for a number of reasons. First of all, we should recognize that no single emotional perspective ever contains the whole truth about another person—or even about ourselves. If we get good at recognizing our own emotions, then when we see someone in a negative light, we can remind ourselves that we're just seeing the person from the perspective of anger or annoyance. We can also remind ourselves that this emotion will pass and that we'll see the person differently before too long.

Emotions that arise out of strong feelings of grasping or aversion tend to produce particularly inaccurate, distorted impressions. They're like fun-house mirrors, bent and twisted. When we grasp at others with strong attachment or longing, we tend to emphasize their good qualities and ignore their faults. By contrast, when we're annoyed or angry with others, we tend to emphasize their flaws and be blind to their strengths and virtues. So we should get in the habit of not being too trusting about our own judgment when we're caught up in such emotions.

Seeing people from the perspective of compassion is particularly valuable to understanding them well. When we're feeling compassionate, we more or less put aside our feelings of attachment and aversion and so are able to see them more clearly. Even if you don't like someone, when you feel compassion for that person your normal aversion is decreased because your heart opens up. And, even if you're usually very attached to someone, when you feel compassion you can see that person's faults and suffering, as well as their good qualities, which decreases the tendency to idealize them. With compassion, we particularly strive to understand the other person's experience, to see things from the other's perspective. Therefore, our view of others when we're feeling compassion for them tends to be particularly realistic.

A FLEXIBLE APPROACH

Still, compassion is also just another perspective. Even as you move from one positive emotional state to another, your view of others changes. Love sees things in a slightly different light from compassion, and the same holds true for joy, curiosity, or simple, calm contentment. The methods presented in this book are designed to help you transform your own emotions. As you use them, you'll note that some emphasize changing your perspective about others in order to shift your emotional state. In other cases, shifting the emotion is done by changing your thoughts or the images in your mind. And others emphasize developing and expanding the affective, feeling component of the emotion itself.

In applying these methods it's important to have a flexible, even playful, approach. I notice that people often take both meditation and psychotherapy very seriously. Of course, both are serious, important endeavors. But when we're working with the mind or the heart, it's best not to get too rigid or serious. The mind is not a computer or a machine. Our emotions are energetic and fluid. To work with them effectively, we need to be intent but also flexible.

When I first was getting interested in Tibetan Buddhism, I took things very seriously. I sat up very straight, listened intently to the teachings, and afterward contemplated them sincerely. I suppose that my previous studies in Western philosophy and religion influenced my approach. The goal, enlightenment itself, was clearly exalted. And so I approached it reverently, with feet bared and mind intent, serious, and analytical. As I spent more time with some of the most revered Tibetan monks—abbots and elder teachers—I found that while their minds were intent, clear, and analytical, they were also remarkably relaxed, funny, and playful. I've found that in working with the mind it is important to take things seriously but also to be flexible and creative.

Working to change our own minds, our emotions, and our ways of seeing the world certainly is not easy. As the story of Avalokitesvara suggests, the process of developing compassion can be challenging and even painful. However, the point of this process is to make ourselves and others happier. The methods presented in the next section of this book are designed to help us cultivate powerful compassion in our hearts. As we experience how compassion leads to happiness for ourselves and others, we are able to place our trust in compassion itself, allowing it to carry us beyond our old limitations and boundaries.

PART TWO

CULTIVATING COMPASSION

The best way to look after yourself is by watching your mind.
The best way to cherish yourself is by cherishing others.

—KYABJE LAMA ZOPA RINPOCHE

FOUR

COMPASSION FOR YOURSELF

True affluence is not needing anything.
—Gary Snyder

You must have compassion for yourself before you can have genuine compassion for others. So as we explore methods for developing compassion, we'll begin by cultivating compassion for ourselves. The goal of cultivating compassion for yourself is to free yourself from suffering. Since showing compassion to others leads to contentment and happiness, you might say that developing compassion for others is a particularly advanced form of showing compassion for yourself. In fact we can develop many different types of compassion for ourselves. In this chapter, I focus on the compassion for yourself that seeks to understand and eliminate the underlying cause of your suffering in order to give you freedom. No one wants to suffer, so in that sense we all innately have some compassion for ourselves. However, in order to develop the deep sort of compassion for ourselves that will be effective in freeing us from suffering, we must look very honestly at the underlying causes of our suffering.

Developing a meaningful, mature sense of compassion for yourself is very subtle psychologically. It's easy to misunderstand this

subject. In all my years of knowing Western psychotherapists, meditation teachers, and sincere spiritual practitioners, I can hardly think of
any who did not seem to get caught up in long periods of confusion or
self-deception when it came to developing real compassion for themselves.

It's not so much that the concepts involved are intellectually
challenging. The difficulty is that our egos have a huge, unconscious
resistance to facing and challenging the real causes of our suffering.
Powerful psychological forces unconsciously hold tight to the very
causes of suffering while pushing away causes of freedom and happiness. In psychotherapy, when patients get close to their deep, core issues—the very causes of their suffering—the unconscious often throws
up roadblocks. At such times, a patient's mind may suddenly jump to
another topic, or he may say that he's confused, that she's lost track of
the conversation, that he's feeling anxious or light-headed, that she's
feeling ill and needs to use the bathroom, or that he's not sure therapy
was a good idea in the first place. If such moments are not handled
carefully, then otherwise brave men and women flee from therapy in
order to avoid facing the pain in their own hearts. We repress those
things about ourselves that we cannot forget but also literally cannot
yet bear to remember. To develop meaningful compassion for ourselves, we have to be willing and able to look deeply at our own suffering and its causes. Doing this is sometimes so painful, heart-wrenching,
humiliating, and terrifying that people avoid it at almost any cost—
even when the cost is terrible suffering over a long period of time.

The same thing happens in spiritual practice. People ordinarily
start off with a lot of enthusiasm for gaining new insights and changing themselves. What happens in our spiritual practice, though, when
we run up against those parts of ourselves that we don't want to face?
If we have a very skillful teacher to help us or if we're at a time in our
lives when we're powerfully motivated to overcome a specific problem, then we may use our meditation or other spiritual practice to

work through a difficult issue. What ordinarily happens, though, is that we distract ourselves. In order to avoid going to difficult places, we develop habits of doing our practice with a distracted mind, of avoiding those aspects of the practice that particularly challenge us, or doing the practice in a formulaic, ritualized way. To avoid facing unpleasant truths about ourselves, we make these compromises without consciously realizing what we're doing. Each time we do this, we lessen the power of our spiritual or meditation practice. We even may begin using our spiritual practice unconsciously as a defense against dealing with our difficulties. As a psychotherapist, I've often worked with patients who used their spiritual practice in part as a way to avoid dealing with emotional problems. In such cases, meditation itself becomes a defense, a tool of unhealthy aspects of the ego. If we make too many unconscious compromises then there is a danger of our spiritual practice degenerating into an empty ritual with all the transformative power of napping or watching television. After many years of psychiatric practice and of studying spiritual practices, C. G. Jung noted, "People will do anything, no matter how absurd, in order to avoid facing their own souls."

If we do not find a way of facing the difficult aspects of our own souls, a way of looking honestly at our suffering and its causes in order to develop a meaningful, mature compassion for ourselves, then regardless of what we do externally, a sense of emptiness or incompleteness will remain in our hearts. We will not become deeply compassionate toward others, and we will not find freedom from suffering in our own lives.

RENOUNCING THE CAUSE OF SUFFERING

The example of Siddhartha, the handsome and wealthy prince who grew up to become the historical Buddha, provides an example of developing compassion for yourself that can serve as a good model for modern Westerners. Siddhartha's father, king of a region of India, exposed him to academic learning and sports as well as to dance, music, and many other amusements. Wanting his son to follow in his footsteps, the king praised the pleasures and responsibilities of royal life while insulating Siddhartha from the suffering of life and from those seriously engaged in freeing themselves from the causes of suffering.

A good student and athlete, Siddhartha enjoyed his life as a prince. He trained for his future responsibilities, and when the time came he got married. Like any normal person busy with daily life, he rarely had time to stop and reflect deeply on the nature or causes of suffering. Up until his early adulthood, Siddhartha lived the life society had laid out for him, and he seemed a picture of mental health and worldly happiness. Beneath the surface, though, his life lacked real meaning or freedom.

Then he had a crisis. The young man who had been overly sheltered by his father was suddenly exposed to human suffering when he finally saw for the first time people suffering from illness, old age, and death. When he thought about how he and everyone in the world he cared about were subject to inevitable aging, sickness, death, as well as "sorrow, lamentation, pain, grief, and despair," he just couldn't go on with life as he'd known it. Realizing that princes and kings were no more immune to the fundamental sufferings of life than laborers, priests, or peasants, he developed an overwhelming sense of compassion. At this point he came across a spiritual seeker of the type one still meets in India, someone who had left home to devote himself wholly to seeking nirvana or liberation from the cycle of suffering. Siddhartha lost interest in anything other than seeking out the cause of suffering in order to root it out in himself and in others. Motivated by such compassion, he left home to study with the greatest teachers of his time and to practice deep meditative introspection, seeking out the cause of suffering within his own psyche. Siddhartha's leaving home to seek enlightenment is sometimes referred to as his renunciation of *samsara,* the ongoing cycle of suffering.

In a sense, we are all like Siddhartha before his renunciation. We're subject to countless different forms of suffering, but we seem not to see it. Like Siddhartha's father, our own society discourages deep introspection, advertising an endless variety of potential distractions. Modern technology gives all of us access to sensory pleasures once only available to princes. The ego is ever ready to follow such distractions, avoiding the discomfort of directly facing the reality of suffering.

Siddhartha had everything when he left home—friends, family, wealth, pleasure, and power. He himself was not yet sick, old, lonely, grieving, or dying. However, seeing the suffering of others had occasioned in him a series of deep insights. He realized not only that everyone is subject to countless forms of suffering in life but also that depending on external circumstances to be happy yields only a paltry and insecure sort of happiness. If you build a house of sand during the low tide, then regardless of whether it's a castle, a mansion, or a shack it will meet with the same fate. By looking honestly at our own experience, we find that much of what we ordinarily label as happiness is ultimately unsatisfactory. Observing our hearts from moment to moment, we may find that not far under the surface of what had seemed pure joy are feelings of insecurity, fear, discomfort, and mental agitation. If we analyze our own experience deeply enough, we may find that happiness born of desire and ego-based compromises is actually a subtle form of suffering. Meaningful, deep compassion for ourselves aims at eliminating both gross and subtle forms of suffering from our lives by seeking out and eliminating their causes.

Siddhartha's giving up his kingdom is a great metaphor for something that each of us can do in any moment of our lives. When we notice our own suffering, rather than distracting ourselves, we can stay with our awareness of that experience. If the ego resists, rebels, or even starts feeling like it's falling apart, we can still refuse to abandon our awareness, and we can honestly analyze our own experience of suffering and its causes. We can look at the role the ego plays in our suffering, and in that very moment, out of compassion, we can practice renouncing the causes of our suffering. No matter how wonderful we thought something was, if honest awareness reveals it as a cause of suffering, then compassion demands that we let it go.

FOUR NOBLE TRUTHS

After he left his kingdom, Siddhartha went on to follow a path of radical compassion, renouncing ever deeper causes of suffering in his quest for liberation. Siddhartha studied with some of the great teachers of his time, but when he discovered that practicing what they taught didn't lead him to ultimate freedom from suffering, he moved on. For some years he practiced extreme asceticism with a group of other seekers. When he discovered that physical deprivations didn't bring freedom, he renounced this as well, much to the consternation of his fellow seekers, who thought he had abandoned his quest for liberation. As we renounce activities that cause us suffering, it's not uncommon to face criticism from others close to us who do not themselves see how those actions cause sorrow.

Soon after abandoning extreme asceticism, Siddhartha walked to Bodhgaya, India, and sat down beneath the bodhi tree, where he resolved to remain until he was enlightened. After seven days in a deep meditation, he finally woke up from the sleep of ignorance and suffering, thereby earning the name of Buddha, "one who has awakened."

When the Buddha decided to teach, the first people he approached were the ascetics with whom he had meditated. Having freed himself from suffering, he was now capable of helping them. His first teaching was on the Four Noble Truths, explaining how to practice compassion for oneself.

The first Noble Truth is referred to as the truth of suffering. To practice compassion for ourselves, we need to see beyond our distractions to recognize our own suffering. The first Noble Truth involves recognizing that we all suffer because of loss, illness, insecurity, conflicts, aging, death, and the ultimately unsatisfactory nature of egoistic life.

The second of the Four Noble Truths is that desire is the true cause of suffering. Translators have used various English words, such as *craving, desire, wanting,* and *attachment,* to refer to the state of mind that serves as the root cause of our suffering. Here, I use *desire, wanting,* and *craving* as synonyms. Of course, not all "desires" cause suffering. Compassion includes a desire for others to be free from suffering, and love includes a desire for them to be happy. The type of craving or desire being referred to here as the cause of our suffering is characterized by a feeling of being incomplete or unfulfilled in ourselves and so looking to and wanting to possess some external object. This external object is usually a physical thing or a person, but sometimes the objects of our desires are less tangible, as when we crave popularity, control, or admiration. We imbue the object or person with an underlying fantasy that having it will get rid of our bad feelings and make us feel whole, complete, and fulfilled. Desire is ultimately a delusion, for it is founded on the belief that perfect and permanent fulfillment can be found in objects that are themselves impermanent and imperfect.

The third Noble Truth is the cessation of suffering, which is described as "relinquishing, letting go, and rejecting that same craving." The fourth Noble Truth outlines the path or skillful approach to achieving that cessation.

The second Noble Truth is really shocking. We spend so much of our lives, moment after moment from waking to sleeping and even in our dreams, following desire. We make huge efforts and endure many hardships in the hopes of finding happiness by obtaining the objects of our desires. Rarely does it occur to us that the very way we go about seeking happiness has been causing our problems.

The problem is that we have never analyzed our own suffering carefully. Deep introspection will reveal not only that desire plays a key role in our intense suffering at times of illness or loss but also that subtle forms of suffering infect our lives continually because of our deluded desires. Feelings of emptiness and craving afflict our hearts as we long for objects, only to be followed by frustration, sorrow, and anger when we don't get what we wanted or by excitement, boredom, dissatisfaction, and disillusionment when we do. When we move quickly from one desire to another, the illusion of desire-driven happiness can be maintained until we experience a major loss. By pausing to look more deeply into our hearts, though, we discover that the entire process was in the nature of suffering from the beginning.

Each of us has certain psychological defenses that block us from facing our suffering and its causes. Even as we read about the pervasive, subtle suffering that accompanies desire-driven living, these defenses may become activated, keeping us from analyzing our own experience. When we gain insights about ourselves through contemplation or meditation, such defenses can also cause us to forget those insights or to put off applying them in our lives. What's needed at such times is a profound sense of compassion for ourselves. Such compassion can keep us from turning our awareness away from the truth and can give us the energy required to break old habits, renouncing the deluded cravings in our hearts that cause our suffering.

INFANTILE LONGINGS

Buddhist teachers recognize that we all ordinarily believe that following our desire will bring us happiness. Lama Tsong Khapa wrote, "We follow desire in the hope of getting satisfaction, but following desire leads only to dissatisfaction.... Through following desire, the mind becomes rough and unpeaceful." Lama Zopa Rinpoche says,

> When you are told that you have to give up desire, you feel as if you are being told to sacrifice your happiness. You give up

desire, then you don't have any happiness and you're left with nothing. Just yourself. Your desire has been confiscated; you have been robbed of your happiness; and you are left there empty, like a deflated balloon. You feel as if you no longer have a heart in your body, as if you have lost your life. This is because you have not realized the shortcomings of desire.

We may have read a lot, we may have meditated or gone to therapy, we may have done all sorts of things in our lives, but we haven't yet analyzed how desire works or where our suffering comes from.

You don't need to be a genius at introspection to discover that desire leads to suffering. Most blues and country music songs are based on this simple observation. Attend any Alcoholics Anonymous meeting or talk with a divorce court judge, and you'll hear vivid stories about the suffering and intense disillusionment that can result from desire. Walking through any casino in Las Vegas at three-thirty or four in the morning also easily reveals the suffering that craving can bring. Freud often observed that human happiness did not "seem to be the purpose of the universe, and the possibilities of unhappiness lie more readily at hand." Although the odds are clearly stacked against us, we continue placing our bets on objects of desire hour after hour, night after night, hoping to hit it big.

Desire is always idealistic. By its very nature, desire idealizes objects. It ignores every fault and only, always, entirely wants to have the object. Desire draws us toward objects like sailors drawn toward the songs of sirens.

Freud and the various psychoanalytic thinkers who came after him did an excellent job of describing how the desires of infancy gradually give rise to just the sorts of ego desires described in Buddhist psychology. In infancy, the main object of the child's desire is the mother, particularly her breast. (Developmental psychologists note that the psychological role of the mother is most often played by the biological mother but that the primary caregiver who feeds the infant, provides cuddles and smiles, and wakes up to hold the baby at night may be some other adult in the infant's life. I use the term *mother* as most developmental psychologists do, to refer to the primary caregiver who plays this role.) An infant doesn't yet have a clear sense of the mother as a separate person. When he's cuddling or nursing, he focuses on the pleasurable sensations he's experiencing so that all sense of separation seems to fade away. This state of early pleasure is seen by the infant as a perfect, symbiotic union. Psychoanalysts note that from very early on, we're willing to deny or ignore aspects of reality in order to maintain the pleasurable fantasy of perfect, symbiotic union. The infant fantasizes that union with the object is perfect, and he splits off, suppresses, and denies anything that gets in the way of this fantasy. When he cannot have what he wants and these defenses fail, then suddenly things go from all-good to all-bad, and he cries, wriggles, screams, and throws tantrums. Frustrated desire turns to rage.

By the age of two or three, we begin to realize that we cannot simply seek a symbiotic union with our mothers whenever we wish; we can't always get what we want. For starters, the mother isn't always available. She has her own desires, interests, and other responsibilities. Also, there are other people—for example, our siblings or our father—who compete for her attention. The point here is that our infantile desires are inevitably frustrated, and so when our tantrums don't work, we learn to substitute other objects for the mother.

Let me give a simple example of how this works. A young girl likes sleeping beside her mother, cuddling up against her warm, soft body. Eventually, her parents insist that she sleep in her own bed. She initially gets quite upset and anxious. She may cry or throw a tantrum. If her parents hold their boundary, though, she'll likely choose a soft blanket or favorite toy to cuddle against. In her bed, alone, she feels the soft warmth of the blanket or stuffed animal, and in her psyche it comes to stand in for her mother. Now her anxiety and agitation decrease, but she suddenly finds herself very attached to this favorite toy. She cannot sleep without it. This is how the ego develops. When we cannot immediately get our desires met, the ego finds compromises or substitutions. Thus our overwhelming desire for the mother gets spread out to countless other objects.

Now, imagine this same girl a few decades later. When her husband goes out of town on a business trip or divorces her, suddenly she cannot sleep well at night. She feels terribly lonely, agitated, and even a bit afraid in her own home when she's alone late at night. All these years later, her fear and agitation are rooted in frustration of the infantile desire for symbiotic merger. Just as she initially sought a sense of comfort and safety in her mother and then in her toy, so also did she seek it in her husband. Somewhere along the way, unconsciously, she substituted her husband for the favorite toy of her childhood. When she cuddled beside him in bed at night, her desirous mind again fantasized a symbiotic union with him that made the world all-good. His absence leads to unfamiliar, regressive, bad feelings of fear and agitation. Her infantile, idealizing mind of desire was still there each night.

Freud once wrote that "a child sucking at his mother's breast has become the prototype of every relation of love. The finding of an object is in fact a refinding of it." From infancy on, each of us has been following desire in the eternal hope of escape from suffering into perfect union with the object. When Freud uses the term *love* here, he means the kind of desire that wants to totally possess and symbiotically fuse with the object. He is describing the same dynamic as the Buddha observed. Whether the object is a lover, a piece of chocolate cake, a new sports car, or a cappuccino, desire unconsciously idealizes the object and grasps in the hopes of finding a feeling of wholeness and lasting happiness in the object. All along, we've been splitting off, denying, suppressing, and repressing our awareness of suffering, fear, impermanence, and loss. At any moment, feeling vulnerable or frustrated can bring our suppressed, negative feelings into awareness.

Losing something we strongly desire can bring it all flooding back. And so we desperately look for other things to desire. As we walk around, our eyes flit from object to object, desiring and seeking more to desire, to keep the whole distracting, frustrating process continually in motion.

If you think deeply about Freud's observation, it's quite disturbing. As we go about our seemingly mature, adult lives, we're actually more like large infants, craving and grasping at things to keep misery and aloneness at bay. It's the same point that Lama Zopa Rinpoche was making—that we feel as though without continual desire we'd be like a deflated balloon, like a person with no heart in her chest.

This is something you can check out for yourself. In every moment of the day you can analyze how desire functions in your mind. When you lie down in bed at night, how do you relate to your partner or even to the bed itself? What role does your television play in your life? What of your car, your clothes, even your self-image as a competent person in your relationships and at work? Do you enjoy these things very purely, with a totally open, relaxed, joyful mind? Or, in some deep part of your mind, do you crave and grasp at these things as a child grasps at his blanket at night, to magically make you feel all right and to keep the darkness at bay?

This is the first, absolutely essential step for overcoming the mind of addictive desire—analyzing your own experiences with compassionate but ruthless honesty. It's very easy to deceive yourself. Freud made all these observations, and yet when people asked him about the psychology underlying his smoking of cigars, he said, "Sometimes a cigar is just a cigar." Later on, he died an incredibly painful death from cancer of the mouth. The cost of self-deception is always your own suffering.

As compassion entails the wish to free ourselves from suffering, we must see our suffering clearly in order to develop compassion. Only to the extent that we see our own suffering and its causes through eyes of compassion will we succeed in eliminating the causes of suffering from our minds.

BECOMING YOUR OWN THERAPIST

We can develop meaningful compassion for ourselves and achieve happiness by decreasing our craving and desire. People often assume that decreasing or letting go of our desire and craving necessarily means giving something up. It does not. Sometimes people think that adopting a specific lifestyle will help us attain happiness and freedom from craving. Unfortunately, there is no formulaic, outer solution to the problem of desire. Craving is a state of mind, and it can be dealt with only through understanding and training the mind itself. Lama Thubten Yeshe says, "If you do not investigate your own mind with introspective knowledge-wisdom, you will never see what's in there." He goes on to say,

> These days, people study and train to become psychologists. Lord Buddha's idea is that everybody should become a psychologist. Each of you should know your own mind; you should become your own psychologist. This is definitely possible; every human being has the ability to understand his or her own mind. When you understand your own mind, control follows naturally.

At the beginning, it can be useful just to become aware of the ongoing flow of thoughts, feelings, and images related to desire that are continually passing through the mind. At first, as you spend time looking within, you may not even realize the pervasive role that desire is playing. You'll notice your mind thinking about work, school, your bills, a phone call you forgot to make, getting the oil changed in your car, your lover, places you wish you could go, and so on. As you observe your own thought-flow, you'll see a continuous sequence of passing thoughts. Now, step back from that sequence and ask *why* you are thinking about most of the things that pass through your mind. When the Buddha stepped back and asked himself this question, his answer was "desire." When subsequent Buddhist practitioners over the centuries asked themselves this question, their honest answer also was "desire." When Freud sat in his consulting room and asked this same question regarding himself and his patients, he also answered "desire." Western psychologists since Freud's time have also noted that most of our mental and emotional life is driven by an underlying sense of wanting or desire. It's not enough, though, that these other people have answered the question through their analyses of their own minds and of the minds of people they knew well. You must answer it for yourself if the answer is to have an impact on you. You have to check up on the thoughts and images that run through your own mind and see whether or not they come from an underlying feeling of desire.

After you've spent some time observing the flow of thoughts and images in your mind and also checking on whether or not desire serves as the motivator for most of your thoughts, you can deepen your self-analysis by choosing a specific desire to look at more carefully. It's good to start with something that you desire often and toward which you feel a fairly deep, almost involuntary, compulsive craving. Typical desires of this type might be for money, praise, attention, sex, alcohol, drugs, or food. You may have many such desires, but it's useful to begin by focusing on just one.

Over the course of a number of days or weeks, spend some time carefully observing how your desire for the object functions. It's a good idea to take notes on what you discover. Does your desire come up most strongly when you're stressed or when you're upset about something? Is it strongest in the morning, during the day, or late at night? Is it typically associated with certain other feelings such as loneliness, insecurity, or feeling tired?

Also try to understand what your experience is like when you desire something but don't yet have it. Notice the sense of longing and feelings of emptiness, dissatisfaction, and incompleteness that go along with compulsive desire. It can be frightening to focus on these aspects of our experience, but if you look deeply you'll be able to see for yourself the almost infantile feelings of neediness I discussed earlier, which underlie feelings of craving.

It's also important to take note of what happens in your mind when you cannot have the thing you desire. This is the point at which desire often gives rise to other negative emotions such as frustration, anger, jealousy, rage, sorrow, grief, and hopelessness. Often we find the experience of not getting what we want so unpleasant that we quickly substitute another desire to distract us from our feelings of frustration. Be sure to take honest note also of how you act when you don't get what you want. On that infantile, often unconscious level discussed earlier, this is the point at which we throw a tantrum. Psychologically, as long as we follow desire, the capacity for tantrums will be present in our psyches. As an adult, how do you habitually act at such times? Do you pull away from others, get sullen, act gruff, or get rude and difficult? Do you lash out at others? Do you get depressed? Does the impulse arise to use unethical means to get your desires met? Most of the very worst of human behaviors—murders, rapes, incidents of child abuse, assaults, thefts, cheating, cruelty, and lies—come from following the uncontrolled mind of desire. Even if you ordinarily control yourself long before you engage in such behaviors, try to see if you can understand through introspection how other people come to such negative behaviors by way of desire. Such understanding can give rise to empathy for others who engage in these negative behaviors and also to humbly realizing that as long as we follow compulsive desires we're not as different from such people as we like to imagine. Such humility is important and can serve as a psychological protection against becoming like the many people we've heard about who appear psychologically or spiritually quite advanced but later are revealed to have engaged in unethical behaviors that harmed others.

After you have looked at your experience of unfulfilled desire, it's important also to analyze your experiences of getting what you want. It's not enough just to read about this subject or think about it a little bit. Most helpful is paying close attention to what happens in your mind at such times. On this subject again the findings of Buddhist meditators and Western psychologists are similar. Both note that getting what you want leads to a brief period of excitement or exhilaration followed quickly by a return to how you were feeling before. For example, if you're sitting at home eating a piece of cake, there's the momentary pleasure and enjoyment of flavors on your tongue. Then the piece of cake is gone, and you think, "What now?" So desire returns, and you have another piece. This can continue until you feel so full that your stomach aches. It's similar when making money. You make a deal, and it's exciting for a brief period. The excitement fades, and you want to make another deal and then another. The point here is not that getting what you want is bad; it's momentarily exciting or pleasurable. The problem is that it never grants any lasting, permanent happiness. Desire does not lead to satisfaction; it leads to more desire.

The cycle of desire giving rise again and again to more desire is one way of describing what Buddhists call *samsara*. Samsara isn't a place any more than nirvana is. When you live in the ongoing cycle of desire and dissatisfaction, that's samsara. When your mind is entirely free from desire, frustration, anger, and other afflictive emotions, that's nirvana.

Once you have deeply analyzed your own desire as I've just described, you can try one more thing. Focusing on the same desire you just carefully analyzed, move now to observing what happens when you try to relinquish or let go of your craving. Westerners and especially Americans have a very hard time with this. We get caught between materialistic desire for objects of the senses and a puritanical rejection of those same objects, but letting go of our craving has nothing to do with either of these.

When we set out to let go of our desire or craving, most of us try to let go of the object of our desire or craving. We deny ourselves those objects in the hope that this will bring us happiness. But if you deny yourself the object while still holding desire deep down in your heart, this can only bring more frustration. We try to let go of the object, but we don't let go of desire itself.

You have to check out the difference between these two approaches in your own experience. Go back to the desire you've been observing up to this point. First, try the typical approach of deciding that you'll just stop chasing after that object of desire—that you won't try to get that object anymore. What happens is that an inner conflict arises. The desire is still in your heart, wanting the object. But also present is the thought that you aren't going to seek the object. So you feel uncomfortable. Over time, this approach can lead to all kinds of problems. It can lead people to feel guilty and bad about themselves. It also can lead people to simply repress their desires. In such cases the desire is still there but the person is now unaware of it. Repressed desires show up in the form of new compulsions, give rise to other psychological symptoms, or eventually resurface with more power than before. This is not what the Buddha meant by renouncing desire, and it's certainly not compassion for yourself.

So the final step of this process of dealing with desire by being your own therapist involves focusing not on the object of desire but on the feeling of desire itself, and just letting go of that. Most of us have rarely if ever tried this. Don't repress the desire. See it there in your own mind with your full awareness, and recognize through your previous analysis that it only causes you suffering. Now view yourself through eyes of compassion, and decide to take care of yourself, lovingly, by freeing yourself from the cause of suffering. With your eyes wide open, just let it go. Doing this well requires some practice and skill. At first you won't get it right. It's a bit like hitting a really good tennis serve or taking a jump shot where the ball swishes the net. At the beginning you try to let go, and sometimes it goes wrong. But with practice you'll feel what it's like to get it just right.

When, in any given moment, you do let go of your desire, it leaves you with just the opposite feeling from what you expected. You experience neither deflation nor excitement. Desire ordinarily takes us out of the present moment, always hoping for something better. When you let go, you find yourself right there in the present moment, feeling whole and satisfied and relaxed. Without desire, there's no tension and no stress. You feel complete, simple, and open to the reality of your life.

People sometimes imagine that without desire there would be no enjoyment. The opposite is true. When you're caught up in craving, you never really enjoy anything very much because your mind is always pulling you on to the next desire and the next after that. When you let go of desire, then you're free to enjoy whatever is right in front of you.

One other thing you'll notice as you get better at letting go of desire is that this gives you much more mental space. Before, the ongoing flow of thoughts driven by desire took up most of your mental energy, leaving little time for meaningful or creative thought. William Blake once made this point when he said, "Were I to love money, I should lose all power of original thought; desire deadens the genius of man." We assume that without desire, we wouldn't have the energy to accomplish much. Again, I say that just the opposite is true. Compulsive desires take up much of our time, and the things we do accomplish under their power rarely lead to satisfaction for ourselves or others. By contrast, when we're free from egocentric desires, we're free to direct all our energy toward whatever we find most meaningful and important. In particular, we're then free to give our energy, creativity, and genius to works of compassion.

DEVELOPING CONTENTMENT

It should be clear by now that developing compassion for yourself by letting go of the causes of suffering in your own mind is not something that happens overnight. With even one specific desire, you need to analyze carefully how it functions and then practice letting it go again and again. Just because you successfully let it go once or twice doesn't mean that it won't come back. The mind does whatever it's in the habit of doing. If you have felt a certain desire over many years, then it will keep returning for a while. The good news is that as you get better at letting go of desires, the process gets easier. Before, you were habituating your mind to desire; now, you're habituating it to letting go and to satisfaction.

It's important to take note of and rejoice in each bit of progress we make along the way. Each moment we succeed in letting go of a desire is a step in the direction of contentment and freedom from suffering. In this sense, a moment in which we let go of desire is more meaningful than one in which we gain some award, wealth, or other object of desire. By taking note of such moments, we can encourage ourselves to continue the inner journey to happiness.

As even one compulsive desire decreases, we give ourselves that much more freedom from suffering. I recall a time when my mother, along with many others, lost a good deal of her savings because of dishonest accounting processes in a large investment company. At the time, she was studying just this subject of letting go of desire. One man who lost his money committed suicide. Another woman got so stressed out and upset that her immune system became compromised, leading to a chronic illness. Now, my mother certainly hadn't given up all her desires or concerns about financial security, but gaining some understanding about letting go of desire allowed her to deal with the loss calmly. She had to change her lifestyle, but these changes did not upset her as she went on enjoying her life in the face of her loss.

Once you understand how to let go of one or two desires, working with other desires becomes easier, as long as you keep up your efforts. A realistic approach is to make gradual progress over the years. As new desires arise, you practice analyzing them and letting them go. Even years later, old cravings sometimes will resurface. At such times, feeling upset or guilty about it certainly won't help. Instead, the idea is to approach your own life and your own mind in a wise and compassionate way, again making efforts to let go of the causes of suffering.

When you decide how to relate to objects of desire, be both compassionate and practical. An alcoholic who lives next door to a bar or has beer and whisky around the house probably will find progress more difficult. Someone with no interest in alcohol will experience no problem with these things. Similarly, someone trying to overcome a powerful craving for sweets might find that having lots of cake and cookies around presents a problem. Over the long run, it's important to know your own tendencies and to treat yourself kindly, putting yourself in situations that make freedom and contentment easier to attain.

Buddhism, like many other religions, has a tradition of periodically offering retreats. Part of the benefit of a retreat is that, in giving you the opportunity to get away from your usual surroundings, you may see the causes and effects of your desires more clearly. When we're always surrounded by the objects that we compulsively desire, we may not even realize some of the ways that our attachment and grasping are causing suffering for us. Many people from a wide range of religious traditions have noted that taking periodic breaks from these objects allows for deeper introspection, which can be helpful in the long-term process of decreasing our compulsive desires and developing happiness.

I also want to mention briefly the role that monasticism plays in dealing with desire. Psychologically speaking, for those who are highly motivated to overcome their desires in order to attain liberation, monastic vows can be a very useful tool in helping them become aware of their desires and make more rapid progress in letting go. The Buddha said clearly that a main purpose for establishing his monastic communities was to provide situations that made attaining freedom from desire most readily possible for his students. More generally, I believe that true monastic renunciates provide a meaningful example to everyone of the contentment and happiness that can come from renouncing desire. You'll recall that Siddhartha began his quest for enlightenment after his discussion with a wandering renunciate. Before meeting this renunciate, Siddhartha had seen the suffering that comes from desire, but he had not yet seen an alternative to desire-driven living. The Buddhist tradition says that Buddhism flourishes only in those nations or regions in which the monastic community exists. This means not that only monastics can practice Buddhism, but that all of us need living examples of people who have found contentment by renouncing desire. We need people like the Dalai Lama, Mother Teresa, or Gandhi to provide examples of a happiness that transcends the normal processes of desire and grasping. In them we glimpse our own potential for such happiness.

As we strive to develop compassion for ourselves, it's important to avoid making "letting go of desire" or "developing compassion for yourself" into new objects of compulsive desire. Becoming obsessive about quickly seeing big results from our efforts is a sign that deluded desire rather than compassion is driving our efforts. Real progress derives from honest introspection, and we cannot analyze our minds carefully when we're hurried. Transforming our hearts is a gradual, organic process, and successfully cultivating compassion for ourselves necessitates a mature and steady approach. If we catch ourselves using our renunciation as a way to feel arrogantly separate from and superior to others, it is a bad sign that compulsive desire is running our practice. Contentment is not like a currency that you can obtain through grasping and hoarding. If we catch ourselves using ideas about our own purity, goodness, or virtue as ways of distancing ourselves from others, we should recognize that we've turned these ideas into objects of deluded desire. Recognizing that we're again caught in a cycle of suffering, we should practice compassion for ourselves by letting go of such grasping.

Even after we have begun making progress in abandoning desires that cause us suffering, we may feel discouraged by the challenges of analyzing and letting go of each of our many desires, one after another. Fortunately, Buddhist practitioners have found that there are additional methods for discovering more moments of genuine contentment free of craving. One of the most powerful means for making progress in letting go of our desires in order to free ourselves from the cycle of suffering is contemplating impermanence. The contemplation of impermanence undermines the psychology of compulsive desire, naturally allowing us to let go of many desires at the same time. If facing impermanence and loss at first seems unpleasant, practice quickly reveals that it is an effective way of progressing in the practice of compassion for ourselves. Tibetan teachers say, "Reflection on impermanence yields inconceivable benefits," including decreasing our desires, giving us great energy for living well, helping us focus on living a loving life, and serving as a direct antidote to our suffering. So in the next chapter I address using the contemplation of impermanence to develop compassion for ourselves and others.

FIVE

MOURNING THE LIVING

*Time gives us a whirl. We keep waking from a dream we can't re-
call, looking around in surprise, and lapsing back for years on end.
All I want to do is stay awake, keep my head up, prop my eyes
open, with toothpicks, with trees.*
                                              —Annie Dillard

E very meeting will end in parting, every accumulation will be
dispersed eventually, and every birth will end in death. In any
given moment, everything inside of and around us is changing.
Our thoughts and feelings flow on in an unceasing stream of consciousness. The air invisibly swirls around us and rushes into and out
of our chests. Subatomic forces interact, electrons spin, molecules col-
lide, and thousands of neurons fire in each blink of our eyes. As our
planet spins around a sun that circles the center of a galaxy that flies
away from other galaxies, our blood keeps rushing through our veins
for as long as our hearts keep on pumping.

Direct observation and analysis reveal a world that is made up of
utterly impermanent, infinitely complex, interdependent events. And
yet, as we eat our breakfast, the fork feels solid, and we ourselves feel
solid. We assume that we exist in a certain way—separate, solid,

permanent, and real. We imagine that we will continue to exist in this way, that we will not die today. We assume that we will not die now.

Believing we exist as solid, separate, permanent entities is a huge obstacle to compassion. When we grasp strongly at this illusion, more and more compulsive desires arise. As we try to block out awareness of our own fragility and of the reality of impermanence, we make huge efforts to maintain a self-image that includes having status, power, and possessions, as though they magically could make us invulnerable. There is no possession or power that can protect us from parting, separation, or death. Desires driven by the underlying fear of loss and death have no end; ultimately they cannot succeed. So the illusion of a solid, permanent entity keeps us from letting go of desire and from progressing in developing compassion for ourselves. By blocking our awareness of others' suffering and by making us feel separate and disconnected from the world around us, this illusion also blocks us from developing love and compassion for others.

I want to be clear that in bringing up the illusion of our existing as solid, permanent entities, I'm not discussing anything terribly subtle or philosophical. In Buddhist philosophy you can find beautifully subtle analyses of the philosophical view of emptiness, which are designed to help meditators become free from a subtle wrong view serving as the basis for all delusions and negative emotions. But here I'm discussing something much more basic. Any person sitting at a breakfast table can look within to find and challenge the illusion of solid permanence that I'm discussing. On any given morning, we can reflect that this may be the last day of our lives or of the lives of those we love. We can see how our minds resist accepting this truth, and we can work through that resistance, resolving to spend this precious day well.

We may imagine that recognizing impermanence will lead to a sense of detachment from others and from life in general. We assume that facing death and loss will lead us to feel down or hopeless. The

Buddha used to send his disciples off to charnel grounds to meditate. This may sound terrifying or depressing to us. The Buddha found that contemplating impermanence cuts through our attachments without leading to detachment; recognizing life's fragility can wake us up, inspiring us to let go of petty desires and to give each moment wholly over to what's most essential. The ego defends against awareness of impermanence; cultivating such awareness can lead us beyond the ego's boundaries and defenses to a deeper and more satisfying level of connection with life and with others.

If we do not face impermanence directly, then we will not remember what's most important in life, and even if we do remember occasionally, we won't be able to live our lives genuinely, in accord with our deep values. Our ego desires and defenses will get in the way, blocking us. Thoreau once wrote, "I went to the woods because I wished to live deliberately, to front only the essential facts of life, and see if I could not learn what it had to teach, and not, when I came to die, discover that I had not lived." If you avoid facing death in a visceral and meaningful way, then you also run the very real risk of missing out on life itself. You run the risk of spending your whole life deceived, caught up in the prison of the ego's fears and desires without even knowing it. If you do not confront the truth now, the terrible regret and ego-driven terror that will arise when you actually face death will be of no use; at that time it will be too late. Realizing this, Thoreau literally left his home and went into the woods to face the essentials of life and death. To live a meaningful life, each of us must step outside the familiar, confining walls of ego defenses and enter our own wilderness, our own charnel ground, to face honestly the truth of impermanence and loss. In the strange cemetery of imagination, mourning ourselves, we suddenly stumble upon what's most essential. Facing loss, we find love.

AVOIDING AWARENESS

Years ago, when I was studying at Kopan Monastery in Nepal, Geshe Lama Lhundrup, the abbot of the monastery, was giving a teaching and mentioned that one could not realize *bodhichitta,* the most exalted state of compassion described in Buddhism, without first having realized genuinely the truth of impermanence. I was a bit shocked when he said this. While I was strongly interested in compassion and bodhichitta, I found the idea of contemplating death, loss, mourning, and impermanence unpleasant. The truth of impermanence seemed self-evident and, therefore, a boring subject for contemplation. It also seemed uncomfortable to spend time thinking about the inevitability of losing everything and everyone I cared about. I asked Lama Lhundrup if I had heard him correctly. He smiled benevolently and said, "Yes, dear, I'm sorry. Without realizing impermanence, you cannot become a bodhisattva."

He was pointing out a fundamental truth, which is that the more deeply we can face the truth about impermanence and suffering, integrating our understanding of these subjects into our lives and personalities, the more deeply compassionate, content, and joyful we'll become over time. Seeing how others continually change helps us let go of our rigid projections about them, and recognizing how they suffer from loss and impermanence helps us develop compassion. Reflecting on our own impermanence helps us stop following the dissatisfied mind of desire whose impulses are seen as without meaning in the face of death. When we don't face impermanence and death, our lives become busy, complicated, and stressful. When we do face them, our lives become simpler and more full of meaning. Our fear of or aversion to facing these subjects is a trick that the mind plays on itself, which keeps us caught in the trap of self-centered, compulsive, neurotic egotism. The illusion that we exist as solid, permanent entities is in fact a trap or prison for our hearts; facing the truth about impermanence is the doorway out.

In order to understand why facing the truth about impermanence helps us be content and compassionate, we must return briefly to our discussion of how the ego and the personality form. From the discussion in the previous chapter, you recall that when children don't get what they want they start finding other things to stand in for the original objects of their desire. For example, the girl who cannot have her mother beside her at night finds a teddy bear or a blanket that stands in for the mother and soothes her.

If we could, we'd always have just what we desire, and we'd try continually to escape from suffering by grasping at the illusory fantasy of perfect, symbiotic union with the objects of our desire. Object relations analysts say that the infant's experience of losing the earliest, fantasized, perfect union with the mother is almost unbearable, giving rise to terror and rage. One child analyst writes, "Awareness of bodily separateness [from the mother] is the heartbreak at the centre of all human existence." The young child who desires contact with his mother when she isn't available doesn't yet have the ability to use memory, reason, and imagination to help deal with the situation. The infant cannot yet think, *Oh, I've been through this before; Mom will come back soon.* He is wholly and terribly in the present moment, which he finds unbearable. Unable yet to realize that an object that isn't present can still exist, the infant experiences absence as annihilation or death. This feeling of separateness and need without any hope is heartbreaking, overwhelming, and terrifying.

This terribly difficult but inevitable experience of frustrated desire is in fact positive for the child's development. Of course, the child cannot remain indefinitely in the illusion of symbiotic union. Child psychiatrist and object relations analyst D. W. Winnicott describes the process that begins with these early experiences of loss as "dis-illusionment." The child's earliest illusions are essentially narcissistic and include fantasies of omnipotent control, grandiose self-importance, perfect symbiosis, and unlimited sensory pleasure. Experiences of frustration are positive in that they cause the child to begin modifying such fantasies, bringing her expectations more in line with reality. They are also positive in that they pressure the child to begin developing healthy coping skills. Melanie Klein, another object relations analyst, says, "The primordial fear of being annihilated forces the ego into action and engenders the first defenses." When the child cannot readily get what she wants, she learns to substitute thoughts for sensory experiences. When she cannot be held by her mother, she learns to soothe herself by remembering being held by her mother. She learns to delay gratification by waiting, she starts using language to ask for what she wants, and she develops complex problem-solving skills to get her needs met more effectively. She also learns how to play and use her imagination, which is extremely important because now she need not rely only on the outside world; she develops a world of inner ideas, images, and resources that she can turn to when faced with difficulties. These early experiences of frustration serve as an impetus for developing the many positive capacities of the human ego, which include rational thought, self-control, use of language, playfulness, problem solving by experimenting with the outside world, and use of imagination.

Forming a healthy ego is an important accomplishment. Not only does it allow us to control ourselves, to understand social realities, and to imagine, it also allows us to understand others' feelings, empathizing with and developing compassion for them. The Tibetan Buddhist tradition, which holds that beings can be reborn in many different realms of existence, says that a human rebirth grants the most useful opportunity for developing the mind in positive directions. The unique capacities of the human ego as described by psychoanalysts make up much of the reason for this special opportunity. Our abilities to control ourselves, imagine, think rationally, and speak give us a special capacity for introspection and self-transformation that any being without a healthy human ego lacks. Tibetan teachers also note that as humans we have just the right mix of happiness and suffering—and mix of stability and loss—to be able to develop compassion.

The healthy ego is an important accomplishment, but the ego's way of relating to the world is still by its nature ultimately unsatisfactory and frustrating. The ego uses its positive capacities mainly to pursue goals driven by desire. At the same time, it strives to block out awareness of mortality, loss, and impermanence. At the core of the ego is the fear of annihilation, loss, and death that drove the ego into existence in the first place. Jung, who was well aware of the positive aspects of the healthy ego, said, "Fear of self-sacrifice lurks deep in every ego." He noted that the ego separates and insulates itself from the dynamic world of change and instinct "only partially, for the sake of a more or less illusory freedom" and that it "represents nothing final."

We were not able to mourn our earliest losses and heartbreaks. Our just-forming egos could not yet make sense of such experiences. Our terror and fear were too overwhelming to be digested or understood. So, out of the fragmented, confusing bits of our infantile experiences of loss, we created a defense, a wall, a bulwark against the awareness of suffering, impermanence, and loss. Freud likens this part of us, which serves to block out awareness, to a "special envelope or membrane resistant to stimuli," describing it as a part of us that died in reaction to early experiences of loss. For the young child, this calcified, deadened part of the psyche served as a protection against getting overwhelmed; it allowed the child to develop. In the adult, it becomes an obstacle to joy, love, and compassion.

This calcification blocks some of our awareness and limits our understanding of reality. It is made up mainly of the illusion of our existing as a solid, permanent entity that I mentioned earlier. The solid, permanent self-image, which is there with us at the breakfast table and as we go about our day's activities, then, is not our true identity. It's a mere calcification, a stony dead zone in the mind. By contemplating impermanence and death, we can wear away this dead zone, retaining all of the ego's positive capacities while eliminating this aspect of the ego, which keeps us from seeing things realistically and keeps us from loving wholeheartedly.

I once spent a couple of days with a gem cutter, watching him cut, grind, and polish precious stones. He began with rocks that looked not very precious to my untrained eye. He held them repeatedly to fast-spinning grinding wheels topped with diamond dust, which produced a high-pitched sound that was unpleasant, but after a time he'd come away with beautifully faceted, precious gems. This is what it's like contemplating impermanence. We begin with our rough and stony egos, holding them up against the diamond wheel of awareness of death and impermanence. You'll see as we go through some of these contemplations that the experience of the ego's calcifications grinding against such awareness can be unpleasant. If we stick with the process, though, eventually we will reveal our own precious, jewel-like capacity for joy, meaning, and love. The end result is more than worth the unpleasantness along the way. Through such grinding, we modify our egos, uncovering capacities in ourselves that our untrained eyes had not been able to see.

MOURNING YOURSELF

Freud and the analysts who came after him were not particularly interested in moving beyond the ego's way of relating to the world. Jung did have some interest in this subject. For example, he noted that many cultures have initiation rites designed to change how the ego functions. In the process of an initiation, participants often face considerable challenges, danger, and even a symbolic death and rebirth. The idea is to bring up the ego's core fears in order to change the participant's ego and self-image. In some cultures, a series of initiations and related spiritual experiences over the course of years can help the ego emerge gradually from its calcifications. The most important thing you can do to start such a process of emergence is to spend time consciously facing and working through your feelings about impermanence and death.

The Buddha sent his disciples to sit in the charnel grounds of India in order to face their own mortality by watching bodies being burned or simply rotting. As they looked at these corpses, they would think about how they themselves and all the people around them soon would be corpses also. The first Dalai Lama upheld this ancient Buddhist tradition in Tibet by doing a meditation retreat beside a large stone where "sky burial" was practiced. In Tibet the cold made burial difficult, and the altitude made firewood too precious to use regularly for cremations. So, much as some Eskimos offered their dead on the tundra to the wolves, Tibetans offered corpses to the vultures as a final act of generosity on behalf of the dead. The first Dalai Lama sat right next to the sky burial stone, watching bodies as they were cut up and eaten. All the while, he thought about how he too would soon suffer a similar fate.

This retreat on impermanence clearly had a powerful impact on him. One could say that as the first Dalai Lama watched these sky burials, he was transforming his own ego, crushing his illusions of solid permanence to dust and then giving his whole self over to compassion. There is a well-known Tibetan practice called *Chod* in which you imagine cutting up your body as the corpses are cut for sky burial. Next, you imagine transforming the shreds of your former body into nectar that grants all beings' wishes. Part of the symbolism of this practice involves sacrificing the old ego with its many desires and defenses, thereby being reborn to a new identity in which the positive capacities of the old ego are retained but its fear and desire abandoned and replaced by wisdom and blissful compassion.

Over the years that followed this retreat, the first Dalai Lama became one of the most renowned and energetic masters of compassion in all of Central Asia. Years later, many people requested that he build a monastery where his teachings could be preserved and transmitted. Though he'd done many retreats, he chose this particular site for his monastery. He built Tashi Lhunpo there, and it became one of the greatest monastic universities in Tibetan history. He placed his own teaching throne just a few feet from the stone slab beside which he once had done retreat. I imagine that he used that stone as a reminder of impermanence and of the time when he ground away his ego's illusions.

In our modern, Western culture, there are no charnel grounds or sky burial stones. Culturally, we are insulated from many of the realities of impermanence and death. Our general lack of exposure to the reality of death reinforces the ego's natural defenses against awareness. The media tends either to avoid the issue of death or to present a barrage of gory images intended to excite and distract rather than deeply move us. Even the funeral industry uses makeup and paint to create an illusion that hides the real face of death. Individually and culturally, if we allow ourselves to remain insulated from the awareness of death and impermanence, we will be unable to discover much of what's best in us.

We do not need to visit an actual charnel ground or sky burial site to begin grinding away the calcifications of our egos. We can proceed by actively directing our awareness to the realities of impermanence and death. I will present a few exercises that allow us to use our reason and imagination to begin wearing down our illusions. By engaging in such exercises, we use positive aspects of our egos to overcome the ego's prisonlike illusions of permanence, thereby granting ourselves greater freedom and joy.

If you haven't tried such exercises before, they may sound somewhat morbid at first. You may find yourself wanting to turn away from the experience of the ego's illusions being ground down. But once you engage in them for a while, you'll start seeing for yourself how they affect your mind and your life in positive ways; you'll begin glimpsing the jewel beneath the ego's calcifications.

First, I'll present a fairly simple imaginative exercise that I often use with patients in therapy. It's best to begin by sitting or lying down comfortably and focusing on your breathing for a few moments to calm your mind. Next, imagine yourself at some time in the future. You can imagine yourself a few hours in the future or many decades from today. You can imagine yourself at different ages each time you do the exercise, but once you choose an age, stick with it for the length of that run through the exercise. Imagine what you'll look like then. Imagine your face, your hands, and your clothes. Imagine what you might be doing at that time and who you might be interacting with. Take some time with this, and be specific. The more clearly and deeply you imagine, the more effective the exercise will be.

Next, imagine your own death. Choose just one method of dying for this run through the exercise, and then you can imagine other methods as you do the exercise again and again. Sometimes imagine quick deaths by way of heart attack, car accident, war, murder, and the like. Other times, go through the process of imagining a slow, drawn-out death by way of AIDS, cancer, Alzheimer's, emphysema, debilitating strokes, and the like. Again, be as detailed and specific as you can in imagining the process of dying. Imagine experiencing the physical pain that usually comes with death and also the pain of parting from everyone and everything you care about.

When you begin engaging in this exercise, you may not feel much. This is simply because your ego defenses are strongly blocking your feelings. Don't imagine that an initial lack of feeling indicates you've transcended the fear of death. Such lack of feeling suggests rather that the fear of impermanence and death at the core of your ego is so strong that you cannot yet handle facing it. If this is the case, I advise stepping back from death and imagining losing something smaller than your life.

Begin by imagining having your car stolen, losing your job, losing your life savings, or having your house burn down. You also may begin by imagining losing someone you love. For the purposes of grinding away at your illusions of solid permanence, it can be useful to begin by imagining unexpectedly losing your eyesight, your hearing, or the use of your legs. Since any one of these losses is much, much smaller than the loss we experience at death, more highly defended people can begin to access the fears at the core of the ego by starting with smaller losses and building up to imagining death. Of course, when we die we lose all of these things and everything else, all at once.

It's often said that at the end of our lives, we look back and take stock of how we lived. This is the final step of this contemplation. From the perspective of the end of your life, imagine looking back. Ask yourself what matters from that perspective. Notice how many of the things that you usually think are important appear as totally empty and meaningless from that vantage point. Again and again, with as much sincerity as you can muster, ask yourself what matters, what is essential in the face of death.

Of course, this exercise is not uniquely Buddhist. Religious practitioners from many traditions have engaged in such imaginal exercises. For example, during the eighteenth century, the European mystic Rabbi Nahman told his students that he had "several times pictured [his own] death; it was so vivid as though he were really dead, tasting the very taste of death." He pictured the scene of his death so clearly that he could smell the terrible smells, hear the weeping, and almost feel his very spirit leaving his body. With the intense feelings that this brought up, he would pray for the power of bravery and love to be able to sacrifice himself for the welfare of others.

I have done this exercise with many different people in therapy and in meditation classes. I cannot recall a single person who didn't, in his or her own way, respond that love, kindness, and compassion were what mattered most in the face of death. Researchers on near-death experiences also say that people who've had such experiences consistently report a greater commitment to being loving. It's often surprising how ordinary people respond to the most horrible tragedies with an almost shockingly altruistic heroism. There is a great deal of evidence to support the Buddhist psychological view that facing the reality of death is an essential means of developing real, spontaneous compassion.

I recall one of my patients, a high-powered corporate consultant, who reacted to this exercise in a way that's not at all unusual. In his home office, he displayed a number of awards and trophies from his days as a college athlete and also from his many professional achievements. Within a week of doing this exercise, he took them all down, replacing them with pictures of his loved ones. He told me, "I've always been so good at making business plans. This week, for the first time, I sat down and began making plans on how to show my love better to my family. All the rest doesn't really matter."

His awards and trophies had been reflections of his ego's desires. They had symbolized his attempts to stave off frightening feelings by building up his underlying feeling of being solid, permanent, and powerful. When doing this exercise broke through part of his defenses, he realized that he could let go of part of this fear-driven self-image, abandoning it in favor of love.

I MAY DIE TODAY

Two variations on this exercise are so psychologically useful that I'd like to share them as well. Again, while there's nothing uniquely Buddhist about these exercises, they are derived from the Tibetan Buddhist tradition. Both of these exercises are simple, direct methods for breaking through ego defenses related to the idea of existing as a solid, permanent entity.

For the first method, you simply place a watch or clock with a second hand in front of you on a table. Choose in advance a certain length of time to devote to the exercise. If you don't, then your ego may try to use concerns over the length of the exercise as a distraction. Now, watch the second hand as it clicks along. Recall that it is absolutely, positively certain that with each click of that second hand, you are moving closer to your death. You have a limited number of moments left, and they are continually passing by like water falling in a waterfall. There's nothing that you can do to stop this. The time left to you is pouring away like water seeping out from your cupped fingers. Your time is literally running out. With each ticking of that second hand, recall that your life is heading unalterably for its end, and repeatedly ask yourself what matters. Don't settle for some pat, intellectual answer. Just sit with the question of what matters, allowing the question to sink more and more deeply into your psyche with each passing second. If your mind drifts away to some other topic, just bring it back to watching the second hand, noticing your life slipping away, and asking what matters. When the predetermined length of time is finished, resolve to spend wisely the rest of the incredibly precious seconds that remain to you.

While this exercise is similar to the previous one, it cuts more sharply against the ego's defenses. In the previous exercise, we are facing death and mortality, but we still can hold to the feeling that it is a ways off. Deep down, we can still hold onto some feeling of solidity and permanence. This exercise pressures us to let go of that feeling from second to second. In the beginning, doing this exercise is likely to feel disturbing. That's just a sign that you're challenging your ego's defenses. If you keep on engaging in the practice over a number of weeks or months, it gradually will have the effect of teaching you to live more and more of your moments free from confining aspects of the ego.

Another method that can be very powerful is done as soon as possible after waking up in the morning. Upon awakening, think to yourself, *How wonderful that I'm still alive; my life is so fragile, and I definitely could have died last night, so it's really wonderful that I woke up and am still here.* Recall the fact that other people in the world did die last night, but you've managed to stay alive for the time being. Also recall that there are so many different factors that easily and quickly can cause your death. So many people die each day. Some are ill and others are healthy, some are old and others are young, but they all die just the same. A car wreck, a heart attack, a stroke, a murder, an accident, or a terrorist attack could take your life today easily. For a few moments, viscerally imagine yourself dying later on today. Think as follows: *It's absolutely true that I may die today, and there's nothing at all that I can do about that fact; therefore, I'm going to live this day as though it may be my last.* Recognizing that today literally may be the last day of your life, decide how you're going to spend this day. Think about what's important to do today, about how you want to go about the activities of your life today, and about how you want to relate to the other people you'll see. End the exercise by strongly resolving to spend your day wisely.

Doing such a contemplation right after waking up can be particularly powerful in granting us glimpses of the jewel-like capacities that usually lie hidden within the ego's calcifications. Ordinarily, when we're asleep the ego at least partially takes a break. Our feeling of existing as a solid, permanent entity is not entirely absent in our dreams, but it is weakened somewhat as we sleep. When we wake up, the ego quickly starts working again. Our solid self-image returns, and our ego starts planning out our day in accord with the desires that continually drive it. As one Tibetan meditator who practiced this last technique wrote, "If you do not meditate on impermanence in the early morning, by midday you will have many desires." By engaging in this exercise, we can intervene before the ego's defenses are fully in place for the day. By remembering the truth about impermanence upon awakening, we challenge the illusory image of our solid, permanent self. Right there in bed in the morning, while this image is in the process of solidifying for the day, we can recognize it for the illusion that it is.

Before this illusion takes control of our day, organizing it around desire, we can intervene. We can replace the illusory image of permanence with a realistic self-image that understands impermanence and focuses on what's most essential.

In the moments when we think about how we may die today, we are letting go of the fears that hide near the core of the ego. Recall that our calcifications were born of overwhelming fear in childhood. Ordinarily, we live with an underlying sense of fear that has been part of the ego since it began. By consciously breaking through our rocky illusions of solid permanence, we start the day by facing our fears and resolving to live fearlessly. Ordinarily, we live driven by compulsive desires, but here we resolve to live consciously with awareness and compassion. Ordinarily, we live our days with an unconscious belief that we're permanent, in control, and terribly important. Here, we begin the day with an awareness that we're a fragile piece of an ever-changing network of interdependent relationships. We begin the day by letting go of rigidity and desire, opening ourselves up to life, to intimacy, and to love.

If you try using this method for a period of time, it will get easier to generate the feelings described upon awakening. As the momentum of your positive awareness grows, you may find yourself starting to wake up some days like Scrooge on Christmas morning after his dream-vision of his own death, when he clasped his own chest, shouted with joy at finding himself alive, and leaped up from bed to begin sharing all that he had and all that he was with others. This is the kind of energy that Thoreau showed for life while living in the woods and that Tibetan lamas show for their lives lived in the face of impermanence. Normally we don't wake up with that kind of energy and joy because we haven't recognized the preciousness of each of our days—even of each of our seconds. If we spend time engaging in these exercises, facing our own impermanence, then such recognition will dawn more and more, and we'll find ourselves approaching each day with compassionate vitality.

ALCHEMICAL TRANSFORMATION

I sometimes describe the process of using these methods to viscerally face your own impermanence and mortality as "mourning yourself." Psychologically, mourning involves withdrawing the energy that we previously had invested in an object through desire and grasping. Freud once wrote that the process of mourning demands "that all libido shall be withdrawn from its attachments to that object." Hannah Segal, an object relations analyst, says, "A successful renunciation [of an object of attachment] can only happen through a process of mourning."

We mourn someone or something only when we've been attached to it. Many people die every day and we don't mourn them. If you don't have any desire, grasping, or attachment for someone, then you may feel sad, sympathetic, or concerned when they're gone, but you won't truly mourn them.

The word *attachment* has different connotations in Buddhist literature from those it has in Western psychological research. When Buddhists speak of attachment, they're referring to a state in which we've directed our desire again and again to the same object so that we've become deeply habituated to craving and grasping at that object. Based in deluded desire, such attachment is seen in Buddhism as a direct cause of suffering. Western psychologists have done a good deal of research on how children become attached to their parents and also on how people become attached to each other in families, marriages, and friendships. Western researchers don't define attachment as a state of mind; instead they define it behaviorally as a strong disposition to "seek proximity to and contact with a specific figure and to do so in certain situations, . . . [such as when one is] frightened, tired, or ill." Researchers suggest that such attachment in children to their parents or between family members is a cause of good mental health and of happiness. So, superficially we may assume that Buddhism and Western researchers have opposing views on this subject. However, a careful reading of the Western researchers reveals that the emotional state underlying the attachment they speak of is often loving affection rather than desire-driven attachment.

What Western research refers to as attachment is actually a mixture of desire and loving affection. When we lose someone or something we've been attached to, we must withdraw our desire energy. However, our loving affection remains. Mourning is best understood as a process of withdrawing our desire-driven attachment and projections until all that's left is our appreciation and love for the one who is gone. In mourning, we burn off our desire energy, distilling the pure, loving affection from our attachments.

We mourn not only people but also sometimes the roles we've played or the images of ourselves that we've held on to. We often invest a lot of our desire energy in one self-image or another, becoming very attached to it. Then, when circumstances force us to disidentify from that image, we go through a process of mourning it. For example, when circumstances force a young person to first take on the responsibilities of adulthood, she may find herself mourning the loss of her childhood, which means she's mourning the image of herself as young and carefree. Similarly, when someone retires from a job that he's had for many years, he often finds himself mourning the loss of the role he played for all that time. The feelings of sadness, loss, and emptiness that come up at such times are similar to the feelings we have when we've lost a loved one. In either case, we're having to let go of something to which we were very attached.

By repeatedly engaging in these methods of facing your own impermanence, you begin mourning the image of yourself as a solid, permanent entity. This image is so intimately tied up with the ego that you could say that someone who engages in these methods consistently goes through a process of mourning her own ego. To the extent that you've mourned the image of yourself as solid and permanent, you become free to develop a more flexible and realistic self-image.

Such mourning also frees up a great deal of energy. As long as you remain attached to your solid, permanent self-image, lots of your psychological energy is spent holding on to and defending that illusion. When you let go of the illusion, all that energy gets freed up, and it becomes available to flow in other, more positive directions. Through mourning ourselves, we pull back energy we unconsciously and habitually had dedicated to attachment, freeing it up to be consciously redirected to love and compassion.

When it comes to mourning other people—to withdrawing our desire energy and distilling the pure love from our attachment to them—we usually do this only when circumstances force us to. For example, if someone we're very attached to dies or decides to break up with us or cut us out of her or his life, then that person is no longer available to fulfill our desires. Our desire energy still tends to flow toward her, but she isn't there. We smile across the table and feel pain at seeing an empty chair; we lift the phone to call him only to realize he isn't there; we reach out across the bed in the night and feel empty as we find only an empty space beside us. This is the essence of the terribly painful process of mourning someone we've lost. We make thousands of small gestures driven by our desire for the other, and each time we find that the other is not there. Each unreciprocated gesture and unshared moment makes us feel our loss again. We continue smiling, reaching out, and turning toward no one; each time our frustrated desire tears at our ego until, very slowly, we stop reaching and looking for someone who is not there. Slowly, the energy that flowed out toward that other person is drawn back. When mourning goes well, our desire and grasping for the person eventually subside, leaving behind appreciation for who the person was, gratitude for what that person gave us, and our genuine love for him or her.

From the perspective of the ego, the painful process of loss and mourning is entirely negative. It frustrates our desires and harms our image of things existing as solid, permanent entities. When people are deep in the mourning process, they often say things like, "I'm falling apart," "I feel like I'm going crazy," "Nothing seems real to me anymore," or "I've totally lost my mind." What has happened is that the ego has fallen apart. The worldview of the ego has been revealed as an illusion. Living from her ego, the mourner unconsciously but deeply believed that things exist solidly and permanently, that those who are here today will be here tomorrow, that she had control over what happened next in her life, and that by following her desire for the other she could find some lasting happiness. The loss of someone we're deeply attached to tears the ground out from under the ego.

Though this experience is entirely negative from the perspective of the ego, it presents an opportunity for someone striving to transform himself and cultivate compassion. Years ago, I knew a lama named Geshe Lama Kunchok. He'd lived for many years in caves, high up in the Himalayas. One day he was asked to share his life story with a group of us Westerners. He sat down, and, rather than sharing any details about his personal life, he started talking about a rare Buddhist teaching about preferring losing things to getting them, preferring insults to praise, and preferring all sorts of difficult circumstances to comfortable ones. He said that he'd tried to live his life in accord with this specific teaching. He was a very bright, simple, direct person who could laugh harder than almost anyone I've ever met. When he told his life story in this way, some people just looked at him, a bit confused, apparently uncomfortable with the idea of enjoying misfortune. For someone committed to deconstructing and transforming the ego in order to live more compassionately, difficult circumstances present a unique opportunity. To someone like Geshe Lama Kunchok, petty comforts are distractions to soothe our infantile desires. By contrast, losses are valued because they undermine the illusion of solid permanence, insults are valued because they strike at the ego's grandiosity, and hardships in the service of others are cherished as chances to supplant narcissism with compassion. For someone grinding away at the ego's calcifications, such life experiences become touches against the diamond wheel of truth, revealing the gem in one's own heart.

Suffering or losing things we desire is not inherently beneficial. If we don't know how to use experiences of loss skillfully, then they may leave us worse off than before. As a psychologist, I often meet with people who are psychologically damaged from dealing unskillfully with experiences of loss. Some never really let go of the person who died or left them; they hold on to anger, longing, or guilt for years or decades, even though doing so only causes them suffering. They may disconnect from those around them, remaining attached to someone long gone. Dwelling for years in frustrated desire leads them to build up thicker and thicker ego defenses until true intimacy seems impossible.

Others are so afraid of facing painful feelings related to loss that they run from one object of desire to another. They use a new person to distract them from the feelings of grief and loneliness related to someone they've lost. By moving quickly from one experience to another without pausing to reflect on their own experiences, they lose the chance to learn from the past. Failing to learn from their mistakes, they are tragically likely to repeat them.

If we want to use an experience of loss and mourning as an opportunity for inner development, we must begin by facing and thinking deeply about our real feelings. The pain that you feel when someone breaks up with you, leaves you, or dies can become an important teacher if you know how to listen to it. Over twenty-five centuries ago, the Buddha talked about the first two Noble Truths—about suffering and the cause of suffering. We may understand intellectually what the Buddha meant, but deep down our egos are still telling us that we're all right, that we won't suffer, that desire will work in bringing us happiness. So when you mourn the loss of someone or something, that's your opportunity to integrate an awareness of the first two Noble Truths into your personality and your life. When you mourn a loss, if you explore your own experience, you can see directly how your ego deceived you and how your desire and attachment brought you suffering.

Facing and thinking about your experiences of suffering during the mourning process can be useful, but after a while it's certain that the ego will assert itself again. Desire again will arise, and you will face a real risk of being deceived again by the illusion of permanence.

I'll give a simple example of how this often works. A patient of mine named Wendy came to therapy because she was "totally falling apart" when her husband left her for another woman. She'd had a number of bad experiences in relationships before her marriage, including one in which a man had been physically abusive to her. Now, with her marriage ending, she felt "like a total failure." In therapy, she genuinely faced and thought about her experiences as she mourned the loss of her relationship. She could see how she repeatedly had idealized men based on relatively superficial characteristics. Driven by her ego's fears and desires, she repeatedly had taken refuge in her relationships with men, looking to them to give her a sense of security, status, happiness, and joy in her life. Following her unrealistic, romanticized desires, she repeatedly had become attached to men who were not good matches for her or who treated her badly. To avoid this suffering in the future, she resolved to change this dynamic. But then, some months later when the pain of mourning had begun to subside, she found herself wanting to go out and meet a new man. She told herself that she was going to look for a different kind of relationship this time. Before she knew it, she was in a relationship with a man who appeared very different from her husband on the surface but who again wasn't treating her well. She said, "I thought I was headed in a whole new direction, but now I'm right back where I was before, in a relationship that isn't working."

Even if we do learn something from the pain of mourning, as the pain subsides there is a natural tendency to follow desire back to a situation similar to the one we were in before our loss. When Freud noticed the incredible strength of people's impulses to repeat what's familiar, he wondered if this repetition compulsion wasn't even stronger than the pleasure principle. Often, we unconsciously repeat patterns of behavior and emotion because they are familiar, even though we can see that they bring us suffering.

It is important to understand that there is another choice. Once you have seen, through mourning, how your own desire brought you suffering, you can choose a different way of relating to others. Once most of your desire energy has been withdrawn from the lost object of your attachment, you can choose to direct that energy out toward another object of desire, which inevitably will lead to more suffering. Or you can direct that energy through the channels of more positive emotions. For example, in working with people who are grieving, I often see how healing it can be when they direct their energy to love in the form of prayer or to compassion in the form of service to others who are also suffering.

Many of us have a difficult time consciously channeling our energies in healthier directions because we aren't good at differentiating between love and desire. I've mentioned that Western psychological researchers often use the word *attachment* to refer to a mix of these two different mental states. The two states have in common feeling interested in and close to another person. Most of our relationships are characterized by a mix of the two. It's important to get good at differentiating between them in yourself. You can practice doing so in your current relationships, watching how the mind moves from desire to love and back again. With desire, the underlying energy is one of grasping at this other person to bring you happiness. The feeling is that you want or need the person in your life or else you won't be happy. With desire, if the person does things you don't like, or doesn't do what you want, you start getting annoyed, upset, or angry. Attachment isn't love, and it doesn't lead to happiness.

With love, the main feeling is warm affection directed toward the other person. You sincerely want the other to be happy, and you take deep and sincere pleasure in doing things for this person. There is no feeling of grasping at the other or of needing something from this person in order to be happy. You're just in the moment, deeply enjoying giving your warmth and energy to the other.

When you've mourned a particular loss, you have the option of directing your energy back out through desire and attachment or through genuine love. Learning to move your energy in the direction of love or compassion doesn't happen overnight. You develop it over time, through practice. It's like an alchemical process. Ancient alchemists held that you could begin with a base material, and through a process of heating it and treating it with chemicals, you could separate out impurities, transforming it into the mystical philosopher's stone. Mourning is like the fire and acid through which the ego is burned and initially purified. Then, by separating out desire and illusions of solid permanence, you alchemically transform the ordinary ego into the pure and golden essence of love.

MOURNING OTHERS

You need not lose someone in order to purify the attachment from your relationship and alchemically develop pure love. Waiting to mourn someone until that person is gone is actually a big waste. Spending the precious time that you have with someone on desire and attachment, you lose the opportunity to share your love while the person is present.

A friend who lost his father not so long ago told me, "I didn't really appreciate him for all those years. I didn't really see who he was." This is typical. We spend most of our time in relationships caught up in our attachment to the other person and also in the fears, insecurities, frustrations, and annoyances that go along with attachment. Our underlying feeling of genuine love is eclipsed by all these other feelings, and so we miss out on sharing our love with others as much as we might. Far too often, when we mourn someone and succeed in letting go of our attachments, we suddenly discover the underlying feeling of genuine love that was eclipsed for so long by our attachments and projections. At this point, we can direct our prayers and good wishes toward the person who's gone, but it's too late to share our love directly with them.

Following on the methods for facing our own mortality discussed earlier, we can spend time thinking about the impermanence and mortality of other people in our lives. You can do this when you're alone or while you're together with a loved one. Look at or think of someone you care about and actively recall this person's mortality. Think as follows: *It's absolutely certain that this person I care about is going to die, and there's nothing at all that I can do about that fact; without any warning or choice, he or she may die during this decade, this year, this month, this week, or even today.* Spend some time focusing on the recognition that this person you care about really could die quite soon. Imagine how you would feel and react if she or he were to die this week or later today. Finally, notice how your feelings for the person shift in the light of these reflections on the person's mortality, and think about what you would want to say to her and how you would want to interact with her if today really was going to be her last day.

When people do this practice regularly in relation to their lover or spouse, they consistently react by becoming more patient with and kind to that person. People often report that after doing this exercise for a while they tell the other more often how much they love and appreciate them, become more patient, and do more to help and serve them. When people do this exercise while thinking of other relatives, it often motivates them to cut through old family problems. They may be motivated suddenly to apologize for their mistakes, express their love more directly, and cherish their loved ones in ways they didn't before.

As with mourning yourself, the key is to viscerally imagine losing the other person and to face your feelings about this as deeply and directly as possible. Facing these feelings again and again serves as the inner fire that cooks the ego, allowing you to burn off your attachments and desires so as to transform your ego, which previously led to a mixture of happiness and suffering, into an inner philosopher's stone of pure love that can bring more and more moments of pure happiness and joy to your life.

Letting go of our desire-driven attachments to others also helps us let go of the idealized projections that go along with desire and of the devalued projections that arise when we become angry because our desires were frustrated. Because of the projections related to our attachment, we can live with others for years without really knowing them. To genuinely love another person, we must let go of our projections and appreciate that person for who he or she is. Mourning the living is one way of overcoming our projections in order to understand and appreciate others. The next chapter presents another method designed specifically to help us see through our projections in order to achieve genuine empathy and compassion.

SIX

SEEING THROUGH
PROJECTIONS

According to Buddhist psychology, each of our experiences in life is accompanied by one of three basic feelings. With every experience comes a feeling that it is pleasant, unpleasant, or neutral. Buddhist scholars classify this basic, instinctual level of reaction to experiences as an "omnipresent mental factor." Feeling that things are either pleasant, unpleasant, or neutral is one of the most fundamental qualities of our subjective experience of the world. It's not something that we can turn off or escape from; it's there all the time, even in our dreams.

There is evidence that even fetuses in the womb may find their mother's voice and other soothing sounds pleasurable. Right from birth, babies instinctually cry out when things are painful. Even animals share this basic level of feeling. You need only watch a cat for a short while to see that it finds tuna or a spot warmed by sunlight pleasurable and that it finds a growling dog or the sound of a nearby, loud vacuum cleaner unpleasant.

In each moment, as our five senses experience objects or as our minds think thoughts, each fleeting experience of an object or a thought is accompanied by a feeling. As you're driving down the road with the car radio on, you may feel pleasure at hearing a few notes of a song, then a moment of displeasure at seeing someone cut in front of you, then neutral as you see other cars driving along beside you, then pleasure at recalling a loved one, and so on.

At this basic level, our feelings are not a problem. They're very simple and natural. When you see the sun adorned by streams of magenta and violet clouds as it sets in the ocean, hear the sound of a stream's water dancing over smooth stones, or remember a time when you viewed an act of pure and selfless kindness, it's natural to feel a sense of pleasure. When you taste food that's gone sour, hear someone shouting out in rage, or smell a noxious cloud of industrial pollution, it's natural to feel that these things are unpleasant.

Our problems derive from how we react to our feelings. For example, when we experience something pleasant, we don't just enjoy it. Right away, we unconsciously begin focusing on the person or thing that we were relating to when the pleasant sensation arose. We create an internal, idealized projection about that person or thing. We block out awareness of negative aspects of the object and focus exclusively on its positive attributes. We start seeing the object in an unrealistic, distorted way, viewing it as more valuable than it actually is. And so we develop desire and attachment. We unconsciously turn each desired object into an imagined Holy Grail, fantasizing that if we can have it all the time, we will always feel good. This is obviously a delusion. The object can never fulfill our expectations. We've taken a pleasant sensation and unconsciously, unintentionally turned it into an occasion for suffering.

In the case of an unpleasant sensation, again we tend immediately to focus on the person or thing that we were relating to when the sensation arose. The mind creates a projection about that person or thing that devalues it. We unconsciously choose to see only the negative aspects of the object, and anything good about it becomes virtually invisible to us. The mind gets agitated, and we feel aversion or disgust. As we hold onto that negative, devalued projection, each time we have to spend a moment near that person or thing, the mind immediately sees it as negative and becomes agitated. Eventually, this agitation and aversion are likely to give rise to emotions such as anger, spite, disgust, and even hate toward that object. We've taken an unpleasant sensation and unconsciously, unintentionally created a situation in which we're almost certain to experience many more unpleasant sensations.

The great Indian Buddhist teacher Nagarjuna says that all of our suffering is caused by our projections and by the negative, agitated emotions that go with them. In reaction to pleasant sensations, we create idealized projections, become attached, and suffer. In reaction to unpleasant sensations, we create devalued projections, become averse, and suffer. In reaction to neutral sensations, we become indifferent; we ignore the object and don't investigate the true nature of our relationship with it; we remain ignorant, and so we suffer. Nagarjuna says that happiness comes from non-attachment, non-aversion, and non-ignorance.

Nagarjuna is pointing out how we can relate to our own experiences and feelings in a skillful way. He's showing how we can go through our daily lives and find happiness instead of frustration and suffering, enjoying our experiences simply, without creating incredibly elaborate complications and problems for ourselves.

A story about two Zen monks who were traveling together can help us understand this point. As they approached a river that they had to wade across, they came upon a woman who asked for their help. She couldn't make it across alone. Without hesitating, the elder monk lifted her up and carried her across. She thanked them, and the monks went on their way. Quite a while later, the younger monk was looking agitated and said to his elder that it seemed wrong and improper to him that a venerable, celibate monk had touched and held a woman to carry her across the river. The elder monk responded, "Oh, the woman? I put her down when we reached the other side of the river, but you are still carrying her."

The younger monk obviously still harbored considerable desire for and attachment to the female form. One can surmise that he unconsciously felt upset or guilty about his own attachment, which then led him develop a feeling of aversion to women, which served as an inner defense against and an unconscious denial of his desires. When he saw his companion helping the woman, both his attachment and his aversion for women got stirred up. Uncomfortable with his own attachments, he next projected them onto his fellow monk. Now the young monk's attachment- and aversion-driven projections distorted not only his view of women, but also his view of his older companion. Because of this projection, he devalued his companion and developed an aversive judgment toward him. In this way, his initial attachment to women created many complex, interrelated projections, attachments, and aversions, all of which led to mental agitation and suffering for him. Each of us does this all the time; we start with simple experiences, and because of our unskillful way of dealing with our basic feelings, we wind up suffering from our attachment and aversion, carrying around many complex projections. By comparison, the elder monk was free from projections, free from attachment and aversion, and therefore free from suffering in this case.

EVEN-MINDEDNESS

The practice of cultivating a mind that is free from attachment, aversion, and indifference, particularly in relation to other people, is sometimes described as developing equanimity or even-mindedness. Some people mistakenly assume that developing equanimity means becoming indifferent toward everything. They think that even-mindedness entails not caring about anything, but this is totally wrong. Even-mindedness means being free from indifference as well as from attachment and aversion. Even-mindedness means that you can help another person cross the river without becoming attached to that person; it means that you care about everything.

Psychologically speaking, I describe this practice as learning to see through our own projections so that we don't get caught up in attachment, aversion, and indifference. This practice helps us to become skillful in dealing with our pleasant, unpleasant, and neutral feelings toward other people so that we don't cause ourselves unnecessary suffering. The more we become free from projections, the freer we are to enjoy life and care for others without creating complicated emotional and interpersonal problems.

The practice of developing even-mindedness is emphasized in the Tibetan Buddhist tradition as an essential element for cultivating strong compassion. Without even-mindedness, you occasionally may develop some compassion toward those you're attached to, but your own desires and frustrations repeatedly will overwhelm your compassion. You cannot develop genuine compassion for someone toward whom you are indifferent or averse. The projections associated with attachment, indifference, and aversion so distort your understanding of others that you are not able to empathize with them or see their suffering well enough to develop much compassion for them. Because of this distorting effect of our projections, Tibetan teachers sometimes liken developing even-mindedness to making a surface flat and smooth before you begin painting a portrait on it. If you try to create your painting on a surface with many bumps and crags, it's not likely to come out looking very nice. Similarly, your empathy and compassion will not progress well if you don't first develop even-mindedness.

One powerful, practical method used in Tibetan Buddhism for developing even-mindedness involves using your memory, reason, and imagination to challenge your own projections, thereby decreasing your attachment, aversion, and indifference toward others. You begin this exercise by thinking of three different people and imagining them in front of you. One of these people should be someone who upsets or annoys you—someone toward whom you feel some aversion and see as an enemy. The second should be someone you like being around— a friend toward whom you feel some strong attachment. The third person should be a stranger—someone you don't know well and toward whom you feel indifferent.

It's useful to start out by just noticing your current, genuine feelings toward these three people. To understand attachment, aversion, and indifference, you have to see how they function in your mind. Notice how you feel that your enemy is really annoying. Focus for a few moments on your negative thoughts about this person, on your feeling of aversion, and on your view that he or she is somehow inherently unpleasant. As you think of your friend, notice how you immediately feel happy thinking about him or her. Notice your particular, positive thoughts about this person and also how you feel so attracted, as though he or she has a certain inherent, magnetic quality. As you think of the stranger, notice how you have almost no energy for this person. Notice your lack of thoughts or feelings for this person, your lack of empathy, connection, or caring about this person. Don't deny or rationalize your feelings in the beginning; just notice them.

A Tibetan practitioner next challenges his projections by contemplating how his relationships with these three people have changed over time. He thinks especially about how relationships change over the course of many lifetimes, so that close friends and family in this life may have been enemies in a previous life, and enemies in this life may have been cherished loved ones before. For people who have strong faith in reincarnation, such contemplations can be very effective. Here, I offer a modified form of the exercise that doesn't require thinking about past and future lives but is still designed to cut through projections. This approach combines some of the subjects a Tibetan practitioner studies with questions developed in Western psychology for becoming more aware of projections.

Thinking about each of the three people in turn, contemplate the following questions: *How did you come to see the person in this way?* Notice how, with your enemy, you had a limited number of interactions, during which you had an unpleasant feeling. Based on these few experiences, you created a negative image in your mind that you projected onto the person. Analyze your own experience sincerely, seeing how your mind created the negative image of that person, devaluing him or her. Do the same sort of contemplation for the other two people, noticing how you created idealized and indifferent projections about them, based on pleasant and neutral feelings during a few limited interactions with them. Notice that this image you carry around about the other person comes primarily from your mind, not from the other person.

Did you always see the person in this way? Notice that your friend and enemy were once strangers to you. At that time, you saw them very differently. Also, perhaps your enemy was once a friend or your friend was once an enemy. In this regard, it can be useful to contemplate how people's feelings for and projections about each other change radically over time. There are countless examples of this. Everyone knows couples who have gone through a bad breakup or divorce. Before they met they were strangers who felt indifferent about each other. Then they met and fell so madly in love that they could barely stand to be separated. At that point they might have been willing to die for each other. After some years of being together, the relationship got worse and worse until the two of them could hardly bear to be near each other. The breakup or divorce was so messy that by the end they practically hated each other. Early on, each saw the other as nearly perfect, almost like a god or goddess. Later on, each appeared to the other like some horrible demon, totally annoying and unpleasant. Which view was correct? Neither. They were both extreme projections—one based on strong attachment and the other on strong aversion. Notice that people rarely doubt their projections. When the couple saw each other as totally marvelous and wonderful, they felt sure that that view was correct. Later, when they saw each other as horrible, they were just as certain of the correctness of this view. By thinking deeply about how your own projections and the projections of other people you know have been inaccurate and have changed again and again over time, you gain the benefit of beginning to doubt your current projections. As you imagine those three people you began with, perhaps you will begin to wonder if your current views of them are correct.

Does everyone see the person as you do? Do other people see qualities in them that you don't? This subject is also intended to help us challenge our own naive confidence in our projections. Think about your enemy, and ask yourself if everyone else also sees this person as negative. Do other people see positive qualities in him that you don't? Is there perhaps a person in the world who loves and adores him? Imagine how that person feels about him. As you compare the other person's view of him with your own, try to feel how your view must be somewhat incomplete and exaggerated.

Regarding the person to whom you're attached, think about how her enemies view her. Think about what her former lovers might say about her. Think of people she has annoyed. Might they see flaws in her that you yourself are blind to? The idea here is not to become critical of the person; it's to become realistic. Being a genuine friend and loving another person includes really knowing who that person is, understanding the difficulties she faces in her life, and helping her through them. To the extent that you idealize her, you're not available to love her.

Also, regarding the stranger in your contemplation, specifically think about others who care deeply for this person. Think about his parents, his friends, and his children, and contemplate for a while their views of him. Try to imagine how many qualities he may have that you are blind to because of your indifference.

If you got to know the other person by empathizing with that person's perspective on the situation, would your view change? This is an extremely important point. When you're attached, averse, or indifferent toward another person, you naturally don't spend time genuinely empathizing with that person. Attachment, aversion, and indifference arise through focusing primarily on our own perspective. We focus on our feelings, and we react to others based on that. It's a self-centered approach. Empathizing with the other person's experiences and feelings is quite different; it leads toward compassion.

When you're angry at someone, you focus on how that person caused you some unpleasant feelings. You may view that person as negligent, rude, stupid, or intentionally cruel. By not checking in with the other person, you allow yourself to hold onto this negative view indefinitely. If you go talk with the other person, specifically empathizing with his perspective, then you often find that his behavior was unintentional or came out of some difficulties that he was facing. If you focus your attention for a time on the difficulties he was facing and on how he was feeling, then your negative projection toward him suddenly may seem a bit petty or harsh. The idea here is not to deny that you had an unpleasant experience; it's to put that experience into context in order to free yourself from the pain of aversion and anger. Letting go of your negative feelings and projections toward others may decrease the suffering you cause them, and it will certainly decrease the suffering you cause yourself.

Empathizing also clearly cuts through indifference. If you spend time really listening to someone and trying to imagine life from her perspective, you cannot remain indifferent to her. Indifference about people develops out of our ignorance about them. Empathy, curiosity, and caring are antidotes to ignorance about others. In actively empathizing with someone, you become interested in her and likely begin caring at least somewhat about her well-being.

Genuine empathy also can help to decrease the idealized projections of attachment. Regarding the person you're attached to, think deeply about the many kinds of suffering she experiences. Listen to her as she describes the problems in her life, and focus empathically on her experiences of loss, sadness, fear, insecurity, and pain. Really try to imagine all of her suffering as she experiences it. Now, try to relate this image of her as someone who has to face so much suffering in her life to your idealized image of her. Differentiate between your compassion and your attachment. Notice that your attachment wants to view her as pure and perfect. Your attachment fantasizes that you will gain a lasting, flawless happiness from her. As you think of the suffering that she faces, does this fantasy seem realistic? Also, does it seem kind? As you think deeply of her as a person who suffers and wants happiness, how does it seem to you when you honestly face the impulse of your desire, which is essentially to use her to gain your own happiness? At first, your attachment may try to masquerade as compassion. You may try to think that you're attached in order to her to help her. This is just self-deception. If you can cut through such deceptions, then empathy will play a positive role in helping you decrease attachment.

Is this person like every other human being in wanting to be happy and wanting to be free from suffering? This final question clearly develops out of the previous one. The idea here is to focus specifically on how all three people are exactly alike in wanting to be happy and to be free from suffering. We are all equal in precisely this way.

From birth on, we're driven by our own desire for happiness and freedom, but we rarely focus our attention on the fact that every other person wants these things just as much as we do. Recognizing this fact forms the basis for equanimity or even-mindedness. Beyond or beneath all of our projections, self-deceptions, attachments, aversions, fears, neurotic longings, and angry impulses is the simple capacity to recognize that we're all basically the same in this way. As you begin to see through your projections, it's very important to spend time thinking about how friends, enemies, and strangers all want to be happy and all want to be free from suffering. If you don't spend time focusing on this truth, then your attitudes won't change much. By allowing this truth to affect your feelings, you become more grounded and realistic in your view of other people.

The idea of even-mindedness is not that you shouldn't have friends. It's not wrong to enjoy spending time around some people more than others. Being even-minded means that you see through your own projections—that you don't take them literally—and that you relate to others with the respect, empathy, caring, and equanimity that come from understanding their equality in wanting happiness and freedom from suffering.

When someone gives you something, looks attractive to you, or otherwise brings you pleasure, your mind still may start creating an idealized projection. But you can see through it. You can recognize that this person is also a human being who wants to be happy and free from suffering like everyone else. You can let go of your projection and simply enjoy your moments with the person. When someone behaves toward you in a way that brings you some displeasure, your mind still may begin creating a devaluing, aversive projection. Again, though, you can see through it. You can recognize that this person is somehow seeking her own welfare just as you yourself are. You can let those unpleasant moments pass by without closing off to this other person, getting caught up in negative emotions that would only compound your own suffering. And when someone brings you neither pleasure nor displeasure, you initially may have an impulse to ignore him. But you can step right through this impulse and look at that person with interest. You can empathize with the other with an open heart.

In this way you can relate to your pleasant, unpleasant, and neutral experiences skillfully. You can live your life with non-attachment, non-aversion, and non-ignorance. You still experience those three feelings, but you don't go on to create negative emotions based upon them. By doing so, you can avoid a great deal of neurotic, emotional turmoil and suffering.

LIKE A DREAM

It's clear that our projections are intimately related to our negative emotions based on our attachment, aversion, and indifference. Buddhism and Western psychodynamic thought agree that when we relate to others through emotions based in attachment and aversion, we inevitably develop projections. Next, I'd like to look more deeply at the role that projections play in our daily lives. This will help us identify additional means for letting go of them or seeing through them.

Tibetan Buddhist practitioners contemplate again and again along the lines described above, using thoughts about how relationships change from life to life to add breadth and strength to their reflections. Their efforts at developing even-mindedness are supported by the more general Buddhist understanding of projection. Buddhist teachers sometimes say that waking reality is like a dream. It's different from a dream in that not only the mind but also the five senses are functioning when we're awake. But still, the mind plays a primary role in constructing our experience of reality. Based upon input from the senses, the mind constructs a certain vision of reality much as it constructs a dream.

Western research into brain activity during sleep supports the view expressed in this Buddhist teaching. When scientists observe brain activity during dreams, they note that most areas of the brain function similarly during dreams and waking life. Of course, areas of the nervous system that take in sensory input and that control motor activities are largely inactive during dreams. However, with most other areas of the brain scientists cannot tell just from watching neural activity whether a person is having experiences or is dreaming those experiences. Dreams seem so real when we're in them because the mind constructs our dreams much as it constructs our experiences when we're awake.

Let me give a mundane example of how this works in daily life. A young man, a patient of mine, walks into a store. He looks up and sees a woman's face across the room. She looks at him and waves. That's his sensory input. But in fact, he is already thinking about what he sees. The eye sees only colors and shapes; "woman," "face," and "wave" are mental constructs. His mind recognizes this particular face. It links this particular visual image to memories and to a label or name. He thinks, *That's Jane.* Now, an incredibly quick, largely unconscious series of mental events occurs. He thinks about how he's been attracted to Jane for some time. Though he now simply saw her face across the room, his mind makes associations to other images of her. He unconsciously links up with an idealized, attractive image of her—a projection based on attachment. There are associations to mental images of her body, her gestures, and her smile, which are also linked to other images in his unconscious of women he finds attractive. He recalls a time a few weeks ago, when they went on a date and kissed. He becomes excited, generating strong attachment. Then, also he recalls that he hasn't phoned her since then. He unconsciously moves to an imagined image of her becoming annoyed and angry at him about this—a projection based on aversion. It's associated with other images in his unconscious of women who have been angry with him and how he fears them. He feels afraid of her potential anger and has a slight impulse to flee. Now he feels conflicted. Based on his attraction, he can imagine going up to her and having a nice interaction. Based on his fear, he can imagine leaving the store quickly or going up to her and having her react angrily. He grows anxious. He notices his own anxiety, and he thinks, *Damn, why am I always like this with women?* He now has linked to a negative image of himself—a projection about himself based on aversion. Based on this image, he starts feeling angry with himself and mildly depressed. A bad mood has started that will last for hours.

As more sensory experiences occur, the mind quickly creates more and more projections. Over the course of a few hours, countless inner images, associations, thoughts, and emotions occur. Even his particular image of a "store" and his indifferent reaction to all the other people in that given "store" were created by his own mind. How he will interact with Jane is almost entirely determined by his emotions and projections associated with her.

There is nothing particularly unique about this young man's experience. We all do this all the time. Based on brief, sensory experiences, our minds label those experiences and then unconsciously create complex emotional reactions, thoughts, judgments, and projections. Our behaviors are then driven by those emotions, thoughts, and projections. This is our reality.

Tibetan Buddhist practitioners are raised with an understanding of the primary role played by the mind in constructing our experience of the world. One Buddhist practice involves carefully observing the mind as it constructs your reality. Often, you start with something simple like observing how the mind relates to a table. You notice that your mind has a certain internal image of a table—a solid object with four legs and a flat top. If you come across a table with six or eight legs, the mind adapts the concept in order to label this also a table.

Next, depending upon your memories and your past thoughts, feelings, and actions, you may go on to create all sorts of internal stories about a given table. One person may think, *Oh, it's such a beautiful antique. It reminds me of my grandmother's home. I wish that I could have one like that.* Another person may see the same table and think, *What an ugly old thing. It's so pretentious to leave these overpriced antiques around. What a show-off.* The person who labels the table "mine" may think, *Oh, she put her drink right down on my nicest table. How terribly inconsiderate! I'll never invite her over again.* A woodworker might think, *What nice quality purple heart. I like how they did the turning work on the legs.* A child may look at the table and think, *Oh, cool, a fort. I'll hide underneath it.* A monk might look at it and think, *Ah, an altar for making offerings to Buddha.* A person who's freezing might think, *Firewood.* A termite might see it as *food.* As you watch the mind, you can see that we can create limitless different projections for any given object. We naively assume that whatever we are experiencing is inherently related to the sensory object—to the pieces of wood that exist out there. In fact, what we see and experience derives mainly from our own minds.

Buddhism and Western psychology agree that what you tend to project in any given situation depends primarily on your own past. Western psychology looks to childhood for the roots of our projections, while Buddhist psychology looks even farther back to experiences in previous lifetimes. Either way, what's important to understand here is that your own thoughts, emotional habits, and actions in the past have been the primary factors in creating your current experience of the world. And every time you react to another person or thing with a particular set of thoughts and emotions, you're deepening your tendency to see a world based on those types of projections. What you thought and felt in the past determines what you experience and how you feel about it now; the thoughts and emotions that you cultivate now will determine what you experience and how you'll feel in the future. Each moment in which you take control of your own mind and develop it in positive directions has incredible power. This is one of the basic ideas that serves as a foundation for the approach of this book: by changing your own thoughts and emotions, you literally can change your world.

IMAGINARY RELATIONSHIPS

Western psychoanalytic thinkers essentially agree with the Buddhist analysis of the power of projections, though Western psychology tends to focus more on the relational quality of projections, looking at how they originate in childhood and subsequently affect our relationships with other people. Jung wrote,

> Just as we tend to assume that the world is as we see it, we naively suppose that people are as we imagine them to be. . . . [We] go on naively projecting our own psychology onto our fellow human beings. In this way everyone creates for himself a series of more or less imaginary relationships based essentially on projection.

Jung's statement here is very much in line with Buddhist ideas. However, he emphasizes an interesting point—that what's being projected is part of "our own psychology." Both he and Freud emphasized that what we project is always part of ourselves. Usually, it's a part of ourselves that we have a hard time dealing with and therefore have repressed, split off, or otherwise pushed out of awareness. We are unable or unwilling to deal with this part of ourselves consciously, and so it comes out unconsciously in our projections.

Buddhist teachers usually emphasize the benefits of recognizing and letting go of your projections in order to be free of their negative effects. Buddhist practitioners certainly try to understand their habitual projections in order to work better with their minds. Still, Jung's emphasis on analyzing your projections to discover aspects of yourself that you haven't dealt with effectively is a useful addition to the traditional Buddhist approach. It can help us take greater responsibility for dealing with suppressed aspects of ourselves and also for correcting the ways in which our projections negatively affect others in relationships.

It's very interesting to catch yourself projecting part of yourself onto another person. It always feels a bit strange. In a way, it's like waking up inside a dream; you suddenly realize that what you thought was literally true instead was made up by your mind. It may occur to you that all the while you thought you were talking with someone else, you were talking mainly to yourself. You may see also that you were coercing someone else to play a role in a drama you unconsciously were creating. It's possible, even likely, that the other person also was relating to the situation through projections of his or her own, but it's important to remember that your main job is to become aware of and work through your own projections. Trying to help another person work through his projections when you're caught up in an unconscious projection toward him is a bit like a person who's drowning in a riptide deciding that she's going to save someone else whom she is not yet sure is in trouble. She's unlikely to help him and may contribute to his drowning as well.

There is no end to the number of different emotions and psychological capacities that people project onto one another. Both negative and positive aspects of ourselves can be projected. For example, jealousy ordinarily develops from projecting negative aspects of the self onto someone we're close to. Jung went so far as to assert, "The kernel of all jealousy is lack of love." Say a man projected a strongly idealized image onto a woman and married her based on his projection rather than on genuine love. Over time, his wife inevitably does not live up to the idealized projection; "having" her cannot bring him permanent happiness. So, as his projection loses energy, he begins feeling a sense of emptiness within himself. Deep down, he wonders if he would be happier with another woman. At the same time, he wants to maintain the image of an ideal marriage. He is still attached to his wife, hoping somehow to find happiness in his desire for her. He is not able to face certain facts about himself—that he lacks genuine love for his wife, that he doesn't know how to give of himself in love, and that he's struggling against impulses to seek happiness through desire for other women. He's unconscious of all these issues. What he notices is that he suddenly feels very suspicious when she comes home late from work. Seeing her around her male friends and coworkers makes him terribly uncomfortable. He imagines that she doesn't really love him and that she's thinking she'd be happier with another man. He has projected his own inner conflict onto her. He starts accusing her, checking up on her, and getting annoyed with her when she's late. She tries to reassure him, but to no avail. No amount of reassurance can work when people are projecting jealousy because they don't doubt the other, they doubt themselves. One of the clear signs that you are projecting is when you have the same conversation or argument again and again with little positive effect. When someone is projecting, no amount of discussion resolves the issue because the people involved literally don't know what they're talking about.

If this man does not become aware of the inner issues he's projecting, he will not be able to stop himself from making his own and his wife's lives more and more miserable as time passes. The solution is for him to admit what he's projecting and then to decide consciously how he wants to deal with his own lack of love and his tendency to seek happiness by following the idealized projections of desire.

Projecting your positive capacities onto others also can also lead to trouble. A graduate student was excited about the possibility of getting to study with a world-renowned professor in her program. She'd read his books and knew of his reputation as an expert in their field. Even before meeting him, she thought he was "a genius." Though very intelligent, this young woman had suffered for many years from low self-esteem and feelings of insecurity. In the presence of the professor she found herself anxious and tongue-tied. She signed up for a class with him, but she found to her great embarrassment that she did worse in this class than in any other. By her second year in the program, she had mixed feelings about studying with this professor. On the one hand, she looked up to him and wanted to be around him. On the other hand, she felt so uncomfortable and insecure around him that she wanted to avoid him. Being of two minds about someone is almost always a sign that you're strongly projecting an aspect of yourself that you're unaware of. The conscious mind is in conflict with the unconscious, and you cannot find a solution because you aren't aware just where the problem really lies.

In this young woman's case, she was projecting her own capacity for brilliance, confidence, and genius onto her professor. The Latin root from which the word *genius* is derived means the spirit or god who guides your destiny from birth; your best genius, then, is your highest, divine destiny. Because of her insecurity and low self-esteem, this woman had not been able to acknowledge her intelligence or other strengths. So, in projecting her own best genius onto her professor, she looked up to him, making him an idol for her own hidden capacities. Given this projection, she felt an almost religious awe in his presence. In reality, she had been able to appreciate his work deeply in the first place because her own talents lay in a similar direction as his. He would have made a good mentor and role model for her if she could have related to him in a realistic way. Her projections kept her from doing so. In projecting her own best qualities onto him, she further disowned them in herself. In order to look up so much to him, she unconsciously placed herself terribly low. The more good she saw in him, the less she could find in herself.

This is the difference between projection and respect. When you have a deep, abiding respect and admiration for someone, relating to that person helps you feel better about yourself. The relationship can inspire and empower you to find and develop your own genius. By contrast, when you unconsciously project your good qualities onto someone else, you lose touch with those qualities. You feel that you're inherently less valuable and good than the other person. Rather than developing, you stay stuck in a position of insecurity and weakness. Clearly, to resolve this problem you need to recognize your projection as a projection, moving from idolizing to respect. In this young woman's case, she was able to do so, and she gradually found in her relationship with the professor the mentoring that empowered her to develop her confidence and progress toward her professional goals.

I'd like to share one more example of projection that is particularly relevant here. This example comes from the life of Jack Kerouac after he developed a strong interest in Buddhism. Kerouac was a very passionate person, and when he discovered Buddhism he became passionate about reading Buddhist books, discussing them with friends, and trying to meditate. He was particularly interested in Buddhist teachings about desire leading to suffering and how our experiences are based on projections and therefore can be described as dreamlike or illusory.

From early adulthood on, Kerouac had suffered from alcoholism and from inner conflicts about his sexuality. After he got interested in Buddhism, he tried to renounce desire by not drinking and by remaining celibate for a time. He took a job living alone in the woods for a couple of months as a fire lookout, trying to meditate and be free from desire. Within a few days of leaving this retreat, he found himself drunk, hanging out at a strip club. It's clear that he was deeply conflicted about how he wanted to deal with his compulsive desires. He had an overwhelming tendency to seek happiness through desire, compulsively creating idealized projections toward alcohol and strippers. And he also had some understanding that these projections were illusory and that his compulsive desires led him to suffer.

During this period, he often would visit with his old friend Neal Cassady (who'd served as the inspiration for the main character in his novel *On the Road*). Cassady had no particular interest in Buddhism. However, Kerouac would keep him up whole nights arguing about the nature of reality. With much passion and frustration, Kerouac would put forth the Buddhist view, saying things like, "Pah! All life is suffering and pain. The cause is *desire*. The world is all illusion . . . period!" Visit after visit, Kerouac would engage in the same argument, getting frustrated but feeling compelled nonetheless to keep trying to convince his old friend of his views.

Kerouac was having the same argument again and again without external results. This is a sign that he was talking to himself more than to his friend. Also, he felt ambivalent about the discussions—another sign of projection. In his arguments, Kerouac was holding to his conscious position that Buddhist teachings on desire and projection are valid. But his behavior showed that on an unconscious level he wasn't at all convinced of the truth of these teachings. Drinking too much, hanging out at bars and strip clubs, hooking up with various women, and desperately seeking literary fame were behaviors that showed he was driven by motives other than Buddhist renunciation. He tended to deny and repress his own doubts. He then projected his doubts onto his friend Cassady. Arguing with Cassady, he was really arguing with himself, trying to convince himself to stop believing in projections and following desire. Because he did not consciously face his own deep doubts and questions, Kerouac remained interested in Buddhism but ultimately unconvinced at the deep, unconscious level. On a relational level, projecting his doubts onto his friend only led to a number of frustrating discussions for both of them. For him personally, though, his failure to resolve internal doubts regarding his own compulsive desires eventually led to his tragic death from complications related to alcoholism.

I mention this example to emphasize how easily compulsive desires and projections can keep us from finding the happiness we seek. Even if we study psychological concepts from the East and the West, it's not enough to just think about them a little bit. If we want them to bring about their intended results, then we must relate to them deeply, again and again. We must face our own doubts and uncertainties; we must challenge our projections and denials in order to develop the kind of compassion and joy that come not just from the conscious mind or from a small part of our personality. If we fail to see through our projections and to develop even-mindedness, there is a real danger that we will allow the self-centered ego to be in control of our efforts to develop compassion. Using a traditional Tibetan metaphor, our compassion will consist of many small puddles that can evaporate easily rather than a deep, expansive, long-lasting reservoir.

These reflections on how we project parts of ourselves that we haven't dealt with adequately provide us with some additional questions that we can contemplate as we try to identify and work though our own projections. As we look at our relationships with friends, enemies, and strangers, we can ask ourselves the following questions:

Do I often feel conflicted or ambivalent regarding my relationship with this person?

Do I repeatedly have the same sort of discussion or interaction with this person without our finding a satisfactory solution?

Do I experience strong feelings about the person that I can't quite explain?

Do I often feel excited, inflated, upset, anxious, angry, or obsessed about our relationship?

If you answer yes to any of these questions, it's likely that you are unconsciously projecting a significant, disowned aspect of yourself onto that person. Once you recognize this, it's important to try to understand what you are projecting. Remember that you may project negative aspects of the psyche, such as your aggression, doubts, fears, or cravings, onto another person, and you also may project positive aspects of the psyche, such as your talents, confidence, strength, and even your compassion. An easy way of getting at what you're projecting is to ask yourself what you feel strongly about in the other person. Is it that person's brilliance, incompetence, anxiety, sexual energy, or anger that you feel most strongly about? Be sure to define clearly the quality that you see and feel most strongly about in this person, for most likely that's the very quality you're projecting.

Once you've identified the quality, it's important to try to catch yourself when you start projecting it again. Recognizing you're projecting and not doing anything about it will make the suffering you're already experiencing even worse. When you work on your projections, it can be useful to take particular note of ways in which you may manipulate the other person to play the role that you're projecting onto him or her. For example, the jealous man pushed his wife away through his accusations, which then made him more jealous. People who project their anger and aggression onto others often unconsciously do things to get others to act aggressively, which makes them feel more justified in projecting the aggression. If you find yourself doing such things, make sincere efforts to stop because your projection is hurting both you and the other person.

Then comes the essential step of dealing consciously with whatever you've been projecting. You do this by recognizing that what you were projecting really is an emotion or capacity of your own mind that you have not been dealing with effectively. This is the hardest part—really admitting to yourself that it's you. Once you've done that, you must spend some time making conscious, reasoned decisions about how you want to deal with or express that part of yourself in your life.

Jung notes that as people make progress at withdrawing projections and integrating those parts of themselves into their personality, the result is a sense of wholeness. When we relate to others based upon projections and feelings of attachment, aversion, and indifference, we tend to feel fragmented and incomplete. We're looking outside ourselves for things we can never find there. It's an inherently dissatisfying way of living. Developing a sense of wholeness and integration in your personality is another way of talking about developing even-mindedness. As we let go of various forms of projection and compulsive grasping, we feel more satisfied, complete, and self-possessed. We no longer need to look outside ourselves to seek happiness or escape suffering. Therefore, we become more and more able to relate to others without coercion and constraint; we become freer to relate to them with a sense of interest, caring, and compassion.

Earlier, I noted that Tibetans liken developing equanimity to creating a smooth surface on which to paint a portrait. The extent to which we've developed even-mindedness largely determines our capacity for accurate empathy. Only when our own minds are even can we accurately perceive and portray others in our lives. The next chapter addresses how, once we've seen through some of our projections, we can begin using empathy to give rise to powerful love, which transforms our relationships into sources of deep contentment and happiness.

SEVEN

LOVING COMMUNICATION

For the most part, no one teaches us how to be an effective parent, son or daughter, citizen, spouse, or good friend. At school, we may study military conflicts, the periodic table of elements, and calculus, but we do not study how to communicate with those we love about our deepest values and needs. We do not learn how to understand and empathize with each other. Breakdowns in communication, in empathy, and in love occur in communities, families, marriages, and friendships every day. Who hasn't felt, at some point in some relationship, utterly uncertain how to proceed?

Many self-help books, workshops, counselors, and even television programs are available to teach you techniques for improving communication or learning to compromise. Such techniques can be useful, and I sometimes teach them to patients who need to develop specific interpersonal skills. However, this chapter isn't about a particular communication skill or technique; it's about changing how you approach communicating with others. When you approach any relationship from an unhealthy emotional perspective and without clear, empathic understanding, then even the best communication techniques are likely to fail. But when you approach communication with the right inner understanding, surprising solutions often present themselves.

Three things are necessary for meaningful, powerfully positive communication. Through introspection, you must be honest with yourself about your own thoughts and feelings; through empathy, you must be as aware as you can of what the other person feels, thinks, and wants; and you must feel a sense of caring or love for the other person. So much of what we say every day is driven by attachment, aversion, and ignorance. We often talk about things that don't have much meaning to us or to the people we're talking with. It is hard to count how many conversations each of us has had in which both people forgot what they'd talked about a month, a week, or an hour after it was over. We also often have conversations with family members or friends that are based on projections: the words of these conversations may be felt deeply by the people saying them, but because they are not based on empathy or genuine love, they lack the power to have a positive impact on the other person or on the relationship. With conversations based on projection, we may find ourselves having the same discussion again and again without any positive results.

The Buddha taught that "right speech" is an essential element of a happy life and of the path to enlightenment. He said that any speech that is essentially dishonest, that puts others down, that is aimed at hurting other people's feelings or creating divisions between people, or that is essentially meaningless ultimately serves as a cause for suffering. Speech informed by empathy and thought, motivated by love and compassion, serves as a cause for positive relationships and for happiness. The Buddha also taught that if you get in the habit of communicating in a meaningful and loving way, then you gradually develop certain inner qualities that give your words power, allowing them to influence and benefit others. Someone who regularly practices right speech develops integrity, character, and self-respect, and these qualities give their speech and even their silence a certain power that cannot be measured but is surely felt.

Both as a Buddhist and as a psychologist, I assert that the vast majority of problems in relationships come from communication that lacks honesty, empathy, or love. When we don't say the positive things that need to be said, when we unconsciously say hurtful or meaningless things, and when we fail to address problems in our relationships directly and lovingly, all sorts of suffering and problems arise. I believe that there are no problems between people that cannot be solved positively through patiently engaging in honest, empathic, loving communication.

THINKING BEFORE WE SPEAK

We often communicate without much mindfulness or awareness. If we're feeling annoyed or angry, we may blurt out words that hurt someone. Often people aren't even aware of what they're angry about. We simply may be in a bad mood or upset about something at work or at school, and we make a harsh, sarcastic comment that hurts those closest to us. Even without speaking, people who feel angry often create an agitated atmosphere in their homes; family members who pick up on their sighs and rough gestures grow tense and fearful so that they wind up walking on eggshells to avoid a conflict. Day after day, small interactions of this kind affect our friendships and our families as termites affect a house; they eat away at the foundation until relationships crumble.

It's similar with communication motivated by other unhealthy emotions. For example, someone driven by a desire to get others' attention and approval at first may seem entertaining. Over time, though, their tendency to interrupt, to try to control the direction of conversations, and to inflate their own self-image begins having the opposite of its intended effect. Eventually, even the energy of their gestures and facial expressions may prove tiring not only to others but also to themselves.

Each of us has tendencies to communicate in ways that don't lead ultimately toward happiness for ourselves and others. The Buddha once gave a discourse to his disciples on how to live a life free of conflicts and problems. He said that before we utter anything we first should know that what we're about to say is "true, correct, and beneficial."

The implication is that we must think before we speak. From a Buddhist perspective, the purpose of communication is to help yourself and others be more awake to what's true and real. One of my professors in graduate school, a psychoanalyst named Dr. Avedis Panajian, once pointed out to me how often people speak in order to distract themselves and others from what's most essential in that moment; we distract ourselves from what's most real in order to lull ourselves and others into a sort of waking sleep. He noted that a good psychotherapist must stay fully awake and always think deeply about the purpose of a statement or interpretation before making it. Simply wanting to say something isn't reason to say it. We first must be clear that what we're saying is true and valid. Even if it is true, we must strive also to be clear that this is the right time to say it and that it's likely to be beneficial. The Buddha is making a similar point. First, we should ask if what we want to say is truthful. We should remember that there are many ways of being untruthful. Large or small overt lies are the most obvious kind of untruth. We may be untruthful also through lack of conscious awareness. For example, someone asks us how we're doing, and we say "I'm fine" because we aren't even conscious that we're upset or angry about something. We then proceed to show covert signs of agitation and anger. This happens every day in close relationships, undermining our own sense of integrity and the other person's trust in us.

Another subtle form of dishonesty that I come across often in psychotherapy is people claiming not to know things they do know. You may ask a person what she really thinks about some important matter, how he really feels about an important person in his life, or what she really wants. The person replies by saying "I don't know," "I'm not sure," or "I'm confused about that" when actually, deep down, they do know. They are simply afraid to admit to themselves or others that they know because this might lead them into deeper intimacy and communication than they are used to. People do this all the time with loved ones, deflecting questions in order to avoid deep intimacy. An honest approach would be either to check in with yourself and then give a genuine answer or to say openly that you don't feel comfortable discussing that issue at that time. Any subtle dishonesty simply eats away at the foundations of our self-respect and of our relationships.

Even if something is true, the Buddha advises that it's not worth saying if it's not likely to be beneficial to yourself or the other person. Our communication should be rooted in love or compassion. Our speech should have meaning and a useful purpose; it should help ourselves and others wake up to what's real and not lull us further into sleep.

So, as the Buddha advised, if we want to live with a sense of integrity and to develop relationships that are not characterized by chronic tension and conflict, then we must cultivate the habit of thinking before we communicate with others. The great Buddhist teacher Atisha advised, "When in company, check your speech; when alone, check your mind." To check whether something is true, we must be honest with ourselves. Rather than habitually giving responses such as "I'm fine" or "I don't know," we must look into our hearts. Often, saying what's really true can be quite difficult or frightening at first. However, facing such difficulties is essential for developing meaningful, satisfying relationships.

A friend of mine recently told me that she felt her relationship with her boyfriend had grown a bit distant in recent months. At first she wasn't sure what to do, but then she approached him about it. She said, "Listen, I really care about you, but it seems like we've been drifting apart lately. I realize that it's partly my fault. I've been angry with you because I feel like you sometimes don't take what I want enough into account. But I haven't told you about it, and that was my mistake. I'm telling you now, though, and I want you to also tell me how you're really feeling. I want us to be able to tell each other what's really going on." She was very brave. Of course, she was aware of the possibility of being rejected by him, but it's only through repeatedly taking such risks that real intimacy and mutual understanding develop. In my friend's case, her boyfriend admitted that he'd sensed her anger, which had led him to distance himself. As they talked through things, he was glad to understand why she'd been angry. Through her committing to being more direct about what she wanted and his resolving to take her feelings into account, they were able to get their relationship back on track.

Cultivating deep honesty in our relationships is essential if we want to develop intimacy with others. However, as the Buddha pointed out, honesty itself is not enough. For example, some people are very honest but often shout at others, speaking harsh and angry words that only hurt others' feelings. Others often speak out impulsively so that even if what they say is true, it doesn't bring about the desired effect because it wasn't delivered in a time, place, and manner that allowed the other person to take it in and make good use of it. To communicate in a way that leads to happiness, we must know that what we're saying is true, and we must also know that it's likely to be beneficial. To know if our communication is likely to be beneficial, we must develop our capacity for empathy.

VICARIOUS INTROSPECTION

The word *empathy* was introduced into the English language in the twentieth century, derived from the German word *Einfühlung*, which meant the ability to feel into another's experience. In psychological literature, *empathy* has come to mean the ability to understand another person's inner experiences. Heinz Kohut, who has written a great deal on the role of empathy in personality development, refers to it as "vicarious introspection." Empathy involves relating our direct observations of and feelings about others to our memories, reason, and imagination in order to develop some understanding of what they are thinking and feeling. Empathy is a skill or ability, similar in some ways to the ability to sing or dance. We're all born with a certain natural ability to empathize. How much we develop that natural ability depends upon effort and practice.

There is a good deal of scientific research supporting the idea that empathy is a key ingredient for healthy relationships. Research suggests that empathy is one of the most essential elements of effective parenting, that it increases pro-social and altruistic behaviors, and that it is a key factor in emotional intelligence. Research also shows correlations between empathy and marital satisfaction, close and secure family relationships, good communication, development of strong social skills, and feelings of compassion. By contrast, a lack of empathy is correlated with higher degrees of anger, aggressive behaviors, sociopathy, child abuse, and delinquency in adolescents. Some researchers suggest that empathy serves as the very root of human morality; our empathic understanding of others' suffering is primarily what helps us choose not to harm them and instead to help them. If we empathically resonate with another person's feelings, then causing them suffering also causes us some suffering, and this serves to restrain our behavior.

Developing empathy requires the bravery to face others' suffering. It should come as no surprise that understanding other people's thoughts and feelings largely entails understanding their suffering. As we gain empathic understanding of other people's inner lives, what we see is much like what we saw in our own minds when we first began looking within. Often, we find that others are worse off than we are. Empathy shows us that many people are almost continually following thoughts of attachment, aversion, and indifference and that they are living lives based largely on projections and driven by afflictive emotions, which inevitably leads to much frustration, exhaustion, and heartache.

As you practice seeing things more deeply, it may seem sometimes as though just beneath the surface appearance of our normal urban or suburban lives lies a wasteland of the heart. On the surface things seem fine, but beneath the surface you may begin seeing the varied, inner landscapes of suffering. Being around people in extreme emotional states, either positive or negative, helps you see such inner landscapes with stark clarity. By empathizing with someone who is more enraged, ecstatic, lonely, terrified, wildly loving, or terribly obsessive than you have known before, you gain the benefit of becoming familiar with a new emotional landscape, which will make it easier for you to empathize with others in the future. As you get to know a greater variety of inner landscapes, your capacity for empathy increases.

It may seem that facing others' suffering will be depressing, discouraging, or overwhelming. Of course, each of us has to proceed into new psychic terrains at a pace we can handle, but in general increasing our empathy leads to positive results. Our relationships with others become based less on projections and more on reality. As we get to know others' minds, we learn to understand and work better with our own minds. As you empathize with people who have spent much time following the mind of addiction, anger, worry, or manic excitement, you gain a greater understanding of what's happening to yourself each time you allow yourself to get caught up in one of those mental states.

It would be difficult to enumerate all the many benefits that come to our lives and our relationships as we cultivate empathy. Empathy is an absolutely essential ingredient for intimacy, love, and compassion. If you are not willing to face others' suffering, then you cannot develop compassion for them.

FOCUSING ON OTHERS

If you want to improve your ability to empathize, the first step is learning to calm and focus your own mind. As long as the mind is caught up in its usual focus on your own flow of thoughts and sensations, it cannot focus on empathizing with someone else's experience. We temporarily have to stop focusing on our own sensations, emotions, and desires in order to pay attention to another person. Freud sometimes spoke of "evenly hovering attention" as a way of describing how a psychoanalyst must pull her attention away from her own desire-driven thought flow to make it available to the patient.

Through practice we can learn to improve our ability to calm and focus the mind intentionally. Many Westerners have seen for themselves how simple mindfulness meditation leads to obvious improvements in these areas. If we regularly spend time focusing the mind on any object, this naturally leads to relaxation and to improved mental focus and control. A great deal of scientific research now supports the view that regularly spending time on such techniques decreases stress, improves immune functioning, decreases anxiety, and increases empathy. I often suggest that my patients regularly spend some time focusing on their breathing, on some peaceful mental image, or on repeating a word or phrase to help them relax, improve their concentration, and decrease the effects of anxiety. Some Catholic patients again take up reciting the rosary for this purpose, just as Buddhists and Hindus recite mantras that calm and focus the mind. As long as they keep up the practice, they consistently report many benefits, which usually include decreased feelings of worry and stress. Many hospitals are now using such relaxation techniques as adjuncts to patients' medical treatment. Regularly spending even a little time on any practice of focusing the mind can be helpful.

Once you've improved your ability to focus your attention, you can use that ability to focus on other people when you're with them. You can develop the habit of looking at people when you're talking with them and of really paying attention to what they're saying and how they're saying it. This is absolutely essential to improving empathy. Wouldn't it be wonderful if children in school learned to calm and focus their minds a little and then also learned to practice sitting down opposite another person and really paying attention to that person for a few moments? Any of us can start today to practice this in our daily lives. You and other people in your life will feel the difference quickly when you simply start practicing calming down and deeply paying attention during conversations. Just looking others in the eyes as they speak and paying close attention can bring an unfamiliar sense of intimacy and understanding. Many of us are so busy that we rarely give our full, undivided attention to anyone, including our closest friends, spouses, or children. As you try just this small practice of giving someone else your eye contact and your whole focus, you may come to the realization that attention is a particularly precious gift.

CONCEPTUAL EMPATHY

To understand and develop our empathy, I find it useful to differentiate between two kinds of empathy discussed in Western psychological research. Borrowing terms from the research, I call them "conceptual empathy" and "resonant empathy." Let's start with conceptual empathy since it's a bit easier to understand and develop.

Simply listening to what someone else says and noticing their tone of voice and gestures is not, in and of itself, sufficient for giving rise to empathy. Consciously or unconsciously, we must relate what we've seen and heard to our memories, ideas, and imagination in order to make sense of it. Recent research suggests that some people, particularly those with autism and other pervasive developmental disorders, may have severe deficits in conceptual empathy. Some researchers refer to this deficit as "mindblindness," suggesting that people with such disorders may be blind to other people's states of mind. For example, if you are talking to someone with severe mindblindness and you say, "I'm worried about my friend Joe, who's ill, and I have to go and check on him," that person might reply, "I'm not worried about my friend."

If you reply, "Yes, you've never met Joe, but *I'm* worried about him and need to go," the person might reply, "*I'm not* worried, *I don't* need to go." You might go on explaining, "I'm quite concerned," and that person would go on just as plainly explaining, "I'm not quite concerned." The issue is that such a person cannot take your statement that you are worried, relate it to his or her own experiences of worrying, and then conceive of the idea that *you* are experiencing the state of mind called worry, which is similar to what she or he has experienced in the past. Such people are blind to the fact that you or others experience subjective states different from their own. Those with severe mindblindness are aware of their own mental states but cannot grasp the idea that other people have minds and experience such states as well.

What people with mindblindness cannot do reveals what most of us do naturally every day in showing a basic level of conceptual empathy. Someone tells you about her thoughts and feelings. You recall similar experiences that you or other people close to you had in the past, and then, taking account of similarities and differences between yourself and the person you're speaking with, you imagine what's going on in her mind. That's a basic form of conceptual empathy.

Most of us engage in this level of empathy all the time. Someone tells us that he's running late, that he's upset about something, that he wants something from us, or that he's sorry, and we understand what he means because we've experienced similar mental states and so can imagine empathically how he's feeling.

Of course, conceptual empathy is always an approximation. We cannot be entirely certain that we're imagining accurately how someone else feels. Based on what we've seen and heard, we're imagining that person's mental state; we're not perceiving it directly. Researchers find that conceptual empathy improves as we put effort into practicing it.

If you want to improve the accuracy of your conceptual empathy, a good thing to do is to check in with the other person, allowing that person to give you feedback on how well you "got" his or her thoughts and feelings. This is easy to do. You simply tell the person what you believe she or he is thinking and feeling, and then you ask if you've gotten it right or if you've missed something. Therapists working with couples and families often have them practice this with each other during sessions. If you ask for and then consider such feedback regularly, you'll get better and better at this basic level of conceptual empathy.

Conceptual empathy becomes much more challenging when you're trying to empathize with a state of mind that is not similar to anything you can remember experiencing yourself, that you haven't empathized with before, or that the other person cannot describe easily. This requires more thought and imagination. It's like entering a new psychic terrain. You need to step for a moment out of your own perspective, cultivating an open, imaginative, almost poetic state of mind. It's a bit like being an actor who imaginally steps into the skin and mind of some new character. You think of what this other person says, and you also think of her gestures, tone of voice, and facial expressions. You imagine being her, saying those things and making those gestures. And you ask yourself what in the world you'd be thinking and feeling if you were she.

In cultivating an imagination that can empathize with the unfamiliar, studying various psychological theories can be useful. I've found that contemplating poetry, novels, biographies, and plays is often just as useful. When striving to develop your empathy or to teach empathy to a child, it's great to use movies, television shows, or books. You can focus on individual characters, imagining and discussing how they may be feeling and what their experience of the world may be like. Storytelling can also be useful for developing empathy. I often do this with children in therapy. We create fictional stories together about people or animals, pausing periodically to reflect on what the characters are feeling and on why they're doing the things they are doing.

Because there is a natural psychological tendency to see things from your own familiar perspective, it can be useful especially to imagine the most extreme kinds of psychological states. One way of doing this is to read books in which characters undergo extreme experiences and to strive to empathize with the characters. Tibetan Buddhist practitioners cultivate their empathic imaginations by spending time actively imagining the various realms of existence described in Buddhist cosmology. They sit with paintings and books describing the wildly different realms, really imagining themselves inside the skin of the beings in those realms. They imagine what it is like to live the life of a dog, a fish, or a worm; also a denizen of hell; a wandering, hungry ghost; or a divine, celestial being, spending a long life in pleasure gardens surrounded by intoxicating flowers and ecstatic symphonies. They even imagine what it is like to be a Buddha, utterly beyond suffering, having omniscient wisdom, eternally radiating infinite, blissful energy everywhere. Practitioners contemplate every sort of realm as viscerally as possible, pushing their minds again and again to the very limits of imagination and thereby expanding their capacity for empathy and thus also for compassion.

I once worked with an intelligent man who often asked himself the right questions about how to make important changes in his life yet repeatedly got stuck in almost obsessive worries so that he could not go ahead and make those changes. We spoke about this dynamic a number of times, but I couldn't quite empathize with his getting so stuck in worry. Then one day I opened up a poem by T. S. Eliot, and his wonderful description of the character J. Alfred Prufrock helped me understand my patient better. Prufrock has "wept and fasted, wept and prayed," asking deep questions. However, his obsessive, ego-based worries always take control of his deepest concerns and spiritual longings, transforming them into petty obsessions. His thoughts about God and the universe are stripped of meaning and power by the ego until they can hardly be distinguished from his tiny obsessive questions like, "Shall I part my hair behind? Do I dare to eat a peach?" His worries are like a drug that lulls him into waking sleep; he feels "Like a patient etherized upon a table." As I read the poem, I suddenly got what happened with my patient. His deepest insights about changes he needed to make in his life were being swept up in the tide of his obsessive worries so that they lost power, and when it came to actually making changes he felt etherized and unable to act. His anxiety distracted him from what mattered, lulling him to inaction. Once I understood the dynamic, I was able to help him keep his insights about what he wanted in life from getting swept up in his worries.

In order to increase our ability with conceptual empathy, we have to cultivate imagination. When we empathize with unfamiliar mental states, it's often useful to spend time imagining what it would be like to live inside that other person's skin, seeing the world through her eyes. When people begin taking time to cultivate empathic imagination, they usually find that it's both an interesting and enjoyable thing to do. I think that being able to see the world from others' perspectives is part of what makes movies and literature so interesting. Think about how it feels to get drawn into a great book or to lose yourself in the drama on the big screen as you watch the performance of a great actor. There is often something liberating and pleasurable about stepping out of your own perspective in order to understand someone else's. This shift of perspective is something that we can cultivate in any of our relationships. Using the empathic imagination can be engaging and pleasurable in the moment, and over time it naturally leads toward compassion—toward the precious wisdom that understands one's own view of the world as merely one of an infinite number of possible perspectives.

RESONANT EMPATHY

Another type of empathy, somewhat different from conceptual empathy, is called by researchers *resonant empathy*. This kind of empathy begins as a largely physiological process, rooted deep in the mammalian nervous system. Biologists and evolutionary psychologists have amassed a great deal of evidence showing that resonant empathy is not unique to humans but is an essential element of our biological makeup as mammals. One social psychologist describes the process well, noting that "witnessing another's emotional state prompts the observer to covertly, internally, imitate the other's emotional cues (for example, tensing our muscles when witnessing someone under stress). The result of this process is the production of similar, though weaker, reactions in the observer."

We are deeply social creatures. We spontaneously resonate with others' emotions as a guitar string resonates with another, nearby string tuned to the same note. More and more research supports the view that from infancy on, our emotions and even neurological development in our brains are influenced powerfully by reciprocal, resonant interactions with the people and even with the other mammals (such as pets) around us. When an infant rests against his mother's body and she is calm, he naturally senses this through her breathing, her facial expressions, and her gentle gestures. He resonates with her calmness, and he settles down himself. When the infant is upset and the mother stays calm as she interacts with him, he naturally learns, through resonating with her, how to begin calming himself down.

Even as adults, we naturally resonate with the emotions of those around us. During a tense scene in a movie, all the viewers in the theater tense their muscles along with the endangered hero and then let out a breath as she or he successfully overcomes a challenge. We're not ordinarily aware of this process. However, it plays a major role in our relationships and in our emotional lives. For example, say that you often spend time around a friend who is anxious. When he speaks anxiously, you don't only hear his words. As he makes fearful facial expressions, you may unconsciously mirror them back to him. As his breathing quickens and his muscles tense, you tense your muscles slightly and breathe a bit more quickly. As you listen to his agitated tone of voice and see his nervous gestures, you begin feeling some anxiety yourself. This feeling of anxiety then affects you as you move on to your next interaction. If you don't realize what is happening, and if you have several such people in your life, over time you can become a more anxious person yourself. By resonating again and again with others' anxiety, you may become more habituated to anxiety. We literally influence each other's emotional lives through such resonant interactions.

I'll give another common example. Say a woman marries a man who is often irritable and angry. When he gets irritated, sighing, breathing heavily, furrowing his brows, and stamping around, she inevitably gets tense and irritated as well. As this goes on, month after month, her tension can develop into physical symptoms such as back pain or headaches. Then, when he gets very angry, shouting with a red face, she also resonates with this. Like him, she too experiences an adrenaline rush. Her physiologic response is similar to his because of her resonant response. How she then reacts to those sensations depends on her predispositions. Her tension may come out as anger, with her shouting back at him. Or, if she is uncomfortable with anger, she may try to suppress those sensations, becoming fearful, anxious, or depressed.

The point here is that for better or worse, with emotions both small and large, each of us responds to others through resonant empathy. This happens between just two people, and it also happens in large groups. Part of the huge energy that we feel at a rock concert or a protest march comes from the resonant, empathic responses gaining more and more power as people pick up on each other's excitement or passion. Singers or speakers resonate with the energy of the crowd, and the crowd then resonates with their increased energy, and so on as the overall energy builds.

Each of us is born with the capacity for resonant empathy, so there's no need to develop it in order to understand other people and communicate lovingly. What we can develop, however, is our awareness of these processes. When you're interacting with another person, try paying attention to your own physical and emotional reactions during the conversation. Of course, it's possible that your reactions are based more on your projections onto that person than on resonant empathy. With resonant empathy, you're responding to something going on in the other person; with projections, you're responding to something in your own unconscious of which this person reminds you. So to use resonant empathy effectively, you need to have become aware already of your tendencies toward projection. When you have a significant emotional or physiological reaction to another person, you check in with yourself to see whether it's likely based more on a projection from your side or on a resonant, empathic response. If it's based on a projection, then working on the projection is the next step in improving your relationship with this other person. However, if it's based on resonant empathy, it becomes a way of understanding this other person more deeply.

In a sense, our bodies are like antennae or satellite dishes pointed at each other, picking up on subtle emotions that the conscious mind is not likely to see. If you begin paying attention to your resonant, empathic responses, then naturally you will wonder why you tend to feel calm around one person, a bit down when talking with another, anxious during discussions with a third, and so on. Sometimes the reasons for your resonant responses will be obvious, and other times they will not.

For example, I recall working with one patient, a successful businessman, who usually came in appearing confident and calm. He talked about things that he wanted to change in his marriage, and he admitted that his own anger sometimes created problems. As I spoke with him, I noticed that I often felt uncomfortably anxious. I looked for some time for any reason in my personal life or in my relationship with him for those feelings of anxiety, but I was unable to find anything that made sense. So one week when he was talking about his anger, I interrupted and said, "I don't believe that anger is your main problem. I think that anger is actually a way that you deal with some deeper feeling of fear or anxiety." He looked at me a bit surprised.

He'd never once mentioned fear or anxiety. However, as we got deeper into his issues during that session, it became clear that he was often anxious that his wife, his coworkers, and even I might see certain flaws that he was trying to hide. His fear was that if others saw these flaws, they would mock and reject him. So he'd get angry as a way of deflecting attention from those other flaws and also of pushing others away before they could reject him. Only by working on these fears was he able to resolve his anger successfully.

You can see that in this case, analyzing my resonant, empathic reaction provided information that conceptual empathy might never have uncovered. If we get accustomed to being aware of our resonant responses to others, we can understand them more deeply and accurately. Being aware of our resonant responses also can free us from getting caught up in negative moods or from developing negative emotional habits based on our resonating with others' negative feelings. When we are aware of the source of such negative feelings, we can take a few deep breaths, turn our minds in more positive directions, and let go of agitated feelings that we've picked up from someone else. Perhaps most important, though, by being aware of our resonant responses, we can develop the capacity to reverse the tide of a negative emotion. Just as we resonate with others, so also do they resonate with us. If the anger or agitation of others can resonate in us, so also can our calm, love, or compassion resonate in them.

REVERSING THE EMOTIONAL TIDE

A brief experience I had in 1989 involving the Dalai Lama demonstrated to me how we can use resonant empathy to understand someone else and to reverse the tide of a negative emotion. At the time, the awarding of the Nobel Prize to the Dalai Lama had just been announced. He was visiting Madison, Wisconsin, to give teachings, and I had volunteered to help with driving some of the people who were traveling with him—his translator and members of the Tibetan government. We dropped the Dalai Lama and the others off at a reception at the University of Wisconsin. It was a formal reception with officials from the university and local government. Another driver and I were standing in a hallway just outside the reception along with a large contingent of police officers that was assigned to protect the Dalai Lama. Suddenly a large young man came storming in from outside. His eyes and his hair both looked wild, and he was wearing torn jeans and a ragged shirt. He began pushing past police officers, insisting that he was going inside to talk with the Dalai Lama. When the police officers blocked him, he raised his voice and pushed harder. A number of officers escorted him away from the door and were trying to calm him down a little distance behind me.

At just this moment, the Dalai Lama's party began leaving the reception and making its way toward the doorway where we were standing. An officer came up behind the other driver and me and said we should be prepared to help the police block the young man and hold him back from the Dalai Lama. I nervously held my ground as the Dalai Lama walked through the doorway just in front of me. I could hear the young man pushing forward behind me. Viewing the situation from a perspective of concern or fear, I noticed my breathing quickened as I prepared for a physical struggle.

The Dalai Lama naturally had his own perspective. He walked quickly out the door and headed directly toward me rather than toward his car. He reached out and gently parted my shoulder and the shoulder of the driver beside me, creating a passage between us. He stepped through it, reached out, and grabbed the young man. Holding the young man's hands in his own, the Dalai Lama smiled broadly, with a warm look in his eyes. He said, "I'm so glad to meet you. Thank you." While speaking, he also touched the young man affectionately. I looked up into the young man's face, and he was smiling, utterly delighted. Turning away from the young man's now happy, peaceful face, I realized that the Dalai Lama was already gone, on his way to the car. I ran to catch up.

This was an excellent example of how to use resonant empathy to understand another person and benefit him. The young man entering that hallway had entered an atmosphere already charged with a sense of excitement and also caution or wariness. When the young man approached with his agitated, aggressive energy, each person present had resonated with him. Muscles tightened, breathing quickened, levels of adrenaline increased. Depending on each of our predispositions, this resonance likely led to a combination of agitation, annoyance, fear, concern, and anger. The young man himself resonated with these emotions, becoming more agitated and angry. Through quick cues back and forth, the agitated energy in the hallway was building rapidly. It was like some resonant symphony of negative emotion, building toward a potentially explosive climax.

Then the Dalai Lama entered the hallway. Without speaking with anyone, he picked up on the energy present, sensing the tense, escalated emotions, and particularly noticed the young man's anger and the sense of longing for contact that lay beneath the anger. Next came the most important thing about this brief encounter. Rather than allowing the resonating, negative emotions in the room to give rise to a negative emotion such as fear or anger on his part, the Dalai Lama responded with compassion. Rather than becoming a victim of his own resonant response, he seemingly used that response to understand the situation. Then he chose to add his own deep feeling of compassion to the emotional symphony in the room. He recognized what was true and then practiced loving, compassionate communication. What might have ended in a violent crescendo instead concluded with a surprisingly gentle, tender melody.

Any of us can consciously use resonant empathy in our daily lives. Through such empathic, loving communication, we can transform many of the challenging interpersonal situations that arise into meaningful, positive experiences. The key to success is often being sure that your loving communication in fact reflects the energy level of the other person. For example, when the Dalai Lama approached this young man, he did so in a very energetic way. He was gentle but also very direct in how he headed for the young man, parted us, and grabbed hold of him as he looked him in the eyes and spoke. His compassionate communication was just as direct, energetic, and powerful as the young man's anger had been. We often think of love and compassion as being somehow weak. In fact, if such positive emotions are to make a difference in our relationships and in the world, then they must be just as strong, direct, and forceful as any other emotions. When love and a negative emotion meet in a reciprocal, resonant interaction, love must be powerful enough to win out, overwhelming the force of that negativity.

POWER BORN OF TRUTH AND LOVE

I believe one of the most important developments to come out of the dialogue between Eastern and Western ideas relates directly to the empathic, loving communication I've been discussing. That development is the idea of civil disobedience, *Satyagraha*, or nonviolent, direct action.

Thoreau, who wrote about this idea in the mid–1800s, was influenced by Buddhist and Hindu thought. Gandhi, who applied these ideas so powerfully in the early 1900s, clearly combined traditional Eastern ideas with an understanding of Western politics, media, and psychology in developing his approach. And Martin Luther King Jr. openly acknowledged borrowing many of his ideas from Gandhi in developing his nonviolent approach to the civil rights movement in America. Over the past four decades, the Dalai Lama has been one of the most prominent world leaders to take on this approach to politics, adding his uniquely Buddhist slant to its application.

People sometimes wrongly believe that nonviolent, direct action is primarily a political tool, but Gandhi, King, and the Dalai Lama all emphasize that the essence of the approach they recommend is love. Gandhi called his approach *Satyagraha,* which he defined as power born of truth and love. To practice Satyagraha, one must strive to understand the truth (primarily through introspection, according to Gandhi, but also through empathy and reflection) and then also to communicate through the force of love. Gandhi clearly viewed his approach to the British government as communication driven by love for the people of India and also for the people of England.

Similarly, Martin Luther King Jr. defined his "passive resistance" approach as courageously confronting evil with the power of love. His approach is rooted in the faith that it is better to be the recipient of violence than the inflicter of it, since the latter only multiplies the existence of violence and bitterness in the universe while the former may develop a sense of shame in the opponent and thereby bring about a transformation and a change of heart.

To apply nonviolent, loving communication, you begin by seeing what is true in a given situation and then develop in yourself a powerful love for everyone involved, and finally you communicate in a thoughtful way based on the power of that love. External actions are only a physical expression of an inner commitment to truth and love.

Love, then, is not to be viewed as something soft or weak. Love has power. King once wrote, "We must use the weapon of love. We must have compassion and understanding for those who hate us." In his view love, compassion, and empathy were powerful forces for good that, when applied with consistency and bravery, could transform any injustice or evil. This concept of direct, active love, which grew out of the dialogue between Eastern and Western cultures, has been a powerful one.

Sometimes people develop conceptual empathy but remain distant and detached from others. Certain Western psychological theorists even suggest this kind of distant empathy as the correct approach for a psychotherapist. In fact, empathy devoid of any sense of caring about the other person goes against our common humanity. At best it causes our empathy to degenerate into a kind of voyeurism, and at worst it gives rise to the manipulative maneuvers of sociopaths. A con man and a child molester are examples of people who can understand another person by means of conceptual empathy but do not care about the welfare of the other; devoid of caring, empathy becomes a mere tool for manipulation. When empathy is combined with a sense of caring for and connection with others, it naturally gives rise to genuine love.

Gandhi's favorite quote from the Bhagavad Gita included the line, "Seeing everything with an equal eye, he sees the self in all creatures and all creatures in the self." When we see self and others as interconnected and interdependent in this way, empathy and love become inseparable. We understand and cherish others as we understand and cherish ourselves. This is a core insight giving rise to both love and compassion by way of empathy. It is presented clearly in the Buddhist tradition, and it is also clearly a part of many other great religious traditions.

From a practical point of view, as we continue cultivating empathy, we recognize more and more clearly how we are all the same in wanting happiness and not wanting to suffer. We also see that others suffer just as we do, and we may recognize as well that we have the same potentials within us that other people have. If we empathize deeply with our enemy, then we can understand why he behaves as he does. This was Martin Luther King Jr.'s greatest insight, in my view. By empathizing with racists, he understood them and loved them and set out to help heal their poisonous hatred and prejudice through the power of love. This is the essence of empathic, loving communication. Through empathy, we understand others, and we find that our own happiness and well-being are deeply and inextricably interconnected with theirs. By empathically understanding others and seeing our deep connections with them, we give rise to a sense of caring, love, and compassion that becomes a powerful force for healing relationships and bringing about happiness.

When discussing interpersonal communication, psychotherapists often talk about the benefits of compromise. Certainly compromises in relationships are often useful. But they are the domain of the ego. Compromises are often the result of a failure or lack of empathy and love. This important point can be understood only in light of the psychology of love and compassion. It has not yet been addressed in a serious way in the Western psychological tradition. Whether a disagreement is between two nations, two religions, two races, or between friends, spouses, family members, or coworkers, a compromise results in both sides giving up something and therefore feeling somewhat dissatisfied. Each side is still stuck in its own self-centered perspective, giving up something to get something else. This is different from a resolution born of empathy and love. Resolutions derived from empathy and love transcend old conflicts and bring about genuine justice, harmony, and peace. In our daily lives, such resolutions become possible when the force of our love transcends the limitations of our desire-driven egos.

When you read the teachings of the Buddha, you find that he did not discuss compromise; he discussed how people can find truth and liberation. Communication in his view was not about finding compromises between people's egos; it was about helping each other wake up to the truth and to find freedom. This is always the goal of loving communication—for both sides to see more clearly what is true and to be more free and joyful. The force of love, born of empathy, leads both parties to see through their illusory projections, which they wrongly believed were some truly existent disagreement, problem, or conflict. This is why the Buddha could assert that communication based in truth and love led to a life free from chronic problems and conflicts.

When both parties awaken to empathy and love, old problems or conflicts are seen as bad dreams that arose during a slumber in egotism.

LOVING COMMUNICATION AT THE MALL

What I want to emphasize is that empathic, loving communication of the sort practiced by great, nonviolent reformers is not something intended primarily for the political sphere. When the Dalai Lama points out that real peace in the world must begin in our own hearts and in our own lives, he is encouraging us to apply empathic, loving communication in our daily lives. We are all one human family, deeply and inextricably interconnected, and any of us who have not yet learned to empathize well with others and to communicate with the force of love will not be able to find peace in our own personal relationships. As long as we approach our relationships primarily from the perspective of the desire-driven ego, we find at best temporary compromises, which inevitably will be marred again and again by conflict.

In any given moment as we're relating with another person, we can pause to cultivate honesty, empathy, and love. We always have the choice whether we'll communicate based on projections and negative emotions or based on empathy and love. My wife, Terry, applied this approach when managing a cosmetics and skin care counter at an upscale department store in California. On the floor above hers, a piano played classical music. Atop the glass counters were lights, mirrors, and plastic units with products to apply any imaginable color to a woman's face. The workers there were young and pretty. One Valentine's Day, Terry noticed an older customer shouting at two of her coworkers. When she went to help out, the woman thrust a near-empty container of eye cream in front of her face.

"This was supposed to get rid of the wrinkles and puffiness around my eyes, but just look at them. Just look! The stuff doesn't work. I want my money back. It's useless."

By this point, Terry and her coworkers certainly were having a resonant response to the woman's anger. They already were feeling tense and annoyed with her. When Terry asked for the woman's receipt, she threw it at her. At this point it would have been easy to respond to her anger with anger. When people approach us in a negative way, we naturally may feel that we don't want to empathize with them and that they don't deserve our kindness. It's so easy to develop unconscious, totally negative projections about them and try to get rid of them. Such moments are ideal times to practice empathic, loving communication.

Rather than getting angry, Terry began empathizing with the woman. Combining conceptual empathy with her resonant understanding of the woman's level of unhappiness, Terry said, "We'll be happy to help you make a return. That's our store's policy. It won't be a problem." She paused for a moment before adding, "Your eyes *are* very puffy today. Is everything all right?"

The woman retorted, "No." There was a long pause during which neither of them moved. They paid no attention to the faint piano music or to the sounds of the shoppers around them. Perhaps there was an openness in Terry's body posture or in the quality of her gaze that expressed sincerity on her part, reversing the negative resonant energy of the situation. Somehow, as they looked at each other, they experienced a moment of genuine connection there in the midst of a mall. The woman softened. Though she certainly hadn't known it when she came in, this was exactly what she was looking for—a connection.

She said, "Really, I've been crying. Every night, I've been crying. You girls don't know what it's like to be getting old, to be alone. It's just terrible." Her eyes welled up with tears. Empathy had uncovered the loneliness beneath her anger, allowing for a deepened sense of intimacy.

Terry said, "It must be especially hard on Valentine's Day." She put the lady's eye cream down and came around the counter. She led to woman to a chair beside the counter and put her hand on her back.

The woman cried softly for a few minutes. Terry noticed that she was wearing a gold cross. When the woman stopped crying, Terry asked about it and they talked softly, together about Jesus, faith, and love. Terry said, "You know, you're not alone," as she hugged the woman. And, as other shoppers passed by beside the lights and the plastic displays, with the ceiling high above them, they prayed together.

Whether we are communicating with a customer, a coworker, a friend, or a family member, we can always choose to empathize and be loving. Even if the person is someone we meet only once, as was the case in this story, we can turn what would have been a meaningless or unpleasant experience into a meaningful and positive encounter. If the person is someone who plays an important role in our lives, then each time we employ the power of empathy and love in our interactions, we make our relationship with that person healthier. People and relationships don't transform overnight any more than old racial or political injustices do. I do not assume that the young man who gained the Dalai Lama's attention immediately overcame his tendency toward agitated anger any more than I assume that this customer suddenly resolved her loneliness through one positive interaction with a salesperson one Valentine's Day. When it comes to people with whom we interact regularly, though, we have a special opportunity. If we practice consistently saying what is true in an honest and loving way again and again over time, it can bring about deep changes for the other person as well as for us. If there is someone in your personal life with whom you have been experiencing a chronic sense of tension or conflict, it may be useful to begin cultivating honesty, empathy, and love in your communication with that person. In that way, you yourself will practice *Satyagraha*—the power born of truth and love.

EIGHT

THE RADIANT HEART

Buddhism and Western psychology agree that the more deeply, intensely, and frequently we allow ourselves to feel any given emotion, the more habituated we become to it. Each time we strongly experience a certain emotion, we increase our predisposition for experiencing that emotion again in the future and for seeing the world from the perspective of that emotion. This is true in the case of negative emotions like anxiety and rage, and it's also true of positive emotions like love and compassion.

It may feel sometimes as though we have no control at all over our emotions. If we have not analyzed emotions deeply, it may seem as though they are singular entities that arise of their own accord. In fact, when an emotion arises spontaneously, this means that it is one to which we've allowed ourselves to become habituated strongly. We do have the power to gradually increase or decrease how much we experience any given emotion. If we don't understand the nature of our emotions and how to work with them, then we may use that power unconsciously to cultivate negative emotions. When we spend time worrying about something, ruminating on a feeling of resentment, obsessing about an event that annoyed us, or longing for some object of desire, we unconsciously are cultivating negative emotions—unintentionally ensuring more suffering for ourselves. By understanding how our emotions work, we can stop cultivating negative emotions and begin habituating ourselves to positive emotions. The more time and energy we invest in cultivating positive emotions, the more spontaneous and powerful they will become, ensuring happiness for ourselves and those around us.

In this chapter, I present a relatively simple and popular Buddhist method for increasing the love and compassion that we already feel. While Western psychology recommends methods for increasing empathy, it has no practical methods to offer for increasing feelings of altruistic love or compassion. Still, Western psychology can help us understand how this Buddhist method works, and we will use it to analyze the various elements of our emotions, explaining how we can intentionally or unintentionally enhance them to bring about helpful or destructive consequences for ourselves and others.

ELEMENTS OF OUR EMOTIONS

On an unconscious level, each of us already knows how to cultivate emotions. We may have spent years unintentionally developing our anger, craving, or insecurity. If we want to understand how to develop powerful, positive emotions, it is helpful to become conscious of what we already know intuitively about cultivating emotions.

We can begin by recognizing that our emotions are not singular entities. Our significant emotional experiences contain a number of different elements, including thoughts, mental images, memories, beliefs, and physical reactions and sensations. These often produce behaviors that then become associated with (and may reinforce) the emotion that gave rise to them. For example, my patient Sam was preparing to make a presentation before a large group of people and was feeling anxious about it. He started out by thinking things like *I don't really know what*

I'm talking about, I can't do this, I'm going to make a fool of myself. These thoughts then triggered a certain negative image that he had of himself as an ineffective, incompetent person unworthy of acceptance or respect. Unconsciously, this image was linked to memories of unpleasant experiences in the past when he felt disappointed with himself and rejected or put down by others. He also held a mental image based on his past that he projected onto others, seeing them as mocking or rejecting. Making associations to these mental images and negative experiences triggered certain exaggerated, negative beliefs about himself, such as *I'm basically not a competent person, I'm so stupid, I'm never good at anything.* As he continued thinking such negative thoughts and focusing on his negative self-image, he began experiencing certain physical sensations. His heart rate increased, his breathing became quick and shallow, his palms got sweaty, his shoulders and neck muscles tensed up, and he even began feeling a little light-headed.

It was only when the physical symptoms began that Sam consciously realized he was feeling anxious. In the past he had focused on those negative thoughts and images so many times that they rose in his mind effortlessly, one after the other. He wasn't consciously aware of the role his past anxiety had played in his current experience; he didn't even notice many of the images, thoughts, and memories that were triggered in his mind. He just thought, *I'm anxious.*

At this point, because of his habituation to anxiety, his physical sensations, thoughts, and images built upon each another, further heightening his anxiety. Noticing his sweaty palms and light-headedness, he thought, *Oh, look how anxious I am, I'm a mess—a total wreck.* Thus his self-image worsened. He began thinking, *Not only don't I know what I'm doing for this presentation, I'm also going crazy with anxiety; maybe I'll wind up fainting; I'm a real nut case; oh, I can't stand this.* The more he dwelled in such negative, fearful thoughts, the more negative his self-image became and the more severe his physical symptoms grew. In the past Sam had avoided giving talks or doing other things that made him anxious, which kept him from having experiences of success that might have counteracted his negative self-image. We can get caught up in cycles like this, nurturing a relatively small, initial feeling of fear until it blossoms into an almost limitless experience of anxiety. By allowing negative thoughts, images, memories, and sensations to build upon one another, we eventually become totally paralyzed by fear. Actually, we can do this with any negative emotion, allowing one element to build upon another until we're overwhelmed.

Whenever we allow negative emotion to build energy like this, a great deal of suffering inevitably ensues. Much of Western psychotherapy is designed to help people work with the various elements of negative emotions and thereby decrease the overwhelming feelings of anxiety, rage, paranoia, depression, or obsessive desire that are running their lives.

Understanding the various elements of our negative emotions helps us see how to work with them. For example, once Sam recognized that his exaggerated, negative thoughts, such as *I can't do this,* triggered his anxiety, he began working at being aware of such thoughts when they arose, challenging them, and replacing them with more realistic thoughts, such as *This will be challenging, but I can do it if I work hard.* He practiced various relaxation exercises so that he'd be able to control the physical symptoms of anxiety when they arose. He also worked at developing a more realistic self-image that recognized his strengths as well as his weaknesses. Once he'd spent some time preparing in these ways, he began making presentations and doing other things that he previously had been too anxious to try. With each new experience of success, his self-esteem improved and his tendency to get anxious decreased.

When you recognize that any given negative emotion is causing you to suffer, analyzing the specific thoughts, images, memories, physical sensations, and behaviors that make up your experience of that emotion will reveal many different ways that you can intervene to decrease its power. Among the major schools of Western psychotherapy, some emphasize intervening with our thoughts, with our internal imagery, or with our behaviors, but all provide methods for decreasing negative emotions.

However, Western psychology has not yet used this understanding of the elements of our emotions to develop methods for increasing positive emotions. This creates a big gap in our approach to working with emotions. The Buddhist method I'm about to present uses an awareness of these same elements of our emotions to increase feelings of love and compassion. Just as we unconsciously can allow the elements of our negative emotions to build upon each other, exponentially increasing their power, so also we can choose to consciously use the elements of our positive emotions to build upon each other, developing more and more powerful love and compassion until they also appear limitless in our minds.

IMMEASURABLE COMPASSION

If you understand the nature of emotions, you can see that there is nothing utopian or far-fetched about cultivating powerful feelings of love or compassion. Someone who is having a panic attack has the subjective experience that the universe is filled with horrific, crushing, suffocating anxiety. Someone who is totally enraged sees the whole world as a terrible place; nothing good is apparent to them, and the response is limitless anger. In a similar way, when we use this method, instead of unconsciously allowing our negative emotions to overwhelm our experience of the world, we are consciously cultivating positive emotions, intentionally developing the feeling of limitless compassion.

Because the power of any given emotion is strongly related to how often and how intensely we experience it, each time we actively cultivate compassion we are habituating ourselves to a positive way of feeling and seeing the world. As you strengthen your familiarity with compassionate thoughts, images, memories, sensations, and behaviors, feelings of compassion will arise more and more powerfully and spontaneously in your mind. As the elements of compassion are very different from the elements of negative emotions, developing compassion will naturally cause your negative emotions to decrease. If you practice this method regularly, then gradually you can make compassion the baseline emotion with which you approach the world. The idea is not that by imagining a universe filled with compassion you'll somehow change the matter on distant mountains, planets, or stars. Instead, the idea is that you'll change yourself and your way of viewing and experiencing the universe around you. Engaging in this method can bring you the inner peace that comes with a decrease in your negative emotions and the joy that comes from sincere compassion.

Begin this method by sitting down comfortably, relaxing, and focusing on your breathing for a few minutes. When we're feeling compassionate, our breathing is usually quite deep and steady. So, even with this first step, we're beginning to evoke part of the physical element of compassion.

Next, begin giving rise to the feeling of compassion toward yourself. Begin thinking *May I be free from suffering.* Now you're starting to work with the cognitive component of this emotion. Just focus on yourself for a while, and keep thinking *May I be free from suffering.* In order to strengthen the emotion of compassion, it's also helpful at this point to begin using memory and mental imagery. Recall times when you were suffering in some particular way, and also specifically bring to mind the image of yourself as someone vulnerable to all sorts of suffering. Briefly imagine how easily you may lose things you cherish, may become ill, or may meet with hardships. As you think of such things, continue thinking *May I be free from suffering.* Continue thinking and imagining in this way until you develop a sense of compassion for yourself.

Next, start thinking about people to whom you feel close. Think *May they be free from suffering.* While you think that, also begin imagining your compassionate awareness radiating out from your heart, reaching out to them, and washing away their suffering. Tibetan practitioners sometimes visualize their compassion radiating from their chest like the warm light of the sun bringing illumination everywhere. It's important to be skillful in working with your emotions to really deepen and increase the feeling of compassion. Think about the people you love, focusing on the specific kinds of suffering that they experience in their lives. Really try to feel energy reaching out from your heart, gently touching them, soothing them, and removing their suffering. If you or other people you know have pets, include them in this meditation. You can also include wild animals that may be in danger or suffering. Some people find it easier to develop strong compassion for animals than for other people. Get to know your own mind, and use your predispositions to work pragmatically at enhancing your positive emotions. It's also good to think of children you know. For a while, continue thinking of various people you're close to, thinking *May they be free from suffering* and imagining compassion reaching out from your heart to them. Try to expand your feeling to embrace as many of them as possible.

Then do the same practice focusing on strangers. Think of all the people in your town whom you don't know, and develop the wish *May they be free from suffering.* Imagine compassionate energy radiating out from your heart, filling your whole town with the warm glow of compassion, freeing beings from suffering. For as long as you can, try to continue expanding your compassion outward, encompassing more and more beings in your compassion. Imagine reaching out to particular places in your nation or in the world, embracing people there with your compassion. Think of children who are homeless, of people who are starving, of those suffering from various diseases, and of people who are oppressed in various ways. Think of people who are going through the motions of life, living lives of quiet desperation; who are lonely and have no voice; who have lost what they loved the most; and who cannot feel compassion even for themselves. When you find that focusing on a specific person or place evokes a stronger feeling of compassion, dwell on that image for a little while, strongly thinking *May they be free from suffering* and strongly imagining the light from your heart touching them and freeing them from pain.

By this point in the practice, the various elements of the emotion of compassion should have begun building upon one another. As you continue with the visualization, you begin feeling a sense of openness in your heart. An image of yourself as open to and connected with others is evoked. At the same time, your repeating the thought *May they be free from suffering* enhances the feeling of connectedness with others. You develop a feeling of cherishing them from your heart. As you develop these thoughts and images, you also develop more of the physical reactions related to compassion; you feel calm and relaxed but also attentive, alert, and open. Your breathing becomes deeper and quite calm. You may feel a sensation of openness in your chest and also of energy radiating through your body and outward. If feelings of sadness or disillusionment about others' suffering arise, this is actually a positive sign that your heart is opening. Don't dwell in the feeling of sadness; just notice it and continue radiating your energy out to others. If you continue focusing on compassion or love, then feelings of sadness or disillusionment simply will get swept up in the wave of positive emotion, adding their energy to that wave.

After you have focused on strangers, next focus on enemies or people to whom you're ordinarily averse, developing compassion for them as well. Enemies can include people with whom you personally have difficulty, people who have wronged you in the past, or people in countries toward which you have a negative feeling. At first you may feel uncomfortable with the idea of developing compassion for your enemies. It's important to understand that developing compassion for them does not mean that you are approving of any harmful actions they may have done. Neither does developing compassion mean that you somehow will be more vulnerable to harm; in fact, cultivating compassion for your enemies is one of the best ways to benefit and protect yourself. Holding on to your aversion, prejudice, and anger toward someone instead causes you suffering. Also, when you're angry at someone, your negative projections allow you to see only that person's flaws, which keeps you from seeing positive attributes that could help you resolve conflicts. It also keeps you from seeing realistically and understanding those to whom you're averse, which actually makes you more vulnerable to them. As others pick up on your anger, prejudice, and aversion (either through your overt expressions or through their resonant empathic understanding of your covert behaviors), they become more likely to react negatively toward you, leading to escalated tensions and even the possibility of violence. Even if you have to stand up to someone, if you remain compassionate this will protect you from getting caught up in negative projections and impulsive behaviors. If your compassion for your enemies were to achieve its goal—if your enemies were free from suffering—then they no longer would have any reason to make problems for you. It's usually people's negative reactions to their own suffering that drives them to act in harmful ways. If they were free from suffering and its causes, then they might stop being your enemies. Often it is difficult people who are suffering the most intensely and who are therefore most in need of compassion.

Continuing with the method for increasing compassion, specifically empathize with the suffering of your enemies and think *May they too be free from suffering.* As you empathically imagine their suffering, see if you can develop a genuine feeling of compassion. Also imagine compassion reaching out to them, overcoming their negative emotions, problems, and suffering. You can imagine them finding joy and taking new, positive directions in their lives.

After spending some time on compassion for your enemies, spend time just imagining compassion going out from your heart to all beings. You can imagine your compassion embracing the entire planet and then radiating out, filling the entire universe. At this point, you think *May all beings be free from suffering.* Really try to expand on the feeling of compassion, imagining that it becomes limitless and immeasurable. Imagine that it radiates everywhere, touching everyone and everything, so that the whole universe vibrates with the energy of your infinite empathy, compassion, and love.

Dwell for as long as you can in the feeling of limitless compassion. When the mind gets distracted and the feeling decreases, you can return briefly to thinking of the various people and other beings for whom you were developing compassion. Think again of specific forms of suffering, generating the wish that those beings may be free and also visualizing compassionate awareness reaching out to them. Once the feeling of compassion has grown strong again, just dwell in the image of a universe filled with compassionate energy radiating out from your heart and in the feeling of infinite, limitless love and compassion.

We all naturally experience some compassion in our daily lives. By engaging in this method, we can make our compassion more expansive and intense, habituating ourselves to seeing the world through eyes of compassion.

RADIANT, RESONANT JOY

If you get good at this method of cultivating limitless love and compassion, you'll find doing it quite pleasurable or joyful. It's similar to the deep pleasure of falling madly in love. When we first fall in love, many different feelings get mixed together. There may be a sense of grasping and attachment as well as a feeling of sexual excitement. When we really fall in love, though, there's also a feeling of deep affection for and closeness to the other person. This often gives rise to a sense of cherishing that person, caring deeply about their welfare. When we feel this way, we often say that we've given our heart to the other person.

I've already explained how desire-based attachment leads to suffering. When people try to base their relationships mainly on attachment and sexual excitement, the relationship either won't last or ultimately won't be very satisfying. By contrast, when we specifically make an effort to develop our sense of cherishing and caring about another, our relationships become more and more satisfying over the years. Consciously cultivating the initial seed of our genuine affection, love, and compassion for the other person is the most effective way to find real happiness in a marriage or other long-term relationship. You can do so by applying to your partner the method of limitless compassion as well as the other methods described in this book.

If you really get into practicing this method as described, you may begin to feel like you're falling madly in love with countless others. Giving your heart away to everyone, you find that rather than having lost anything, you've gained a more expansive and joyful sense of yourself. It's as though you took away the grasping, attachment, and excitement but kept the deep sense of affection and joy of falling in love, and then you multiplied that affection and joy by infinity. That is the pleasure that can come from practicing the radiant heart method well.

According to the Buddhist and Hindu teachings on karma, a person who engages in this method is said to create the cause for taking rebirth in a heavenly realm, as a divine being. They say that hate serves as a cause for a hellish birth, while love and compassion serve as causes for divine births. Whether or not we believe in rebirth, I think that we can see for ourselves that hate creates a hellish existence in this life. If even one or two people in a family are overwhelmed with hatred, then a beautiful home may feel like hell to the people living in it. Similarly, if we really get into the practice of cultivating the energy of vast love and compassion, it will create a sort of divine existence even in this life. Think for a moment of how the world appeared to you and how you felt about things when you were first falling madly in love with someone. You may think that way of experiencing the world cannot be recaptured or maintained. But the deep pleasure we experience and the inspiring beauty we see when we give our hearts away results in fact from affection, love, and compassion; by gradually cultivating these qualities in ourselves, we can come to live more and more in the divine realm of heartfelt love.

I have noticed that sometimes as Westerners start getting good at this practice and develop some feelings of deep joy or bliss, they either grasp at those experiences or they feel guilty for being so happy. Grasping and guilt both destroy joy. Grasping is a result of our old feeling, based in desire, which imagines that there's a limited supply of good things. We must beware of such inner materialism, which undermines compassion and leads us back into the unending cycle of desire and frustration. If you catch yourself grasping in this way, the antidote is just to remember that your joy or bliss is a result of love and compassion. Grasping at it, you distance yourself from love and compassion, thereby ensuring that your joy will decrease. If you want more joy, then continue to cultivate love and compassion for others, and positive results will continue. The Dalai Lama sometimes refers to this point as wise selfishness, noting that if we want to be wise about achieving our own welfare, then we can do nothing better than cultivate compassion for others.

If you start to feel guilty about being blissful, then it's important to address this directly as well. Many people who begin intense practices for cultivating love and compassion and then stop don't realize it, but they're afraid of feeling too good. They may feel that they don't deserve to be blissed out, or they may fear that getting too happy will make them different from other people. But feeling guilty or afraid about feeling good will only get in the way of your developing love and compassion. The skillful way to relate to positive feelings is to let them further increase your love and compassion. Psychologically speaking, if you're stressed out and miserable, there's not much you can do for others. The more wisdom, bliss, energy, compassion, and joy you have, the more you can give to others. The idea is to develop our own inner qualities continually while at the same time giving more and more of ourselves to others.

Even before we begin engaging in specific tasks to help others, our developing love, compassion, and joy do benefit those around us by way of resonant empathy. Many people have noted that it's often very pleasurable and energizing to spend time around great practitioners of compassion like the Dalai Lama. This is partly because we pick up on their incredible bliss and joy by way of resonant empathy. I've found that spending time with great practitioners is one of the main ways to discover positive potentials in myself that I never knew were there. This is one of the reasons that reading Buddhist teachings in books is not sufficient if you really want to practice seriously. Through resonant empathy, we can get a taste of feelings of freedom, bliss, and energy that we cannot realize through reading. Once we recognize those potentials in ourselves, we can begin working to cultivate them.

The more we develop compassion and joy, the more others benefit empathically from our presence. Even if we don't act out negative feelings, just walking around in a state of intense rage or anxiety will upset some of the people around us as they empathically resonate with us. Similarly, just walking around in a state of intense compassion and joy will make some of the people around us feel better. If we want to be of benefit to others, then it's our responsibility to cultivate contentment, happiness, and even bliss in ourselves.

RADIANT FREEWAYS

To develop intense, overwhelmingly positive feelings of love and compassion, it's best to set aside some quiet time to engage in the full method as described above. Once you've gotten used to the method, though, it can be helpful also to incorporate some elements into your daily routines. For example, many people have found it useful to engage in a simplified form of this method while out walking around their neighborhood or town. Notice the people and the animals around you as you walk. Try to empathize with what they may be going through, and then think *May all these beings be happy; may they be free from suffering,* and imagine compassion going out from your heart and benefiting them. In this way, a walk around the neighborhood or around the grocery store becomes a meditation on love and compassion.

A nun once told me about a time she was walking at night near a meditation center, worried about something. Suddenly she bumped into her Tibetan lama, who was also walking alone. She said, "Lama, what are you doing out here at night?"

He said, "Oh, I'm walking around looking for sentient beings who need help." He was meditating on love and compassion.

She began walking on but then thought of her worry, turned around, and said, "I'm a sentient being; I can use some help." The lama smiled broadly, and they began walking together.

You also can practice the radiant heart while driving. I know a number of friends and patients who, while driving, have used simple forms of this practice with positive results. One patient named Daniel really hated his commute. For a few years he unconsciously had been using his drive home from work to cultivate agitated anger. He regularly spent his commute thinking about frustrations with his boss and contemplating how he wished he could change jobs. Through habit he had built up a negative image about his boss, his job, and his commute until he was feeling quite averse and annoyed. Then if traffic was thick or another driver inconsiderate, his annoyance would flare up into real anger. He'd sigh and tense up, sometimes giving dirty looks to other drivers. He'd think about how badly other people drove and how much he disliked living where he did. Occasionally he'd get so mad that he'd shout inside his car. By the time got home, his neck and shoulders were tense and he was very irritable. One day his wife told him that she and the kids felt really anxious when they heard him pull into the garage. They never knew what to expect, and the kids were growing away from him because they feared his irritability and anger.

This conversation with his wife led Daniel to realize that he needed to make some changes. He started working out to take better care of himself, and he also started taking some time to himself just after getting home to calm down and get into a better frame of mind. Then one day we talked about the idea of his using the drive home to cultivate love. The opposite of agitated anger is joyful love, and so this is an ideal antidote to anger. He was open to the idea, and so while driving home he began using the method described earlier in this chapter. He tried to empathize with the other drivers, imagining that they wanted to get home just as much as he did. He also empathized with his boss and coworkers, wishing them happiness and success. He imagined compassion reaching out from his heart to people at his work and to all the other drivers around him, wishing to protect everyone from all kinds of accidents, anger, and suffering.

I think Daniel used the method for only ten or fifteen minutes of his hour-long commute each day. Still, after just a couple of weeks he reported that he was coming home in a much better mood. He no longer needed to take time to himself after getting home. He said, "I didn't realize how uptight I was getting. Just starting to empathize with the other drivers around me made me realize how I'd been projecting my frustrations about work onto them. Giving them dirty looks, I was probably even increasing other people's stress, so that they went home to their kids in a worse mood. I never thought I'd become that sort of person. Now I do my driving meditation, and then I put on some music and just use the drive to think better thoughts."

He didn't need to tell his wife and children that he'd shifted his attitude. They quickly picked up on the change in him. As his kids resonated with his new emotional presence, rather than skulking away to their rooms, they began hanging around the living room near him. When his youngest son started running up and hugging him after he'd walked in the door, Daniel knew that love really was supplanting anxiety and anger.

If you want to habituate yourself to compassion, causing it to arise spontaneously and powerfully in your mind, it's best to set aside a few quiet minutes per day to engage in the complete method. Even applying it in small ways as you drive, wait in line at the bank, shop at the grocery store, or listen to a friend can be very powerful. At the very least, your doing so will make it less likely that you'll wind up getting frustrated and making other people's days worse as they resonate with your agitation. Better yet, you may begin being more openhearted and joyful as you go about such mundane activities, so that you inspire the other people you meet.

JOYFULLY DOING THE DISHES

One of the most popular religious images in Central Asia is of Tara, the female Buddha of compassion. She is radiant, green in color, and is shown seated but with her right leg outstretched, as though she is in the process of getting up. This is an iconographic representation of compassionate commitment. She is radiant, focused, and energetic. Tara's left leg in the pose of meditation suggests the necessity for an ongoing, inner focus on developing compassion in your heart, while her outstretched right leg reflects her absolute commitment to compassionate action. She is ever ready to leap up and actively help someone in need. This is how it feels when we develop a feeling of compassionate responsibility. We don't focus exclusively on the outer world, running around frenetically and exhausting ourselves. Instead, we allow our actions to flow naturally from the compassion in our hearts, and those actions then enhance our feelings of compassion.

Westerners often believe that the commitment to help others is something overly heavy and ponderous. We may feel that our responsibilities are a big burden that our egos must carry. The more responsibilities we take on, the more stressed we become. But commitments and activities born of genuine compassion don't cause stress; they cause joy.

We can be very busy doing things we want to do, and we find it not at all stressful. When we commit to meeting a friend to play tennis, swim, go out to lunch, and do some shopping, we don't find it stressful because we're committing to doing something we want to do. We feel stressed when we do things that we don't really want to do but feel that we have to do for one reason or another. For example, many people feel stressed about their jobs because they don't really want to work but they have to work to get money. This is a compromise made by the ego—we do something unpleasant to get something in return later. When our commitments in the service of others feel heavy and stressful, this means that that those commitments are driven not by compassion but by ego desires that aim to get something in return.

Early on in our development of compassion, taking on too many external commitments is often more a sign of pride—a desire to look good or saintly in others' eyes—than a sign of deep compassion. If we want to become truly compassionate people, then we must begin by setting aside time and energy for cultivating compassion in our hearts.

Once we've made some effort at developing the feelings of love and compassion, it can be helpful to practice doing small, compassionate actions for people at home and at work. It's particularly important to do these actions mindfully; as symbolized by Tara's posture, part of our focus should be on our inner state of joyful compassion, and part should be on helping the other person. By taking joy in our own growing compassion and in how our actions benefit others, we can continue inspiring ourselves so that compassion gives rise to action, which in turn inspires more compassion. By gradually learning to do such actions with our whole heart imbued with sincere love and compassion, we naturally will become able to take on greater responsibilities for the welfare of others without finding them particularly heavy. Such a gradual approach also allows us to develop our inner resources so that we do not feel depleted by our efforts for the welfare of others. The next chapter provides a method for greatly enhancing our inner resources so as to find joy rather than exhaustion in our compassionate service to others.

NINE

GRATITUDE AND INNER WEALTH

Feelings of gratitude for all that we have and for the care, generosity, empathy, and love others have shown us are foundational not only to our capacities for love and compassion but also to our ability to feel good and satisfied with our lives. Etymologically, the word *grateful* implies a feeling of fullness and thankfulness for all that is great—in others and also in ourselves. Feeling gratitude, we are joyful and gracious regarding that which has been given freely to us.

When I teach developmental psychology, I often have the students reflect on and then share with each other times when others showed them particularly meaningful kindness. Within a few minutes, the students are smiling broadly, laughing, and feeling suddenly closer to each other. As we think of others' kindness and grow grateful, our feelings of fullness allow our compulsive desires and ego defenses to relax. We become more open to others. And only when we acknowledge what is good or great in ourselves do we become capable of consciously sharing it with others.

When we feel depleted, empty, or exhausted, it's easy for many different negative emotions to develop. At such times we certainly don't feel good about ourselves, and we may even feel as though we can't handle our lives or we lack something at our very core, leading to fear and anxiety. We may feel that the world around us is impoverished, lacking in sources of meaning, joy, or sustenance, which can lead to feelings of hopelessness or depressive sorrow. If we do see good things in the world around us when we feel depleted, then feelings of envy can arise easily. When we're feeling empty we often develop many desires for external objects that can never fill us up emotionally, ultimately leading to feelings of frustration and anger.

Gratitude is just the opposite of feeling depleted; it predisposes us to many different positive states of mind. When we're feeling grateful, we focus on what we have rather than on what we lack, and this leads to feelings of satisfaction and contentment. Recalling the kindness that others have shown us naturally reminds us of how others have valued and seen the good in us, which can inspire us to see the good in ourselves, leading to healthy self-esteem and self-confidence. Object relations analysts also note that thinking of others with gratitude allows us to identify with them and to internalize the love and kindness they've shown us, enhancing our ability to feel good about ourselves and to feel love for others. Thinking of others' love and compassion can cause us also to resonate empathically to such emotions, evoking them in ourselves. Buddhist psychology notes that cultivating gratitude helps us feel more connected to others and also helps us develop feelings of loving affection, compassion, and the wish to repay or pass on the kindness we've been shown.

In this chapter we'll explore how we can develop feelings of contentment and compassion by actively cultivating gratitude. Some insights from object relations analysts will help us to understand the psychology of gratitude, and we'll look at a few methods for developing gratitude inspired by Western psychology and also by a Buddhist method popular among Tibetans that involves "recollecting the kindness of all mother-beings." Before getting into such methods, though, I'll discuss some cultural factors that for modern Westerners may get in the way of cultivating gratitude.

In order to develop gratitude we must think about and share stories of kindness and love. Often this entails thinking about the past, focusing on those who have made sacrifices on our behalf. While we may share such stories occasionally, our discussions, along with our modern media, more often focus on current news of dangers, conflicts, crimes, and scandals. We focus less on what is greatly meaningful than on what is exciting and less on what is kind than on what is current. Recent psychological research indicates that Americans tend to be unduly fearful, grossly overestimating the likelihood of various types of crime, accidents, and other negative events. Our exposure to negative events in the media leads us to focus on such things more than is useful or healthy. As we spend time thinking unrealistically about what's wrong, we fail to see what's right. As we spend time thinking about exciting or upsetting news, our days pass without our taking time to develop gratitude.

The advertising we're exposed to daily also tends to lead us away from feelings of gratitude. Advertisements are designed to make us want things we don't have. The role of advertising is usually to discourage contentment, sparking desire to have something new, more, or better. The ubiquity of advertising in our culture can add fuel to our inborn tendencies toward desire and discontent, keeping us from developing our capacity for satisfaction. Distracted by our desires, we fail to relax into feelings of satisfaction and appreciation, which are foundational for developing gratitude.

Another cultural obstacle to gratitude and compassion that affects many people is the sense of isolation and disconnection from family and friends that often accompanies our modern lifestyles. Feelings of connection and affection are essential to the psychology of gratitude.

Allowing ourselves to become disconnected from other people goes against our very nature. From an evolutionary perspective, our tendencies to connect with and care about each other have been essential to our survival as a species. We've survived by working together, and our children have survived because of the powerful human disposition to care deeply for others of our kind.

The word *kindness* derives from *kind,* which shares the same etymological root as *kin* and *gene.* Like many other mammals, we humans have a strong, inborn tendency to be kind to others of our kind, particularly to our kin, to whom we're genetically linked. Bonds of love, affection, and gratitude always have been essential to our survival and are also essential to our psychological well-being. When career and lifestyle choices lead us to feel isolated, we not only disconnect from other people, we also disconnect from many of the best capacities of our own hearts.

We don't necessarily have to change our lifestyles in order to reconnect with our innate capacities for gratitude, love, and affection. When I first began spending time with elder Tibetan monks, I was surprised to find that some who had spent years in remote, solitary retreats could be incredibly warm, open, and loving. By using methods like those presented in this book, we can cultivate the best qualities of our hearts wherever we may find ourselves.

One thing unique about humans as compared to other mammals is that we can choose to expand our sense of kinship as wide as we like. Recent genetic research suggests that all of humanity shares a common, ancient ancestry. Most of our genetic makeup is shared not only with all other people but even with other animals who share our common ancient ancestors. Based on this research, we are all quite literally related. Now that we can see images of our planet from space, it should not be so difficult to contemplate the simple fact that we are all kin, sharing a comparatively small and clearly precious home that's spinning through the vast expanses of space. How broadly we expand our sense of connection—who and what we identify with—is up to us. Some highly narcissistic people think of and cherish only themselves. Other people expand their sense of identity to their family so that they cherish them and feel responsible for their welfare too. Others expand their sense of identity to include their town, their city, their nation, or their planet, making considerable efforts and sacrifices on behalf of those with whom they identify.

So although a modern lifestyle that leads us to live apart from family or old friends can be an obstacle to developing gratitude and compassion, it need not be one. Distance need not undermine our feelings of affection, connection, or gratitude and even can serve as a positive reminder of the value of expanding our sense of kinship wider and wider, thereby also expanding the kindness in our own hearts.

The idea of viewing ourselves as deeply connected with others brings up another important obstacle to developing gratitude. We modern Westerners, especially Americans, often have a strong desire to see ourselves as independent and self-sufficient. Focusing on gratitude to others for their kindness and support can seem to us like a sign of weakness and dependency. Actually, gratitude is not a sign of weakness; psychologically, gratitude is a sign of inner strength and successful individuation.

Psychologically, ideas of existing as utterly independent, self-sufficient beings usually serve as defenses; we try to see ourselves as self-sufficient in order to deny deep, unresolved desires for dependency and symbiosis left over from early childhood. A superficial self-image of independence and strength often hides underlying fears of affection, intimacy, and gratitude. When we haven't completed the process of individuation successfully, we fear that deeply experiencing our connections with others will lead to losing our sense of individuality and autonomy—to being swallowed up by our unconscious and potentially overwhelming neediness and desire for symbiosis.

Healthy individuation means that we can experience our individuality and autonomy and can discover our unique interests, goals, and strengths within the context of our true ties of connection and interdependence with others. Buddhism strongly emphasizes that we exist interdependently, inextricably connected by complex relations of causality. Denying our interdependence means that we deny who we really are and how we actually exist. Healthy individuation, which recognizes our interdependence, allows for a compassionate, mature sense of ethics, taking responsibility for how our actions affect others. Dr. Martin Luther King Jr. addressed the link between interdependence and ethics when he wrote,

> Injustice anywhere is a threat to justice everywhere. We are caught in an inescapable network of mutuality, tied in a single garment of destiny. Whatever affects one directly, affects all indirectly.

The nature of this inescapable mutuality has only become clearer since Dr. King wrote those words. Economic, political, and social events occurring in one part of the globe quickly affect those thousands of miles away. New inventions, ideas, businesses, and forms of art and music spread rapidly from one continent to another, as do violence, hatred, and diseases. In many practical ways, our own welfare and the welfare of others are deeply interdependent. We may be in the habit of viewing ourselves as unconnected to many of our fellow humans, but contemplating the reality of our interdependence can help us develop the feeling and the insight that we are all one human family, with each of us responsible to the others for weaving the garment of our shared destiny.

It is unfortunately true that those who most need to experience more affection, intimacy, and gratitude often fear it most. Object relations analysts describe how these positive experiences allow us to develop enough security and confidence to succeed in individuating.

Affection and gratitude allow us to develop enough trust in ourselves and in the world that we can overcome our fears, successfully individuate, and work responsibly and lovingly as individuals in interdependent and intimate relationships.

OBJECT RELATIONS AND GRATITUDE

The developmental process of separation and individuation usually begins during the second year of life, as we move from a world of sensations and instinctual impulses into gradually recognizing ourselves and others as separate entities existing in time. The importance of this developmental period to our overall mental health and particularly to our capacities for intimacy and mature, loving relationships can hardly be overstated. Gratitude plays an absolutely essential role in whether or not we come through this period well.

As the child develops an awareness of her parents existing separately from herself, she becomes capable of imagination and conceptual empathy. These new abilities make life more complicated, allowing all sorts of new emotions to emerge. Only when we recognize that others exist separately from us can we feel thankful to them for their kindness or wish that they be free from suffering. This recognition also allows us to envy others for what they have, hate them for not doing what we want, and fear that others may abandon or harm us. We need only think of the tantrums and nightmares that children exhibit between the ages of two and six to understand how terribly overwhelming these early experiences of negative emotions can be.

Melanie Klein and other object relations analysts describe an inner struggle that takes place in the child's psyche during this period of her development. On one side of this struggle are negative emotions such as frustration, fear, envy, hate, and rage. We all experience such emotions during this period of our lives, but if we get too caught up in them we begin feeling very bad about ourselves and the world, leading the whole process of individuation to go awry. People who have not found their way successfully through this stage of development often experience chronic feelings of emptiness, discontent, and confusion. Their self-image is often unstable, and their impulsive acting out of their negative emotions often wreaks havoc on their relationships.

What is it that keeps most people from following this negative developmental track? Love and gratitude are the primary forces on the other side of the struggle in the child's psyche. Just as early, unpleasant experiences give rise to negative emotions, so also do positive experiences of affection and pleasure with the parents give rise to the positive emotions of love and gratitude. As the child develops stable, internal images of the parents and develops conceptual empathy, she gradually realizes that her very survival has depended and continues to depend upon the kindness of others. She realizes that her experiences of feeding, cuddling, being kept warm, being soothed, and being kept safe all derive from the kindness of her parents. At this stage, she particularly focuses on the primary caregiver, a role most often played by the biological mother but also sometimes played by other adults in the child's life. In healthy development, at this stage the child feels a deep sense of appreciation, affection, and gratitude to this parent for loving and caring for her. Just as she earlier responded to the mother's smile with a smile of her own, so also does she now respond to her love with her own feelings of love and gratitude.

Of course, the child also experiences many moments of frustration, anger, and deprivation. The ideal setting for her development is not a perfect home or world. D. W. Winnicott coined the phrase "good-enough mother" to describe what children need to develop in a healthy way. The child needs to experience some frustration but to have more good, affectionate, pleasurable, loving experiences than bad, frustrating, agitated ones. In this way each of us learns how to deal with challenges while also developing a sense of basic trust that we can find a meaningful and satisfying place in the world and that life can be worth living. The child's love and gratitude toward the parents also allow her to develop the capacity to trust other people. As experiences of gratitude repeatedly win out over envy or hate, the child realizes that intimacy with other people can present challenges but is ultimately meaningful and satisfying. In this way we learn that we need not fear connecting through love and affection with others.

Just as early experiences of love and gratitude lead to a sense of basic trust in the world, so also they lead the child to begin trusting in herself. Because of her gratitude and love, the child learns to control her aggressive impulses. She also learns that even when she does act out, the relationship with her parents can be repaired by way of apology, love, and kindness. Therefore, the child develops deeper and deeper trust in her own abilities to be in the world and in relationships with others. Recognizing her own capacities for love and relatedness, the child begins feeling good about herself.

The child's gratitude to her parents also leads her to feel how much love, affection, compassion, and care she has received from them. Psychologically, this leads to a feeling of fullness; when we recognize and appreciate all the love we were given, we truly receive and integrate it into our personalities. Even as adults, when we develop feelings of gratitude it is this feeling of fullness that arises. When we develop sincere gratitude toward someone, it can feel as though that other person's kindness was poured into us, filling our hearts. If we don't develop gratitude, our hearts remain closed and we cannot truly feel or take in the kindness others do offer. Failing to take in the love offered by others leaves us feeling empty, insecure, and impoverished. Klein makes an extremely important observation in this regard when she writes, "With people in whom this feeling of inner wealth and strength is not sufficiently established, bouts of generosity are often followed by an exaggerated need for appreciation and gratitude, and consequently of persecutory anxieties of having been impoverished and robbed."

This is often the underlying root of compassion fatigue and burnout. We may appreciate the value of compassion and generosity, but on an unconscious level we still carry around feelings of inner poverty derived from limitations in our early experiences of love and gratitude. Therefore, we may give more than we feel that we have. Cultivating gratitude is a powerful means for counteracting fatigue and emotional poverty, allowing our hearts to fill up so that we can love and be generous to others without expectations or bouts of exhaustion.

DEALING WITH UNRESOLVED ISSUES

I've found that it's important for Westerners to be careful in how we go about beginning to cultivate gratitude. If we have suppressed feelings of deprivation, mistrust, envy, or rage left over from the early process of individuation, these can be stirred up when we begin working at developing gratitude. For example, I've often seen intelligent Westerners learn a Buddhist meditation that involves remembering the kindness they received as children in order to develop gratitude, only to find themselves suddenly overwhelmed by feelings of deprivation, insecurity, and anger that they've never worked through from their own childhoods.

Many Westerners, including some psychotherapists, hold mistaken views about how to deal skillfully with such issues when they do come up. It's important to work through such feelings without dwelling in them. If people were abused or neglected, or if they experienced some painful or traumatic events in childhood that are having specific, negative effects in the here and now, then skillfully addressing those developmental issues can help them. However, there are also side effects to dealing with those issues, just as surely as there are side effects to taking medications. Facing negative feelings from our past in order to let them go can be healing, but dwelling in such feelings unnecessarily further habituates us to them, giving them more power over our lives.

There is nothing *inherently* valuable about exploring childhood issues either in general or as they relate to our life currently. I've seen many patients who spent years exploring negative and traumatic childhood incidents with very little positive effect. I've even come across a number of psychotherapists who have been through years of their own therapy but still don't seem particularly content or loving in their own lives. I'm certainly not suggesting that we shouldn't explore issues from childhood. I have a deep appreciation for developmental psychology, and I've often seen people benefit a great deal from uncovering a specific developmental issue and working through it. The point is that we have to know what we're doing and why we're doing it; we have to be clear that the ideas or insights we're developing promote health, love, and happiness.

Wilfred Bion, a brilliant object relations psychoanalyst, once pointed out that any given psychological idea has value in a situation only if it is true in that situation and also is useful in promoting health. Many people overlook this absolutely essential point. Bion's assertion is very much in line with the teachings of the Buddha, who on a number of occasions refused to answer people's questions, noting that discussing things they were bringing up would not help listeners awaken or be liberated from suffering. The Buddha insisted that he would present or discuss only ideas that would help people attain happiness and awakening; anything else was simply not worth our breath or our thought.

To see why we have to be careful not to dwell in negative emotions as we work through old issues, we can look at the example of Sarah. As a child, Sarah sometimes felt angry and even enraged at her mother for being neglectful and making demeaning, cruel comments. Afraid that expressing these feelings to her mother might lead to further abandonment and cruelty, Sarah suppressed them and directed her anger toward herself instead. Unconsciously she thought many negative things about herself, put herself down, and blamed herself for her mother's rejection and anger. Over the years, this unconscious anger developed into depression and low self-esteem. Now, for Sarah to resolve her depression and low self-esteem successfully, it will be useful to go back and recognize that she didn't do anything wrong as a girl and didn't deserve the anger that her mother directed at her or that she directed at herself. In the process of working through those memories, a side effect is likely to be that Sarah now will feel the old anger at her mother that, as a girl, she was too afraid to express or of which she was not even totally aware. The old anger at her mother is like dirt in the wash water that comes out when you clean an old blanket—its coming out is a good sign. However, if Sarah becomes attached to that anger, it will only cause her further suffering.

This often does happen. In the process of therapy, people often get stuck in such negative thoughts and feelings about their parents. Therapists may encourage this by dwelling primarily or exclusively on memories of negative incidents with the parents, on encouraging more expression of the anger than is necessary for resolving the presenting problems, or in mistakenly believing and sharing the idea that the expressing the anger is what helps the patient heal. What is actually healing for Sarah is resolving and letting go of her poisonous anger at herself. Replacing it with anger at her mother will only create a new source of suffering; a healthier approach for Sarah is to let go of the old anger at the parent, stop directing anger at herself, and move forward toward positive goals in her life as it is now.

When we are striving to resolve unhealthy patterns in our lives, facing painful memories from the time when those patterns first arose can be very helpful. However, when the dirt of old, negative emotions related to those memories comes out, it is important to recognize those old feelings for what they are and to let them go. Buddhism and object relations theory have interestingly similar views on how and why holding onto such negative feelings only causes you more suffering.

They also have similar views on the uniquely positive contributions that forgiveness and gratitude can make to our own happiness.

CULTIVATING GRATITUDE FOR WHAT WE HAVE

The simplest, easiest way to begin cultivating gratitude is to focus on what we have in the present. We can focus on the good things in our lives, developing feelings of satisfaction, joy, and appreciation. I sometimes suggest that people list some of the good things in their lives. Too often we don't appreciate and see the value of what we have. I realized this myself when my father became disabled with multiple sclerosis and I suddenly appreciated the incredible value of being able to walk, hold a book, dial a phone number, or hug a loved one. Simple things are often more precious than we know.

The idea here is not that we deny what's wrong in our lives but that we spend time consciously focusing on and appreciating what's right. We can begin by listing the physical things we're able to use and enjoy. Recall that many other people don't have what you do and also that you may not always have these things. Really rejoice in your good fortune. Then also take time to appreciate the less tangible things you enjoy, such as your relationships, health, capacity for positive emotions, freedom, intelligence, knowledge, and so forth. It's also good to spend time rejoicing in the many opportunities you have to do good, meaningful things with your life, such as gain new knowledge, overcome unhealthy emotional patterns, and help or be loving with others. People sometimes think that taking joy in the good things we have and do is selfish. Of course, arrogantly asserting that we're better than others is selfish, but rejoicing is not. If we don't take joy in what we have or in the good things we do, our lives become joyless and we increase the likelihood of feeling depleted, exhausted, and burned out.

Another simple way of cultivating gratitude is to take time to be thankful for the kind things people in our lives do for us each day. It's also important to be direct with people, asking them for what we want and then being gracious and thankful when they give it to us. One self-defeating pattern that often appears in people when they're in a state of inner poverty is that they do not ask for and accept meaningful support from others. Some time ago I was working with a woman named Cynthia who had become so stressed, overwhelmed, and depleted that she'd had something of a breakdown at work. That Friday I asked her about her plans for the weekend. She said, "I don't know. I have to clean the house. It's a real mess. And I have all these errands to run. Oh, and I also have some work I've brought home with me to make up for getting behind this week." It had not occurred to her to focus on taking care of herself or to ask her family for support at this difficult time.

When I suggested that Cynthia take time to relax and also ask her husband and teenage daughters for support, she said, "But he's been stressed out too, and I can't possibly burden my children!" I noted that she didn't usually see it as a burden when her husband or children asked her for help, and I wondered aloud why she assumed that they would see her as a burden. People who are feeling a sense of inner poverty are often blocked from asking others for help for a couple of reasons. First, they're caught in feeling that they are bad and not valuable; therefore, they feel that they don't deserve help and support. Second, even if their adult mind deems the people around them trustworthy, the less mature part of their mind lacks this basic trust. This part of the mind derives from their early feelings of frustration, hurt, and anger; it is afraid that trusting or relying on others will lead to the pain of being rejected, neglected, or abused.

The solution is to face our insecurity and fear and then to practice asking for, accepting, and appreciating help or support from others. For example, Cynthia admitted that she felt too insecure and "uncomfortable" to open up fully with her family. I asked her, "Well, then, how much kindness or support can you bear to ask for and accept from them?" She decided that she could tolerate asking her husband to take care of some of the errands she'd planned to do, asking her kids to help more than usual with cleaning the house, and also explaining some of what she'd been feeling to her husband and asking him to arrange a relaxing family outing for Sunday afternoon.

Her husband and kids had already picked up on her stress level, and they were relieved when she gave them concrete ways to help. After they had a pleasant, family weekend together, I asked her why they'd responded positively to her requests. She found it difficult at first to admit that they'd been happy to help because they all loved and valued her. People who are caught in a sense of inner poverty often don't take in compliments and don't focus on others' love and gratitude for them. This only reinforces their sense of depletion and self-devaluation. If we want to change this inner pattern, we not only must ask for and accept support, we also must allow ourselves to appreciate it. When others compliment us or do something kind for us, we should pause to reflect on what has just occurred, really taking it in. Seeing what others value in us can serve as a mirror, allowing us to find and value the good in ourselves. Appreciating what is good in ourselves is not a sign of arrogance or pride; it is a foundation for self-confidence, stability, and inner wealth. When others are kind or supportive to us, we should spend time taking note of and thinking about what they've done, allowing it to touch our hearts. In this way, we can give ourselves the gift of dwelling in feelings of appreciation, warmth, affection, and gratitude. The more we dwell in such feelings, the more we and those around us will benefit from the sense of contentment and openness that these feelings bring about.

GIFTS FROM THE PAST

While appreciating what we have and being thankful for kindness we receive in the present can help counteract feelings of inner poverty, these methods usually are not powerful enough to generate a deep and lasting sense of inner wealth. Object relations and Buddhism agree that if we want to radically increase our capacities for love, generosity, and compassion, we must turn our attention to the kindness we've received in the past. My own observation is that when people contemplate kindness they received as children, this affects them most powerfully.

I often ask patients and students to share stories about the people who were most kind to them during their early years. For anyone in a helping profession, for anyone planning to be a parent, and for anyone who wants to live a compassionate life, it's absolutely essential to think and feel deeply about the kindness you have received from others in the past. The memory images in your mind associated with these experiences powerfully affect how you think and behave later on when you feel love and compassion for others. These early experiences also form much of the foundation for patience, stability, openness, intimacy, and affection that you must have to care for others in the future.

Tibetan meditators often begin their practices by thinking with gratitude of each of their teachers and mentors. They say that forgetting the kindness of even one person who helped and guided us can become an obstacle to our inner development. We may forget other things, but if we're interested in developing love and compassion, then each instance of someone having shown us genuine kindness—of their having given us something of their heart—is worthy of being remembered with honor and love. If we wish to develop our sense of inner wealth and compassion, we must cherish our memories of grandparents, aunts, uncles, mentors, teachers, and old friends who lovingly shared what they had, what they knew, and who they were with us. We should honor such memories by reviewing them in our minds, writing them down, and sharing them with those we love. Failing to cherish a true act of kindness is like discarding a precious gift, leaving ourselves poorer. By contrast, if we do invest time in recollecting such stories with a heart open to gratitude, we almost certainly will be surprised by the feelings of happiness, contentment, and fullness that result.

INNER PHILANTHROPISTS

Object relations analysts and Buddhist masters agree that an extremely powerful and transformative way to develop inner wealth, strength, generosity, and love is to cultivate gratitude for the kindness shown to us by our parents, especially our mothers. Any Tibetan lama would agree with Winnicott's statement: "It seems to me that there is something missing in human society. Children grow up and become in their turn fathers and mothers, but, on the whole, they do not grow up to know and acknowledge just what their mothers did for them at the start."

When Tibetan lamas teach Westerners about meditating on the kindness received from their mothers, some in the audience inevitably become uncomfortable. Some say that their mothers were not kind to them—that they were abusive or neglectful. My experience with patients in therapy suggests that some people cannot tolerate such contemplations. The amount of hurt, unmet desire for nurturing, confusion, envy, or rage left over from childhood is so overwhelming that trying this kind of contemplation can be too upsetting.

In such cases, it may be best to emphasize the methods already discussed, leaving aside the practice of developing gratitude for parental kindness. However, even for people who were neglected or abused as children, being able to work through such old negative feelings in order to achieve a level of forgiveness and gratitude can be extremely helpful and healing. One of my patients who had been beaten and neglected as a child could not recall ever having been held or nurtured. When her older brother told her about his memories of their mother cuddling and caressing her as an infant, this moved her to tears. When I work with children who were abused and then lost their parents to death or incarceration, I often find that they hold tightly to each little memory of kindness they received. Memories of a small toy received at Christmas, a weekend drive to the beach, or an evening being cuddled in front of the television set serve as life preservers to which such children cling. Their starving for love makes them value each fragment of a loving memory, seeing the mundane as dearly precious. For those who were abused or neglected, it's an individual decision whether or not they can bear to work through their painful feelings in order to forgive and feel gratitude for the specific kindnesses that helped them survive psychologically.

For most people, who did have ordinary, good-enough parenting, there is great benefit in spending time contemplating, acknowledging, and developing gratitude for what mothers, fathers, or other primary caregivers did for us at the start. Even if we cannot remember our first few years of life, it is not so difficult to imagine what others did for us when we were infants and toddlers. The idea here is to imagine how it must have been. We can imagine how, when we were in the womb, our mother avoided unhealthy food and drink, took extra care of herself, and underwent many hardships to ensure our healthy development. Then our mother underwent incredible pain and hardship to give birth to us. After we were born, our parents surely gave up lots of sleep and comfort in order to feed, change, and soothe us. We can imagine how many thousands of times they fed us, changed our dirty diapers, and bathed us. We can imagine how their holding us, cuddling and rocking our young bodies, was just as essential as milk to our early development. We also can imagine how their talking and singing to us not only gave us great comfort but also helped our young brains to develop, laying the foundation for our later abilities to speak and to reason. In brief, we can contemplate, imagine, and remember all the many things they must have done to keep us alive, to feed and clothe us, to keep us safe, to teach us, and to care for us from before we were born until we were able to care for ourselves.

Then we can recall their various acts of kindness as we grew older, such as teaching us to walk and speak, guiding our education, buying us many things, protecting us from dangers, and showing us how to survive in the world. The idea here is not to idealize our parents or to pretend that they were perfect. Instead, we can recognize that despite their imperfections and the stress and challenges they were facing, they still did their best to help us with no benefit to themselves aside from the joy of seeing us happy.

If you meet up with resistance as you engage in such contemplations, check out whether it's based on some of the issues discussed earlier, such as your holding on to a superficial image of independence and self-reliance or your stirring up old, unresolved issues from childhood. Each of us came through the individuation process and landed somewhere on a continuum between inner poverty and inner wealth. If we don't address the issues that underlie our resistance and we give up on cultivating gratitude, we ensure that we'll stay just where we are on that continuum. Ultimately, our resistance is rooted in our own underlying feelings of poverty, and it's only by addressing these that we can discover our potential for increasing feelings of love, compassion, contentment, and joy.

In Tibetan Buddhism, once practitioners are able to generate a deep sense of gratitude to their parents, especially to their mothers, they go on to expand this sense of gratitude infinitely. To Westerners this idea may sound strange, but I think we can understand the psychological principles involved. Based on their belief in rebirth, Tibetan practitioners reflect that over countless previous lifetimes they have had countless previous mothers, each of whom also did her best to nurture and care for them, just as did their mother in this life. Of course, practitioners could reflect just as easily on how, over the course of infinite previous lives, others also played the roles of enemies or strangers, but the choice to focus on mothers' kindness is pragmatic, aimed at developing an infinite sense of kinship and gratitude. By spending time regularly for months or years imagining how they received limitless love and kindness over infinite expanses of time, meditators gradually develop an inexhaustible sense of gratitude, love, affection, and inner wealth. That is the goal of this meditation—to move yourself to the extreme end of the continuum of inner wealth so that you can give of yourself limitlessly to others without feeling exhausted.

We need not be Buddhist or believe in rebirth to learn to use our imagination to cultivate vast gratitude and inner wealth. What's essential is spending time contemplating the feeling that you are the recipient and receptacle of limitless love and kindness. Those who believe in God can spend time focusing on the feeling that God has poured his infinite love into his creation, including themselves. And any of us can recognize that the kindness and nurturing we received from our kin depended on our parents having given us all the love and care they could, and so on. We can think of each small act of kindness we've received in our lives, and then we can multiply that by the seventy-five hundred generations of *Homo sapiens,* the more than one hundred thousand generations of humans, and the millions of generations of mammalian parents who cared for their young with all their might, and we can see ourselves as the living, breathing manifestation of all that unthinkable kindness. By combining the various methods in this chapter, any one of us can develop vast feelings of kinship, loving affection, and generosity. Each of us can move ourselves gradually as far as our imaginations will allow along the continuum of inner wealth.

I remember once hearing that when the Carnegies began practicing philanthropy their wealth was so vast and was increasing so quickly that they couldn't find charities fast enough to keep up. No matter how busy they were giving money away, their wealth grew faster than they could give it. I think this is a great metaphor for what the heart of a bodhisattva is like. By cultivating sincere and powerful gratitude, each of us can increase our inner wealth until we reach a point where we move beyond our own tendencies to feel depleted, burned out, or exhausted. We can become true inner philanthropists.

TEN

THE KEY TO HAPPINESS

*Narcissists do show a lack of concern for others, but they are
equally insensitive to their own true needs.*
    —Alexander Lowen, M.D.

In this chapter I present a practical technique for working with unhealthy patterns in our lives, turning them into causes for happiness.
I call this technique "the key to happiness." The insight at the heart
of the key to happiness—the idea we use to help us understand which
of our thoughts, feelings, and actions lead to happiness and which lead
to suffering—is derived from Buddhist psychology. Perhaps the most
famous proponent of this psychological insight in Buddhist history
was the great Indian Buddhist teacher Shantideva, whose name literally means "Peace-god." Shantideva once wrote,

Although wishing to be rid of misery,
They run towards misery itself.
Although wishing to have happiness,
Like an enemy they ignorantly destroy it.

We all naturally want to be happy. However, Shantideva explained that when we approach life in a self-centered way, focusing primarily on our own protection, security, possessions, and well-being, happiness always eludes us. Seeking happiness in this way unintentionally but inevitably leads to insecurity, loneliness, neediness, and misery. By contrast, when our approach to life is based on love, empathy, and compassion for others, happiness flows to us in an ever-increasing stream.

From my perspective as a psychologist who has studied Buddhism for many years, I believe that for ordinary Westerners this is the most significant and practical insight in all of Buddhist psychology. Although Shantideva's point is quite simple, it's easy for us to misunderstand it for cultural reasons. The point being made here is essentially a psychological one. Although there are many good philosophical and ethical reasons for being compassionate, put them all aside. Put aside any religious or theoretical questions on the issue. Then approach the question of human happiness from a purely pragmatic, scientific perspective. Analyze your own life and the lives of those around you. If you look at things in a deep, careful, objective manner, you'll find that self-centered, self-protective, narcissistic approaches to life consistently lead to suffering while genuinely loving and compassionate approaches consistently lead to peace and happiness.

The Dalai Lama has taught this many times in his travels around the world. He often explains that compassion is the main source of happiness on a personal level as well as in relations between different social or political groups. Many people agree that compassion, like going to church on Sunday or giving to charity, is a good thing. However, people are so in the habit of seeking happiness outside themselves that it's extremely rare for anyone to even consider taking this idea literally—which is how it's intended—and experiment with cultivating compassion as the main path to happiness in their lives.

This technique, the key to happiness, is a practical way of experimenting with the idea of finding happiness through compassion. I often use this method with my patients. You need not take anything on faith. Begin by choosing a specific, narcissistic pattern in your life that's causing you suffering. Then apply this psychological method to that pattern in a structured way in order to see for yourself how to find happiness by freeing yourself from narcissistic self-concerns.

UNDERSTANDING NARCISSISM

From this chapter on, each method presented is aimed essentially at helping us abandon our own narcissism in order to be happier and to succeed in cultivating compassion. Psychologically, narcissism is the biggest obstacle to developing compassion. So it's important to be clear about just what narcissism is.

Tibetan Buddhist teachers often speak of "self-cherishing" as the main, inner cause of our suffering. For a long while I was confused about this. The idea of cherishing and caring about ourselves seems essential to our well-being. It seemed to me that by wisely cherishing ourselves we would take care of ourselves, take time to relax, work at self-improvement, make efforts at letting go of negative emotions, and also cultivate compassion and other positive emotions. Only after years of study did I realize that when Tibetan teachers were speaking of self-cherishing, they meant narcissism. In narcissism what is being cherished and held to strongly is an inaccurate and superficial image of the self. Narcissistic self-cherishing involves cherishing an illusion at the expense of the real.

There is a psychiatric diagnosis called Narcissistic Personality Disorder for people who are so attached to a superficial and grandiose self-image that they appear arrogant, lack empathy, require excessive admiration from others, act exploitative or entitled, disregard others' needs, and have unrealistic expectations in a range of social situations.

From a Buddhist psychological perspective, this disorder is just an extreme version of the basic narcissism that exists in all our minds, serving as a principal cause for the suffering and problems in our lives. In the ancient Greek myth from which narcissism draws its name, Narcissus is unable to love others, and he falls in love with his own image reflected in a pool of water, at which he stares so long that finally he falls in and drowns. This is exactly how narcissism works. We become entranced and enamored with a superficial image of ourselves—a mere reflection—giving much of our energy to that image. All the energy given to that image is unavailable for dealing with life or loving others. And our attachment to that image entrances or hypnotizes us so that we fail to see many of the realities in front of us, ultimately leading to our own suffering.

One psychiatrist correctly observes, "Narcissistic patients can sometimes maintain an inflated sense of their importance and uniqueness for days or weeks at a time." The problematic question is this: Who among us does not sometimes maintain an inflated sense of our importance in the scheme of things? Self-cherishing or narcissism is characterized by a network of incorrect views about the self, including some already mentioned, such as the view of ourselves as solid, permanent entities and the view of ourselves as being utterly independent and self-sufficient. However, the delusion at the very root of narcissism is the belief that our own comfort and status are more important than they actually are in the scheme of things—that our own happiness is independent of and more important than the happiness of others.

Narcissism does not necessarily involve overt arrogance. Working with our narcissism can be tricky because many of us are very good at unconsciously doing a sleight of hand, substituting one superficial image for another to keep ourselves distracted from reality. For example, many spiritual practitioners have underlying, narcissistic fantasies of quickly achieving great realizations or enlightenment that we imagine will bring us great pleasure, freedom without responsibility, popularity, power, and admiration. We may couch the obviously narcissistic elements of such fantasies in acceptable, spiritual terminology. However, when there's some danger of our actually becoming aware of the grandiose and self-centered nature of such fantasies, we then may project the idealized qualities we grasp at onto some teacher or guide, taking on the role of a humble disciple. In this way we hold on to the fantasies while denying any narcissism (to others and to ourselves) by overtly playing a *role* of humility.

The problem is that such spiritual practice still isn't real. We're playing a role of humility without actually learning to be humble; secretly we're still holding onto our narcissistic fantasies. We may even play the role of compassion as a way of hiding our narcissism from ourselves; then our focus is not on others' welfare but on an idealized image of our own great generosity and altruism. If someone points out what we're doing, an unskillful narcissist will become enraged at that person, revealing the superficiality of his apparent humility and compassion. One danger is that those of us who are better at narcissistic sleight of hand may even agree with such a critic, grasping next at a self-image of an all-bad penitent. On the surface, such feelings of regret may seem genuine, but again we are really just playing a role or wearing a mask. Beneath the surface of such repentance, often unconsciously, narcissism is still fantasizing; it covertly whispers, *See how aware, patient, and repentant I am; I am really the humblest person of all, which shows that secretly I'm the best of all.*

This is just one example of how narcissistic sleight of hand can work. The masks or roles we can take on are endless. Whether we're attached to the image of ourselves as grand or terrible, as successful or miserable, as something or nothing, cherishing that image blocks us from seeing the reality beyond such images, from engaging with life in a heartfelt way, and from feeling genuine compassion for others. Looking honestly at yourself and seeing through such roles often isn't easy. C. G. Jung once wrote, "People will do anything, no matter how absurd, in order to avoid facing their own souls." The hardest thing about using the key to happiness is finding the bravery to see through your own narcissistic images in order to face reality. The hardest thing to do is let go of the reflection with which you've become so entranced before you fall in and drown.

ANALYZING AN ISSUE

The first step in using this method is choosing a problematic issue or pattern that causes you some significant suffering in your life. There's no need to worry about whether or not narcissism underlies the issue; if a pattern causes you emotional turmoil and suffering, then some form of narcissistic self-concern lies at its core. It's best to choose an issue that has caused you trouble for some time so that once you've chosen it you can begin thinking about your history with that issue, the role it plays in your life, the direction your life is going because of this issue, and also how this issue affects the lives of other people you know.

When a patient named Richard was facing the issue of loneliness, we went through just this sort of reflection and analysis. Sleet was falling outside when he came in one night a few weeks before Christmas. His black, wool jacket and gray scarf were wet and dotted with ice as he took them off, sat down, and said, "I'm like Scrooge this year."

He went on to explain that he'd been trying to avoid his own feelings of loneliness by avoiding any reminders of Christmas. He said, "All of my decorations are in a box in the back of a closet. I haven't even put out one, and I'm not going to. I play tapes in my car instead of the radio so that I don't have to hear any Christmas music. I don't go anywhere near the malls. When people at work bring up their plans, I change the subject or get away fast. I won't talk with them about it." Speaking quickly, he added, "And I ordered stuff for Zack and had it shipped on the Internet. I'm not going to see him." Zack was Richard's eleven-year-old son who lived about two hours away and who Richard was seeing once a month since his divorce from Zack's mother. For a brief moment as Richard mentioned Zack, I wondered if he might break into tears. He smiled instead and said, "So, don't talk to me of charity. Are there no poorhouses? Bah, humbug!"

I was careful not to smile too broadly at this. His use of the Scrooge story and his humor were both ways of talking about what was going on with him while also striving to keep his feelings of loneliness at bay. He talked about his conflicts with his former wife and how his frustration with her was keeping him from trying to work out plans to visit with Zack over the holidays. Part of his pattern was isolating himself and then feeling lonely.

In analyzing the role that this issue played in Richard's life, we spoke about his past. He noted that he could recall a number of years when he'd felt even worse than this year. He talked about the year just after his divorce, when he'd found his loneliness totally overwhelming during the holidays. He reflected, "I wasn't as good then as I am now at being alone. I've had practice now and gotten better at it. Someday I'll be as good as Scrooge himself at getting away from people or keeping them away from me."

"And also getting away from your feelings?" I asked. When we engage in narcissistic defenses, as Richard was doing, blocking out aspects of external reality, we also block or deny aspects of ourselves.

Then Richard talked about a winter fourteen years earlier, the year that both of his parents had died in a car accident. "That was a year before I met my ex. I wasn't dating anyone. They'd both died that summer. I suppose that was my worst Christmas ever. Talk about being alone. God, I still miss them." He slumped in his chair and rested his head on his hand; then he said, "You know, life and death really suck."

We sat in silence together for a couple of minutes. Loneliness, anger, and resentment were palpable as ghosts, hovering in the room between us. I waited for some time, letting them hover. Then I said, "Tell me about what it is that you miss."

Richard smiled just a little. He told me about good times he'd had with his parents when he was young. His mother often had invited the extended family to their home for Christmas so that the house was filled with children, toys, and food. His descriptions of her kindness and generosity evoked earlier discussions we'd had about his gratitude to and love for her. She'd been at the emotional center of his life until her sudden death. He still harbored regrets for not having expressed his love for her more openly before she died. He also spoke about the first few years of his son's life, when things had not been too bad in his marriage. While they were not close to extended family, Richard did feel that he and Zack's mother had succeeded then in sharing some of the genuine joy and closeness with their son that he'd felt in his own boyhood.

As Richard shared these memories, he stared at a blank area of the wall, above and to the left of my head. It was almost as though he could see vague images of his memories there, as his physical gaze helped his mind's eye see into his past. After he finished sharing these memories, I said, "Well, you began today with Scrooge, and we've covered Christmas present and past. How do you see Christmas future?"

He smiled crookedly as he hesitated for a few moments. Then he said, "Okay, I can see it now. My aunt Jane, who I usually visit now on Christmas Day, is nearly ninety. A few years down the road, she'll be gone. And so I guess I'll be alone every year. I'll be more and more isolated. I'll become more cantankerous and moody. Finally, I'll die alone."

Many people feel particularly lonely during the winter holidays. However, Richard's problems were not unique to the season or to his personal situation. Like so many of us, Richard was having a hard time facing his unpleasant feelings directly. One of Freud's great insights was that when we aren't yet able to face such issues and they remain in our unconscious, they continue to haunt us. Richard was haunted by the loss of his parents, by regrets for things he hadn't said and done with them, and by his own inability to embody in his adult life the love and warmth that he'd had with them as a child. He was also haunted

by an underlying sense of himself as having failed as a husband and father. All of us are sometimes haunted by losses, doubts, insecurities, or
regrets. As a therapist, I've often been deeply moved by people's bravery in being willing to face their own ghosts in order to change their
lives for the better. I respected Richard's willingness to discuss and
work through difficult issues related to his past.

There are many therapeutic techniques for helping people become
more aware of difficult feelings and uncovering unconscious patterns
that we may act out in relationships. However, becoming more self-
aware, by itself, does not ensure that we will become healthier or happier. I've known many people who tried various self-help methods
and went to therapists for years, repeatedly gaining new insights
about themselves while still continuing to live out unhealthy patterns
in their relationships. When we gain a new understanding about ourselves, we then need to know how to transform our feelings and
change our relationships in order to make things better. Looking honestly at a given issue, analyzing the role it has played in our lives up
until now and the direction it's taking us as we move into the future, is
only the first step in using the key to happiness. Analyzing the issue is
a bit like checking out a wall with a locked door. The next step is finding a key; once you have the right key, it's easy to put it into the lock,
turn it, and open a door. This technique is designed to help us look at
our old patterns through eyes of compassion so that we can see the
exact point at which to turn or transform our old patterns, opening
the door to happiness.

SEEING YOURSELF THROUGH
EYES OF COMPASSION

Once you've identified an issue and taken an honest look at the role it
plays in your life, the next step is to look at the same problematic issue
through eyes of compassion. That is, you analyze your experiences re-

lated to this issue, asking which of your thoughts, feelings, and actions have led to suffering and which have led to happiness. In doing this, you particularly check up on the role that narcissistic, self-centered, self-protective approaches have played, comparing them with the role that a more open, compassionate approach has played (or might play if you haven't tried it) in the issue at hand. Buddhist psychology asserts that if you check carefully, you will find that narcissism has played an essential role in your problems or suffering. As one famous Tibetan verse puts it, "Cherishing ourselves is the doorway to all torment."

It will take some time and effort to work out exactly which of your thoughts, feelings, and actions increase your suffering and to discover the role that self-cherishing plays in your issue. It may be useful to write things out in a journal or talk them over with a good friend. It's very important, though, to be honest with yourself in assessing your own self-centered, self-protective efforts for happiness and how they may lead unintentionally to the very suffering they were initiated to avoid. In your process of self-analysis it may be helpful to ask yourself the following questions:

What is the image of myself I'm grasping on to in these situations?

Am I really empathizing with and feeling compassion for others?

What possible solutions am I just not seeing?

How might my efforts at protecting myself or gaining happiness for myself be causing me more suffering?

Charles Dickens's character Scrooge went through just this sort of process. Having reviewed (with some supernatural help) his past, present, and likely future with regard to a pattern in his life, he uncovered the narcissistic core of that pattern. Scrooge was actually an extreme characterization of attachment to a very common narcissistic fantasy.

He was terribly attached to the image of himself as wealthy and powerful. Whether we're actually wealthy or not, if we sometimes find ourselves thinking, worrying, or fantasizing about money when the money will not help us or some other person in a clear and specific way, then we're probably entranced by the same narcissistic image as Scrooge. When we get entranced by this particular image, we may even start believing that happiness could come from wealth. Even if we don't admit it to ourselves, at such times we also believe that our own wealth and happiness are unrelated to or even opposed to the wealth and happiness of others. We feel as though true happiness and power correlate with the numbers in our bankbooks. We almost see some reflection of security, power, or greatness for ourselves in the faces of those great men pictured on our coins and bills. I suspect that this common, narcissistic fantasy has provided the motivation for putting the images of powerful men on our money from Caesar's time until today. The point here is not that there's a problem with wealth, possessions, or power; it's that, when you look carefully, you find that seeking a self-centered happiness in them never works for long. Through self-analysis, Scrooge learned that living in accord with such narcissistic fantasies, seeking his happiness through greed, was only leading him to misery, while sincere, loving affection and generosity might lead him to genuine happiness.

In many ways, practicing the key to happiness is quite simple. What makes it challenging is the entrancing power of our belief in our narcissistic fantasies. Most of us live out our lives without ever seriously challenging our illusions. Sometimes, like Narcissus, we'd sooner drown than let them go. When people told Scrooge that his attachment to wealth was excessive and was causing him suffering, he thought them fools. When any of us is caught up in a narcissistic image, it can be difficult to pull ourselves away in order to see reality.

In Richard's case, the image by which he'd become entranced was of himself as a failure. Believing in this exaggerated mental picture, he thought he was protecting himself from suffering by distancing himself from others. This blinded him to how his self-protective distancing caused him great pain and loneliness while also reinforcing the image of himself as a bad father and an unsuccessful man. This is a common dynamic with narcissism—we try to protect ourselves but succeed only in protecting or shoring up an unrealistic image that in fact causes us more suffering. Wishing to be rid of misery, we steer, through narcissism, toward suffering itself.

Nancy, another patient of mine, was powerfully invested in another common narcissistic image. From childhood on, she'd grasped at an image of herself as the perfect woman with the perfect family. She felt that the more closely she and her family could approximate this perfect image in which everyone was always sweet, harmonious, neat, efficient, and nice, the greater their happiness would become. Her faith in this belief made her unable to see that the pressure she put on herself exhausted her and that her attempts to coerce her husband and kids to fit this image caused them to get angry and pull away from her. Her efforts in the service of an imaginary perfection were undermining the truly valuable relationships she already had. When her family members told her how they felt, she responded that she was trying to be a good wife and mother—trying to help them be happy. She could not empathize with their perspective as long as she held to the mistaken view that happiness would come from living out that perfect image. When we're caught up in self-cherishing, we cannot empathize well with others because we inevitably see them only as they relate to our narcissistic image, not as they are.

People often don't realize that attachment to a narcissistic self-image usually underlies anxiety. When someone feels anxious about meeting new people, dating, or giving a presentation, they often say they are afraid that they won't know what to say, that they'll look stupid, or that they'll make a fool of themselves. Our real problem at such times is that we cannot bring ourselves to say, "So what?" Unconsciously we're enamored with some unrealistic self-image, and we're terrified that a real experience with shatter it. In psychotherapy, when a narcissistic person experiences genuine anxiety, discouragement, or sorrow, this is often a first sign of progress. When we are anxious, this may mean that reality is being given an opportunity to break through denial; we fear losing our illusions. When we are discouraged or sad, we may be becoming disillusioned with one of our old, narcissistic defenses.

So, as we begin looking at our patterns through eyes of compassion, striving to see through our illusions to the narcissistic delusions at their core, we should not be afraid if we encounter some resistance or bad feelings. In fact, they are a sign that we're on the right track. When we think we've uncovered a core issue but haven't met with any real, difficult feelings, this usually indicates that instead we've done a sleight of hand, substituting one narcissistic fantasy for another. The more entranced we've been with a given image, the greater will be our resistance to seeing the truth. This is why it's important to begin with a pattern that has caused us considerable suffering for some time. Remembering our suffering can provide the motivation we need to work through resistance.

NOT DEFENDING THE CAUSE OF SUFFERING

As we work to view ourselves through eyes of compassion, we must beware of the tendency to defend the very narcissistic image that causes our suffering. It may seem surprising, but this is what we often do. Tibetan Buddhist teachers speak of self-cherishing because we really do cherish, treasure, honor, and defend these illusions about ourselves.

When someone directly contradicts or insults the narcissistic image we grasp at strongly, we usually disagree or get angry. When those we're closest to see through our illusions and point out our self-centered mistakes, we quickly get defensive, and if they don't stop we may become quite angry or enraged. If we look at those arguments in which tempers flare and voices are raised, we'll find that most are sparked by our feeling that someone else has injured the narcissistic image we cherish in our hearts. In those moments when a loved one's words run contrary to our illusions, we must choose which we cherish more—the loved one or the illusions. We can have healthy disagreements with those we love, but when we become defensive, moody, agitated, or enraged, this is a sign that we're choosing illusions over love.

We're often so habituated to narcissistic defenses that we will protect them even from our own compassionate self-analysis. Tibetan teachers advise that one solution is to bring to mind repeatedly the many disadvantages of self-cherishing while also recalling the true advantages of love and compassion. When using the key to happiness, we must practice over and over seeing ourselves through eyes of compassion, allowing the insights we gain to really sink in. Narcissism leads us to think habitually, often unconsciously, certain inaccurate thoughts, such as: *Just get more wealth and you'll be secure; pull away from others to keep yourself safe; show others how spiritual you are and you'll feel better about yourself; live up to your image of perfection and then you'll be happy.* We must become aware of such thoughts and counter them with realistic views. Though the voice of our narcissism sounds familiar and friendly, we must stop listening to it and practice instead seeing precisely how we create our suffering.

Sometimes your narcissism will lead you to pretend that you see the faults of narcissism. It will want you to say the words without truly seeing. If you do, then "letting go of self-cherishing" will just become another trick in your repertoire of illusions. The only solution is the hard work of actually seeing that when you identify with a superficial image, your heart closes in upon itself. The solution is to see how cherishing such images makes you chronically insecure, striving to defend and prop up something that part of you knows is actually an illusion. You must see for yourself how narcissism generates exciting illusions while causing you to waste the precious days and hours of your life with concerns that are not worthy of you. Looking with eyes of compassion, you have to see through your illusions to how self-cherishing undermines your relationships, leaves you joyless, and imprisons your heart.

WALKING THROUGH THE DOOR

Once you've looked at an issue in your life and analyzed just what self-centered dynamic is causing you suffering, the next step is to change things. Changing old habits always takes some sustained effort. So it's important that you've done the earlier steps well, analyzing the issue so that you deeply understand why change is worth the effort. Once your motivation is firm, any old pattern can be changed. Old habits gain their momentum because we've thought, felt, and behaved in that way over and over in the past. Such patterns are not inherent parts of us; they *can* be changed. Once we've gotten started, each bit of effort that we put into changing gives momentum to a new and healthier pattern.

It's important to understand that using the key to happiness mainly involves changing your thoughts and feelings. One Tibetan text on overcoming self-cherishing says, "Change your attitude while remaining natural." The point is that we shouldn't put on a show of change for ourselves or for others. When we're caught up in narcissism, we're not really natural; playing a role keeps us from being genuine. Overcoming narcissism involves letting go of such roles, relaxing, and expressing who we really are. This allows us to be vulnerable, heartfelt, and intimate with others.

When we first begin putting aside our masks, we may feel overwhelmed by our sensitivity to the world. We should not be afraid of this. Allowing things to touch us more deeply is a sign that we're beginning to open up to reality.

What's essential is this: each time that we catch ourselves beginning to think and feel along the lines of our old pattern, we must stop. Then we must replace that old pattern with a new one grounded in compassion. If we catch ourselves trying to protect ourselves by distancing, then we have to stop, remember that following that old pattern only causes us suffering, and actively strive to open up to others. If we catch ourselves pushing for an illusory perfection, then we have to stop and strive to be accepting and loving. If we catch ourselves wanting to hoard wealth, then we have to let go of such impulses and cultivate an attitude of affectionate generosity toward others. Using the key to happiness means that once we've identified a narcissistic attitude that has caused us suffering, we let go of it and actively cultivate its opposite.

When I suggest cultivating the opposite of our old attitude, I'm not recommending that we substitute a new image for the old one. The idea is not to develop an image about generosity or compassion but to be, in fact, generous and compassionate. This is an area in which Western psychology can learn something valuable from Buddhism. Too often we help people give up some old, harmful pattern without giving them tools for approaching that area of their lives in ways that bring real joy. Stopping the old pattern decreases suffering but does not by itself bring happiness.

As you begin developing a new approach, the main thing is to work with your mind, developing some real enthusiasm for being with others in new ways. Then, with these new thoughts and this new feeling, you might try some new behaviors, such as giving to the people around you. But work on your mind first; just giving things away without changing mental habits will not be effective. Your old thoughts and feelings will lead you to resent giving those things away, and because you won't find happiness in the new approach, you'll give up. In my experience, it's best to focus more energy initially on cultivating your new thoughts and feelings while changing your behavior only gradually—remaining natural. As you begin doing the new behavior, really get into it, allowing yourself to enjoy the process. Then your behavior will change naturally over time as your feelings of genuine joy increase.

Each of the remaining chapters will present additional methods for cultivating compassion by overcoming narcissism. Only to the extent that we pull ourselves away from being entranced with narcissistic images can we see others for who they are, genuinely appreciating and loving them. Freeing ourselves from narcissism allows us to find real joy in compassion for others and to avoid drowning in our own illusions.

ELEVEN

THE INNER ENEMY

Some time ago I received a gift from Nepal of a vivid, colorful painting of a wrathful Buddhist deity. There are many such deities in central Asian Buddhism. This particular one is known in the Tibetan tradition as an emanation of the Buddha of Compassion. I hung the painting in the bedroom, and one morning I woke up and stared at it while still lying in bed. I noticed his bulging eyes, his bared teeth, and his mouth, which looked as though it were open in a loud shout. His hair was wild, and he brandished an ax and a sword. He was dancing within the dance of red-orange flames, which themselves seemed to be a manifested aura of his fierce, overwhelming energy. As I looked into his wild, intense eyes, I wondered how this, too, could be the face of compassion.

If we have limited exposure to the psychology of compassion, it's easy to associate altruism with an approach that's always gentle, soft, and "supportive." In fact, it's inappropriate to limit our view of compassion in this way. A loving parent whose child is about to run out into a busy street may look rather like the deity with bulging eyes and fiery energy, shouting and running to save the child's life. Or when one finds out that a child is being molested, a mild and soft approach toward the molester is unlikely to be the most compassionate approach. Sometimes real compassion demands an active and even fierce response.

The Buddhist tradition from the beginning has recognized that the path of compassion sometimes requires the fierce, brave heart of a warrior. The Buddha himself and his earliest disciples were sometimes referred to as *Arhats* or "Enemy-Destroyers." At first glance, such an epithet might sound peculiar when applied to a Buddha. After all, Buddhist saints cultivate limitless love and compassion for all sentient creatures. So who or what would the "enemy" be that the Buddha and his disciples destroyed? While we may answer this question on a number of different levels, put simply, the enemies of any Buddhist practitioner are the ignorance, narcissism, and mental afflictions in his or her own mind. The successful practitioner utterly destroys these inner enemies.

All those who sincerely wish to cultivate compassion arrive at moments in which they must be very brave, even fierce, in their practice. An approach that avoids conflicts and shies away from intensely battling inner or outer obstacles leads at best to mediocre results and at worst to a pseudo-compassion that may cause as many problems as it solves.

Some people rationalize their psychological laziness, avoiding challenging issues while thinking they're being compassionate toward themselves. If compassion is the wish to free someone from suffering, then compassion toward yourself means actively freeing yourself from the outer conditions and the inner, negative thought patterns and emotions that cause your suffering. Being patient toward the causes of our own and others' suffering is not kindness. Dwelling in negative thoughts and destructive emotions is actually a form of self-hatred; stopping them is compassion. Being compassionate toward yourself often entails being fierce or ruthless toward your own narcissism and toward your negative emotions in general. These are your true enemies, which hide in the recesses of your own mind. Your narcissism and mental afflictions only lead to sorrow, relationship problems, self-pity, anxiety, grief, and exhaustion; they only harm you and others. When it comes to dealing with the afflictive emotions in our own minds, we should be like that fierce Tibetan deity of compassion, ruthlessly cutting them with the sharp sword of insight and then dashing them to pieces with the unbreakable ax of skillful, compassionate action.

KNOWING THE ENEMY WITHIN

The roots of this next method, which I refer to as "battling one's inner enemy," can be found in many of the world's great religious traditions, particularly in the life stories of their saints. In the Buddhist tradition, the Indian master Shantideva advocated a form of this method; he spoke of inner "enemies such as hatred and craving" and vowed that "holding a strong grudge, I shall meet them in battle!" Tibetan Buddhist teachers note that for someone striving to develop compassion, self-cherishing is the principal inner enemy to be defeated. Hatred and anger are obvious enemies of compassion, but in daily life the simple tendency to cherish our own self-image, comfort, security, possessions, and status more than we cherish others is the real enemy that chokes the very life of compassion.

The first challenge in applying this method is to realize that we can live our whole lives without ever becoming aware that this inner enemy, our own self-centered narcissism, even exists. Problems arise in our lives, and we don't think deeply about the cause or we spontaneously blame other people or outer circumstances for our troubles. It never occurs to us that the biggest obstacle to our happiness, the main cause of our suffering, is hiding within our own minds.

Compassion entails being deeply concerned with others—cherishing them and working for their happiness. Narcissism entails being concerned with yourself—cherishing yourself and working for your own happiness. Buddhism and most schools of Western psychology agree that narcissism lies at or near the core of ordinary people's psychology—of our psychology.

Yet ordinarily we don't notice our own narcissism, and our friends, family, and culture support it. We wake up and think about what we will do today, what we want to eat, and where we need to go. If our spouse, friend, or coworker acts in a way that contradicts our wishes, we feel irritated. If we get stuck in traffic, we feel annoyed. When others praise us, we like it; when they put us down, we feel upset. We enjoy receiving things but obviously dislike having them taken away or stolen. We like when others give us things and speak sweetly to us but really dislike being yelled at, lied to, or cheated. And as we go about our days we naturally spend time thinking about how others view and treat us, about our finances and retirement planning, about our health, our diet, our weight, our self-esteem. We may think about our exhaustion, our depression, our fears and worries. We think about our good times in the past, and we plan to relax, see movies, work out, go to dinner, take our vacations. This is all normal, human, narcissistic functioning.

I'm not saying that any of this is necessarily wrong. What I am asserting is that in the midst of our normal, daily lives there may be something in our own minds and hearts that cheats us, blocking our own and others' happiness. And we may never see it because it seems so very normal. Perhaps some parts of ourselves that we see as normal and essential to who we are in fact block us from being more compassionate, loving, creative, content, and joyful than we've yet imagined we could be. The lives of saints and philosophers from many different great traditions contain a period of battling with aspects of themselves before attaining a new level of insight, love, rapture, altruism, or bliss. I'm not suggesting that anyone has to change anything about themselves that they don't want to change. I am suggesting, though, that anyone seriously interested in cultivating compassion will reach a point at which she must search her own soul to find the enemy within who blocks her way.

If we wish to battle our narcissism, we must first come to know it well. When you want to battle an outer enemy, the first step is learning his strengths and weaknesses so that you can strategize about how and where to attack him. Similarly, if you wish to conquer your inner enemy, you must understand clearly how it functions in your life. Only by knowing your narcissism well will you understand which of your thoughts, feelings, and behaviors should be abandoned and which should be increased.

As narcissism always involves some self-deception, it takes effort to get to know this enemy in our minds. The great Indian Buddhist teacher Dharmaraksita wrote a brilliant poem titled "The Weapon-Wheel Mind Training" about how to understand and battle "our real enemies: selfish concern and self-cherishing." Dharmaraksita is like an incredibly precise and wise psychotherapist in describing the many attitudes and behaviors that arise when we allow narcissism to abide in our hearts. We don't begin the day intending to be self-centered or to cause suffering for ourselves and others. Yet our narcissism is there so often, causing misery. How can we become more aware of this in order to fight against it?

Dharmaraksita explains that usually it's in the little things that we can see how we cherish our self-image and comfort more than we cherish others. When we avoid difficult or annoying tasks, hoping that others will do them instead—leaving the garbage, the dishes, or the cat litter for someone else—this is a clear sign of our narcissism. Acting kind, friendly, or charming in order to get others to do what we want indicates that we cherish ourselves more than others and are willing to use them to our ends. When we look down on or ignore those who are less intelligent, attractive, wealthy, or powerful than we are, or when we court the attention of those above us in a social or business hierarchy,

this strongly suggests that we're more concerned with narcissistic ap-
pearances than with knowing who others really are or having compassion for them. If we annoy other people with our habits, say things to
hurt their feelings, compete to get ahead of them, seek their admiration, or strive to be the center of attention, what can this mean but that
we believe our own happiness is more important than and independent
of the happiness of others? When we find ourselves hoarding what we
have and not wanting to give, feeling arrogant about some of our own
qualities, trying to appear better than we are at something, complaining about other people, telling small lies out of convenience, or getting
angry at people for not doing what we want, we can be fairly certain
that we're under the control of narcissism.

Dharmaraksita refers to narcissism as a demon, a "sly, deadly vil-
lain," and a "self-centered butcher" who slaughters our true, spiritual
aspirations. He says,

> As it's true what I have said about self-centered interest,
> I recognize clearly my enemy now.
> I recognize clearly the bandit who plunders,
> The liar who lures by pretending he is part of me;
> Oh, what a relief that I have conquered this doubt!

Dharmaraksita is sharing an important psychological point here.
As we make progress in understanding narcissism as an inner enemy,
we must stop identifying with our superficial self-images and our narcissistic defenses. As long as we identify with our narcissism, feeling
this is me, it's who I am, we cannot battle it effectively. If you don't first
break through your identification with narcissism, there's a danger
that your efforts at battling your inner enemy will degenerate into a
form of self-hatred. When you still identify with your narcissism, seeing the faults caused by narcissism leads you to think *I'm so terrible,
I'm so bad.* Then, trying to work against your narcissism feels like

striving to destroy yourself. In fact, all of this is just another narcissistic sleight of hand. We're just unconsciously substituting a new superficial image for our old ones; we're still preoccupied with ourselves. To use this method effectively, we must get to know our own narcissistic tendencies well, and we must recognize that our inner enemy is not really who we are. Only by disidentifying from the inner enemy will we recognize that fighting against it is a compassionate approach to achieving our own welfare and also to benefiting others.

THE FACE OF MY ENEMY

Of course, the idea of an inner enemy is a metaphor. It's not that we literally have other people inside ourselves. Engaging in this method, one is personifying an inner quality, pattern, or tendency, imagining it as a separate person. Buddhist teachers over the ages have used various metaphors that suited their times and cultures to describe their battles with the inner enemy. Ancient Indian teachers often used the image of military conflicts with enemy armies; traditional Tibetans sometimes used the image of struggles to exorcise evil demons; and modern Tibetan teachers use the image of strongly resisting malevolent dictators to illustrate the process of this inner battle. Intentionally using a metaphor, personifying one's inner qualities, can be psychologically useful in various ways.

Jungian analysts have long noted that "*personifying* is crucial to religious and psychological experience." It is as natural as sleeping and dreaming, for our dreams are filled not with people but with personifications. Every night our psyche spontaneously creates the inner characters that populate our dreams. In our religious lives as well, we cannot seem to help personifying the divine, so that God is seen as a father in heaven, the earth or the church as a mother, and the dark underworld is populated by demons or the monsters of our nightmares. Buddhism also uses many metaphors to describe the Buddha, though it insists that one not take them literally. (The Buddha himself said that those who knew him through his physical form didn't really know the Buddha; one knows the Buddha by perceiving the true nature of reality for oneself, and anything else is just a metaphor pointing toward the direct experience of wisdom.) The psychological force behind literary fiction, theater, and movies is also largely our natural interest and joy in seeing human qualities personified in stories. Even in popular culture, the psychological force behind the sports and entertainment industries is the natural need to personify. Whether we look back to Marilyn Monroe and Elvis or to the latest sports heroes, singing divas, irreverent comedians, or film goddesses, it's clear that we are less interested in knowing such stars as people than in having them embody or personify certain archetypal human qualities for us.

When we use metaphors or personifications, we're externalizing parts of ourselves. We're seeing our own inner qualities projected outward. When we do this unconsciously and in the service of narcissism, it is often destructive. The world of narcissism is so empty and joyless that we project our narcissistic images outward and make them bigger than life, creating big distractions from our own boredom and discontent. We may do this with a famous star or with someone in our own lives, seeing that person in terms of some idealized, grandiose image or in terms of a devalued, wholly negative one. In either case, we have created some illusory drama to distract us from the tedious reality of self-centered living. When we relate to others through such narcissistic projections, we are using them like objects for our own narcissistic purposes. We don't wish to know them as they are, and so we don't feel real love or compassion for them. This is why famous people can go so quickly from being adored to despised; it's all a narcissistic drama that has little to do with who they really are. When we're using others as objects for our narcissism, we don't empathize with them, and so we often are not aware when our actions harm them.

However, the natural tendency to personify need not be negative. Buddhism and Jungian psychology agree that projecting can be healthy if done with awareness. For example, Buddhists cultivate the tendency to personify their own best capacities for wisdom, skill, artistry, and compassion in the figures of deities and past masters as a way of evoking and getting to know more about those qualities in themselves. However, the Buddhist practitioner does this with an awareness that projections are projections.

Jungians find that it can be beneficial to take note of the characters we find intriguing in dreams, literature, or movies. Often those we feel strongly about personify qualities in ourselves that we have not dealt with consciously. We may project our narcissistic greed onto one character and our capacity for joyful creativity onto another. By taking note of these projections, we can become more aware of such qualities in ourselves and then deal with them consciously.

Jungian analyst James Hillman writes, "Personifying helps place subjective experiences 'out there'; thereby we can devise protections against them and relations with them." Through conscious effort, we can use the mind's natural tendency to personify inner qualities to help us become more aware, to get to know the unconscious forces that often drive our lives.

When we imagine some previously unconscious inner quality as an enemy soldier, a cruel dictator, or a malevolent demon, we immediately gain the psychological benefit of disidentifying from that inner quality. By imagining it as a figure with a face and a name, we gain distance from that quality and become able to see it as separate from our identity or sense of self. Of course, it's not that the quality suddenly disappears from our minds. The quality remains, but now we can be aware of how it affects our feelings, behaviors, and relationships.

Personifying our inner qualities sounds a bit theoretical, but in fact it is a simple and practical method that I use often with my patients. For example, Erin always wanted other people to like her, and so she spent her waking hours continually trying to do what other people expected. This led her to feeling resentful and exhausted. One day Erin found an image for this quality. She said, "I'm like a human pinball, bouncing from one demand to another. I'm so busy bouncing off bumpers that I never stop to think where I want to go or what I want to do." From then on we used "human pinball" whenever we talked about her becoming distracted and bouncing quickly from one thing to another with no internal sense of direction. Before, she had simply identified with this as her way of being in the world—as essentially who she was. Now, as Erin set aside time to think about the direction she wanted to take in her life, she sometimes caught herself: "Oh, I was busy last week, running around, and suddenly I thought, 'I'm becoming the human pinball again.' So I just stopped and took some breaths and got in touch with my own feelings. I thought about what I was doing and why; I'm not going back to being a human pinball." This metaphor became a tool for her, to keep her from falling back into that old pattern.

Another patient named June often found herself stressed out, anxious, and tired. Particularly when she was stressed, June tended to get into big arguments with her husband. When she first came to see me, she described her exhaustion, noting how hard and stressful her work was and how little her husband helped out at home. After a while, June was able to recognize that her own perfectionism was playing a big role in creating her problems. She wanted to be a perfect therapist and a perfect mother and to have a perfect home. And she was including her husband in her pattern, expecting him to be perfect as well. June had begun identifying her inner enemy, compulsive perfectionism. To encourage her to personify this inner enemy, one day I asked her what she'd be like if she continued identifying more and more with her perfectionism so that down the road it totally ruled her life. She winced as she said, "Oh my gosh, I'd be such an uptight nag. I'd never be able to relax, and I'd always be bothering my poor husband

and kids." She hesitated, visualizing this negative personification, and then she laughed as she said, "Eventually, I guess I'd wind up an uptight, nagging old witch."

Psychological research shows that people tend to view their own motives and behaviors in unrealistically positive ways. We tend to ignore our faults and to view even negative behaviors as positive or normal when we are the ones doing them. Exaggerating our negative traits somewhat and then personifying them can serve to counterbalance this tendency. When June visualized herself as an old, bitter, nagging witch, she gained insight at the feeling level about how negative was her compulsive perfectionism. This motivated her to work harder to stop living and interacting in that way. When she caught herself being overly hard on herself, pushing herself too much, or giving her husband and children a hard time, recalling the image of a scowling, wrinkled, crooked-nosed, nagging witch served as a quick prompt to change.

So, as both Dharmaraksita and Jung have noted, personifying one's inner enemies grants us a number of benefits. It helps us decrease the extent to which we identify with negative qualities as aspects of ourselves. It also can serve to counterbalance an unrealistically positive assessment of our own thoughts and behaviors. Simply bringing the images to mind can serve as an immediate prompt to change. As the process of personifying is natural and often enjoyable, it's also a way of bringing more spontaneous energy to our inner work. Toward this end, it's important to use an image that feels personally interesting and meaningful. Finally, personifying such inner qualities is also a way of getting to know them more deeply and accurately, and knowing one's enemies well is essential to battling them effectively. We are habituated especially to seeing our destructive, narcissistic qualities as positive. Developing a good personification for these qualities can help us to see and remember exactly how they cause suffering for ourselves and others.

A BATTLE PLAN

Once you have identified your inner enemy and personified it, the next step in this method is to create and implement a battle plan. When we're entering into an inner battle, we should work hard to create plans for various contingencies with a sense that victory is necessary and ultimate failure is unacceptable. Like good soldiers, we should be both cunning and brave. Buddhist teachers note that inner enemies are not like outer enemies; they have no place outside the mind to hide and regroup. Once they're routed from your psyche, they cannot return to fight again. Therefore, one should fight fiercely and ruthlessly to destroy them.

You might begin by taking on some specific negative issue or enemy such as perfectionism, arrogance, laziness, or compulsive craving. Or, if you are particularly brave, then you can take on narcissistic self-cherishing itself. If your goal is to develop joyful compassion, then these other issues are like the soldiers in the enemy army, while narcissism is the dictator who rules that army.

As you begin making your battle plan, it's important to be sure that you're not identifying with the narcissistic issue you're setting out to fight against. Wrathful compassion directed at an inner cause of suffering is totally different from self-hatred, which is actually just another inner cause of pain. Self-hatred involves being narcissistically attached to a very negative image and dwelling in destructive emotions, while fierce compassion entails letting go of narcissistic images and overcoming unhealthy emotional patterns. With self-hatred we feel bad about ourselves and grow discouraged, while with wrathful compassion we develop increased confidence and energy. So we must be precise about who our inner enemy is, imagining his face and demeanor while also recognizing that he is not us. I find that it's useful to cultivate feelings of love and compassion for ourselves and others as we begin our inner battles. If you can feel genuine compassion for yourself while being ruthless with your inner enemy, this is a good sign that you've succeeded in breaking your identification with the narcissistic pattern you're battling against.

It's also important to begin by taking on an enemy we can handle. By conquering one unhealthy tendency, we grow in the confidence, strength, and skill needed to battle others. This is much better than trying to overcome all our narcissistic tendencies at once, only to feel defeated and give up. We must be realistic and compassionate with ourselves, taking a long-term view in our battles against our delusions.

In psychotherapy, I find that my patients are often content to take on one or two enemy soldiers, winning themselves a bit more contentment and connectedness, and then calling a cease-fire with narcissism and allowing things to rest there. For example, Erin, who'd been feeling like a human pinball, created a battle plan that involved spending a few minutes each morning thinking about what was most important for her that day, saying no to someone at least once per week, asking someone else for something each week, taking a day to herself each month, and catching herself (and stopping) when she started to feel like a pinball. By implementing a relatively simple battle plan like this, Erin was able to feel more relaxed and to start getting in touch with her inner voice. From her perspective, this was a sufficient victory.

By contrast, religious practitioners of various traditions have been more likely to take on the inner dictator, narcissism itself. There are many, many stories in the Buddhist tradition of meditators' remarkable and heroic efforts in their inner battles. Here I'll use the example of a Westerner who chose to battle narcissism itself in his quest for compassion. I feel that using examples of big and somewhat extreme battles are useful both to readers who wish to battle the dictator and those who simply wish to fight a soldier or two.

Francis was a bright, imaginative, fun-loving young man whose early life typifies many of the qualities of normal, everyday narcissism. The son of a wealthy businessman, he often used the money that his parents gave him or that he earned by working for his father to throw wild parties with his friends. By the time he was twenty, he rarely missed a party in town, and he himself often threw lavish parties, "ordering whatever food and drink he liked and inviting any attractive girl willing to risk her reputation" into his and his friends' company. He had a number of girlfriends but avoided settling down. A bit vain (and perhaps proud of his family's wealth), he wore the finest clothes. Though he was generous toward his friends, he felt a spontaneous disgust toward sick, homeless beggars who seemed to serve as a reminder of unpleasant human frailties. Though his father wanted him to join the family business, Francis loved stories of romantic adventures, so he often thought of joining the military or finding other means to seek out exciting experiences. If Francis was a bit immature or irresponsible up this point, he certainly wasn't a bad person. He was really pretty normal, concerned with pleasure, friends, and excitement. Internally, like most of us, he had a certain degree of preoccupation with maintaining a positive self-image and reputation as well as with finding a life for himself that might lead to adventures, enjoyment, wealth, and even fame.

It was during this stage of his life that, in and around his home in Assisi, Francis began experiencing unusual dreams and visions that seemed to call him toward a deeply religious life—and that eventually led to his canonization as one of the great saints of Catholic history. I focus here not on the religious or theological content of his transformation but rather on its psychological content, as he went from being a normal, self-centered person to someone overwhelmed by ever-flowing love and compassion.

Early on in his process of inner transformation, Francis gained the insight that lies at the heart of the method described in this chapter. In Western psychological terms, it is the recognition that your capacity for genuine love and compassion is inversely proportional to the extent of your narcissism. That is, the more psychological energy you invest in your own superficial self-image, comfort, security, and pleasure, the less you have to give in deep love and compassion. Putting this same point in terms of Buddhist psychology, the more caught up you are in self-cherishing and in attachment to the affairs of this life—to wanting praise, wealth, pleasure, comfort, and fame—the less ability you have to cultivate altruism. The well-known Prayer of Saint Francis expresses the insight as follows:

> O Divine Master, grant that I may not try to be comforted but to comfort, not try to be loved but to love. Because it is in giving that we receive, it is in forgiving that we are forgiven, and it is in dying that we are born to eternal life.

In order to combat his own self-cherishing, Francis essentially used the method we've been discussing. In his dreams, prayers, and contemplations, he personified his self-cherishing sometimes as a proud, arrogant knight (like the man he previously imagined he'd become) and at other times as demons tempting him away from the path of compassion.

Francis's battle plan against his inner enemy was clear and uncompromising. It was designed to strike swiftly and directly at all the key elements of the narcissism with which he previously had identified so strongly. If his approach seems overly extreme to you (as it did to many in his own time), then read his story as a warrior might read the stories of great heroes of the past. Even if one would not follow the specifics of his battle plan, it provides an model of inner heroism.

One of Francis's first attacks on his own narcissism focused on his aversion for the sick. He had felt an aversion especially to those with leprosy, a disease that simultaneously destroyed one's health, appearance, and social status. Previously he'd gone to great lengths to avoid lepers. Now, he must have struggled against his own fear and revulsion as he first approached a leper, gave him a coin, and kissed his hand. He then went to a hospital for lepers, giving each individual some money and exchanging kisses with him. A powerful, inner warrior, Francis began his great battle with a direct strike at his self-cherishing.

Self-cherishing is not a foe that's easily vanquished. However, Francis kept up his battle. A few years later, for one brief occasion, Francis's aversion for lepers reasserted itself. One of his fellow friars, Peter, invited a leper to share a meal with them. Francis initially gave Peter a hard time about this. Somehow the idea of eating together had triggered his old aversion. Quickly catching himself, Francis apologized to Peter and then went directly to the leper and shared his meal with him from his own bowl. The leper's hands, with which he took his food from the bowl, were covered with festering sores; Francis was uncompromising in his battle.

Francis wrote out his battle plan in the form of rules that he and his fellow friars would follow. Each element seems to have been designed to counter radically an element of his former narcissism. Previously he had been attached to his family's wealth; now he created a rule that he never again would have any money at all or possess any property or wealth. Previously he'd been vain, loving beautiful clothing. Now, he renounced wearing shoes, and he clothed himself only in a plain, rough tunic. Striving to cherish others more than himself, he often gave away his only tunic to others, wandering naked until someone offered him another piece of cloth. Previously he'd planned to become a soldier, fighting to gain fame and glory. Now, he refused to retaliate when he was attacked violently as he wandered, homeless, through the roads of Italy. I am struck in particular by his willingness to abandon even his own autonomy, promising obedience to a number of popes who appear to have had less wisdom, altruism, and intelligence than he himself did. When in the grips of narcissism, we want control, praise, gain, health, and comfort. Again and again throughout his life, Francis accepted losses, severe humiliations, beatings, and serious illnesses with equanimity, as means to greater and greater victories in his inner battle for compassion.

If the radical example of a medieval saint seems a bit remote, then let me briefly share a more modern example of another unusually brave inner warrior. Roger Kunsang, an Australian who became a Buddhist monk as an adult, didn't have an easy childhood and even was involved briefly with gangs in his late adolescence. When he first came to a Buddhist monastery and understood the sort of inner battle required to conquer self-cherishing, he left, hoping to avoid the challenges of such a struggle. His teacher, Lama Yeshe, met him as he was leaving and said that was fine because clearly he'd be back. Lama Yeshe saw the heart of a compassionate warrior in Roger before he saw it in himself.

Some time after Roger became a monk, he found himself in a position shared by many other modern people. He was working full-time for a business (one that financially supported a number of altruistic projects), and he was so busy with the demands of his job and other tasks of daily living that he could hardly find time for meditation and prayer. He approached one of his teachers, Lama Zopa Rinpoche, about this problem, and Rinpoche advised that it could be solved if he simply cut back his sleep to two or three hours per night. Then he could meditate and pray for others through most of the night while still fulfilling his work responsibilities (also for others) during the day.

For many of us, sleep deprivation brings up seemingly overwhelming feelings of self-cherishing. We become irritable, moody, and childishly cranky when tired. Interestingly, St. Francis followed a similar schedule to the one suggested to Roger; he also prayed almost all night and worked for others all day. When Roger first tried this attack on his self-cherishing, he began falling asleep in strange places. One day, while standing at a teller window at the bank, he suddenly fell across the window, sound asleep there in the middle of the bank. Another day, when at a nice dinner party, he slumped over, suddenly asleep, with his face landing in a plate of food. Most of us would have given up at this point. Soldiers bear many severe hardships in external battles, and ordinary people bear many difficulties in order to earn money. And yet we generally don't want to bear hardships when cultivating the inner qualities that lead to a lasting happiness.

I recently saw Roger as he was working to prepare a venue for a teaching by Lama Zopa Rinpoche. I was aware that he'd had very little sleep for the previous few nights, as he'd been awake doing various tasks to serve his teacher and help other people. I also knew that he'd been up early that morning, as he is every morning, for prayers and meditation and also to work together with Lama Zopa Rinpoche on various projects. At around seven in the evening, as he was working at preparing things, his robes brushed against a candle and caught on fire. Without flinching, he slapped the fire out and continued with his work. He seemed as focused and wholly present with his work for others as a soldier in a battle. Many hours later, at around four in the morning, I was feeling exhausted when I looked over at Roger. He was sitting with the burn marks on his hand, with a hole in his singed robes. As he jumped up energetically to serve others yet again, with a light in his eyes and a lightness in his steps, I could imagine the fiery energy of a fierce deity of compassion and could see the joy and freedom that come from compassion gaining victory over narcissism in ones's heart.

NO QUICK, EASY PATH

Whether one is striving to overcome a specific, destructive, narcissistic pattern in one's life or striving to transform one's entire personality, as in the examples I've just shared, battling one's inner enemy requires bravery and sustained effort. One practical method used by Francis and Roger was creating behavioral rules for yourself so that when narcissism prompts you to follow some unhealthy habit the rule will be there in your mind to stop you. This is an important psychological function of many religious vows or pledges—to create inner boundaries that keep us from wandering back into old, narcissistic tendencies. Of course, there is no set of behaviors that will necessarily undermine our self-cherishing. Many people have worn simple clothing or slept little for narcissistic reasons. What helps is finding rules that go against our own narcissistic impulses and taking them on joyfully, motivated by genuine compassion. We must be skillful in planning out how to keep ourselves from repeating old, destructive habits.

Freud once noted that the compulsion to repeat what's familiar is so strong in humans that it often overrides the pleasure principle itself. That is, when a pattern of thought, feeling, and behavior is familiar, people often repeat it even if it clearly is bringing them more suffering than pleasure.

I often talk with people who have gained an absolutely clear insight that a current pattern is their inner enemy, bringing them and those around them only suffering, and yet they're terrified to change. Giving up their old approach—letting go of that enemy—feels like losing a part of themselves or losing their best friend. Moving into a new way of being seems terrifying, like stepping off a cliff. I suspect that everyone who is serious about inner work feels that way sometimes. At such moments, we must remind ourselves not only that our old approach brings suffering but also that we have the capacity for something better. Buddhist masters advise that we should be easily satisfied regarding external comforts but should not settle for less than we're capable of in our inner development. When we feel hesitant or afraid, we must generate a warrior's sense of our own dignity, integrity, and self-respect, not settling for less than the joy of compassion's victory over narcissism. If we want to be kinder and happier, then it's essential to face our difficulties, to toss aside our inner enemies and move ahead firmly. This is the way of strong, even fierce, compassion.

Many Western psychological researchers have noted that when narcissism begins experiencing a defeat, a temporary increase in negative feelings such as depression or anxiety often arises. When we're engaged in an inner battle, we should not be discouraged by such feelings but should take them as signs that the battle is progressing well. For example, I recall working with a very self-centered, arrogant teenager who had been treating his parents and peers badly for years. When his parents confronted his negative behaviors, and when they and his school began implementing strict consequences, he became quite depressed, feeling genuinely sad and losing interest in things. His parents became worried about this, thinking they should stop confronting his negative behaviors and put him quickly on antidepressants. I explained that this depression was the first sign that their approach was working. D. W. Winnicott calls this sort of depression "disillusionment"; one feels sad because one is losing certain grandiose illusions about one's own importance. We feel sad or anxious when we lose the illusions that we're more important than other people; that our life will or should always be easy and pleasant; that time won't eventually take away all that we are and all that we have; that others exist in large part to serve our needs; or that our interacting by being demanding, manipulative, or enraged will lead to satisfactory results. These depressive feelings are developmentally positive; they indicate that we are getting more in touch with reality. The path away from narcissism and toward compassion is also a path away from illusions toward reality. If we allow feelings of depression, anxiety, or disillusionment to cause us to flee back to our narcissistic illusions, then we only ensure our long-term suffering.

Over the years I've repeatedly been moved by the Dalai Lama's personal descriptions of the great efforts it takes to bring about inner development. Once in Los Angeles, someone asked the Dalai Lama what was the "quickest and easiest" way to enlightenment. I'll never forget what happened next: the Dalai Lama bowed his head and began to cry. It struck me that such a question probably would be asked only in the United States, as though spiritual development could be gained as easily as fast-food hamburgers. The search for quick and easy results is itself a manifestation of narcissistic arrogance. Eventually the Dalai Lama explained that there is no "quick, easy, or cheap" method for real, inner development. Though he would admit to having made only limited progress himself, he spoke about his own strong, sincere efforts over many, many years to develop patience and compassion in the face of so many losses for himself and his people. Then he spoke of the great Tibetan saint Milarepa, who the Dalai Lama has taken as a role model. Milarepa underwent many hardships early in his life in order to obtain Buddhist teachings. Then he spent many years living alone in high, Himalayan caves. He had only a single white, cotton cloth to protect his body against the Tibetan winters, and his skin eventually turned greenish from his subsisting so long just on melted snow and wild nettles. The Dalai Lama told of Milarepa's final meeting with his greatest student, Gampopa. After having given Gampopa many different spiritual teachings, Milarepa said that he had one secret, very profound teaching that was "too precious to give away." So he sent Gampopa away, but when Gampopa had walked so far that he could barely hear Milarepa's voice, Milarepa called him back. Milarepa then praised Gampopa's qualities as a student, explaining that in fact he would share his final and most precious, secret teaching. Milarepa then lifted up his robe, exposing his naked body, which was covered with many hardened calluses. Milarepa explained that there was no teaching more profound than this: it is only through bearing the hardships of persistent and strenuous practice that one gains deep, good qualities and enlightenment. As a result of his efforts, Milarepa was able to sing, "I am the one who always adheres to kindness; With great compassion I have subdued all evil thoughts," and also,

What happiness to sing the victorious song,
What happiness to chant and hum,
More joyful still to talk and loudly sing!
Happy is the mind, powerful and confident.

The Dalai Lama noted that whatever happiness and good qualities he has developed arose from following this precious and profound teaching of Milarepa's. To the extent that each of us is able, we too must put effort into defeating our inner enemies, achieving minds with great compassion, happy, powerful, and confident.

In this chapter we studied the inner work of differentiating from and battling our inner enemies. As our understanding of narcissism develops, it becomes clear that following self-cherishing rather than compassion creates much unhappiness in our relationships. Each time we choose to cherish an image rather than another person, we create suffering for ourselves and also for those close to us. In the next chapter we explore how to battle our narcissism in the context of relationships. We learn how to use conflicts in relationships skillfully so that we can keep difficulties from creating suffering for ourselves or others and can use them instead to harm our inner enemy.

TWELVE

JOYFULLY LOSING
AN ARGUMENT

When others, out of jealousy,
Mistreat me with abuse, slander and scorn,
I will practice accepting defeat
And offering the victory to them.

—Geshe Langri Tangpa

Whether a conflict arises between nations, neighbors, or spouses, it's only natural for both parties to want to win. Conflict arises when we feel that we aren't getting what we want and that our interests are at odds with someone else's.

The emotional perspective from which we view a conflict largely determines our approach. If we have strong craving or desire, then we may act in a fiercely competitive manner, striving to achieve our goals regardless of the other person's needs. If we feel angry, then we may be aggressive, perhaps even intentionally harming the other person to get what we want. If we are jealous, we look for some way to get what the other person has. If we're anxious, we may try to compromise or even give in to escape from our own discomfort. People who are both aggressive and fearful (passive-aggressive) may even lose an argument intentionally in order to use it later against the other person.

There is no way to approach a conflict from the perspective of compassion. When viewed through eyes of compassion, seemingly solid problems dissolve like mirages. Conflict implies that our interests are at odds; to compassion, our interests are intimately interconnected. Think of any argument, any interpersonal problem, in your own life, and then imagine seeing it through eyes of compassion. Imagine viewing it from the perspective of the Dalai Lama, who speaks with love of those who stole his country. Imagine viewing it from the perspective of Gandhi, who prayed for the man who shot him; of the Buddhist saint who gave his body to feed a starving tiger and her cubs; of Jesus, who prayed for those who killed him. When we look through eyes of compassion, we find that arguments are rooted in our own narcissism. Of course people's opinions and interests can differ. However, such differences need not lead to conflicts, anger, or hatred unless we cherish our own interests and opinions more than we cherish our own and others' happiness. When we have deep compassion, we can appreciate our differences, and so our disagreements lead to dialogue rather than arguments.

Of course, most of us don't walk around each day seeing the world through the eyes of a saint. Our problems usually appear very solid and real. In this chapter, I offer a method for dissolving conflicts and problems by means of compassion. I call it "joyfully losing an argument."

A GIFT OF GOLF BALLS

This story was told to me by George Farley, a fellow student of the renowned Buddhist master Lama Zopa Rinpoche. Some years ago, George was involved in planning and fund-raising for a large event in Sydney; the Dalai Lama was to come and grant a Kalachakra initiation for the first time in the southern hemisphere.

One of George's tasks was to raise awareness and funds by meeting with groups to explain the meaning of the upcoming ceremony. One such dinner was for roughly a dozen people at the home of Wendy and her husband, Stuart, a bright and good-hearted psychiatrist.

The guests were intelligent, and the conversation flowed easily. People asked George many questions about Buddhism. Then, over dessert, Stuart told a story that was clearly disturbing him. He had a very nice, new BMW that he cherished. Some months earlier he had been sitting quietly at home when he heard a crash in the street. Looking out the window, he saw that his much-loved sedan had just been rear-ended by his neighbor. He rushed downstairs and into the street in time to see his neighbor's car pulling up the street and disappearing into his garage. There was a good deal of damage to the BMW. After taking a few deep breaths, Stuart went to the neighbor's house and rang the doorbell. There was no response. Repeated ringing and door thumping were met only by silence.

When the neighbor continued avoiding Stuart, he submitted the bill to his insurance company. They eventually sued the neighbor with Stuart as a witness, and the neighbor had to pay about $5,000 for repairs to the BMW.

A few weeks after the court case Stuart found that the brand-new paint job on his treasured car, which had been paid for by the settlement, had been gouged deeply: someone had dragged a sharp, metal object along the entire length of his car.

Of course, Stuart suspected his neighbor. However, lacking proof and wishing to avoid further conflict, he had the car fixed, paying for it himself. A week after having the car fixed, he found yet another deep gouge running the length of his car.

At this point the vandalism was really beginning to get under Stuart's skin. He went to see his neighbor, who not only dismissively denied gouging his car but also threatened to sue Stuart for harassment and slander for coming to his door with the issue.

Stuart felt trapped. Having gotten his car fixed for a third time, he was fearful and worried that it would get damaged again. He felt annoyed and angry, even indignant toward his terrible neighbor. And the problem only seemed to be growing. Stuart found himself repeatedly checking out his window, hoping to catch his neighbor in the act of damaging his car again.

Unsure about how to handle this ongoing conflict, Stuart asked his dinner guests, "What would you do? We love living here. We simply haven't the room to build a garage, so our cars have to be parked in the street. Frankly, it's driving me crazy. If I catch this bastard in the act, I won't be responsible for my actions."

People suggested all sorts of options, from hidden cameras to extra-sensitive car alarms. During the discussion about how to handle this conflict, George was quietly wondering what a Buddhist approach might be. He asked himself what his teacher, Lama Zopa Rinpoche, would do. Suddenly he knew.

George said, "Stuart, what you have to do is buy him an expensive gift, take it to him, apologize sincerely for all the trouble you have caused him, and ask for his forgiveness."

Naturally, there were lots of strong reactions to this suggestion. The dinner party got very lively after that. Wendy, Stuart's wife, said, "Over my dead body. This guy is a low-life, and we're going to make sure he gets what he deserves." Most of those present agreed that George's suggestion was an unrealistic and overly altruistic approach.

What seems reasonable and realistic to a person depends heavily on their perspective. Very intelligent people can remain blind to options that are right in front of them. Often, people's fear, anger, or insecurity causes them to waste decades by obscuring choices that could transform their lives quickly. Luckily for Stuart, he wasn't this sort of person. He had that too rare kind of inner bravery that allowed him to step outside himself. Inspired by George's suggestion, he looked beyond his own hurt and worried perspective. Seeing both his own and his neighbor's suffering as ultimately and intimately interconnected, he took a brave leap into the perspective of compassion.

Stuart remembered having heard that his neighbor was an enthusiastic golfer. So he quickly went out and bought half a dozen ridiculously expensive golf balls, the sort that are too expensive and indulgent for most people to buy for themselves. He gift-wrapped them carefully and beautifully. The gift as well as the extent to which he'd transcended his own narcissism were both extravagant. He went to his neighbor's house and rang the bell.

His neighbor was naturally wary and tense to find Stuart standing in his doorway. But Stuart smiled sincerely, and with an abundance of goodwill he sincerely apologized for his past accusation, gave the neighbor his gift, and asked for his forgiveness. His neighbor just stood in the doorway, dumbstruck, holding his golf balls.

At this point, regardless of his neighbor's response, Stuart already had transcended their previous conflict. In intentionally making himself vulnerable to his enemy, he had moved beyond his own vulnerability and fear. In embracing compassion, he had succeeded in joyfully losing an argument.

About an hour after receiving the gift, Stuart's neighbor showed up on his doorstep. It was clear he had been crying and was still choked up. He said that no one had ever shown him such kindness and that he was deeply sorry for all the problems he'd caused. He made a commitment to being a good neighbor and, still on the verge of tears, offered to do anything he could to help Stuart in the future. From that point on, they became good, friendly neighbors.

LOSING AN ARGUMENT WITHOUT LOSING YOURSELF

C. G. Jung once noted that Western culture tends to be extroverted, focusing most of its attention on outer phenomena, while Asian cultures, particularly those influenced by Buddhism and Hinduism, tend to be more introverted, focusing more of their attention on inner, psychological phenomena. There's some truth to Jung's insight, and so there is a danger that Western readers will focus too much on the outer level when trying the practice of joyfully losing an argument. That is, we may use this method to justify giving in to other people without actually changing our attitude. In fact, lots of people already behave this way. Wanting to be liked and accepted by others, they suppress their own desires in order to pretend they're just the people they imagine others want them to be. When behaving in this way, people may appear patient and kind on the surface as they gracefully allow others to have their way. A person who lacks self-respect and fears being abandoned or hurt can engage in an incredible degree of self-sacrifice. However, losing an argument because you want to be liked and accepted is neither joyful nor compassionate.

Giving in to others out of fear is a common dynamic in abusive relationships. It's really just another form of narcissism—identifying with the superficial image of what you think others want in order to gain their acceptance. Like other narcissistic approaches to seeking happiness, it does not work. When we suppress aspects of ourselves and play a role to gain others' acceptance, we undermine real intimacy. We aren't being genuine with the other person, and eventually we become resentful and tired of playing a role. People who engage in this form of narcissism are sometimes referred to as martyrs or as codependent. Engaging in self-sacrifice out of fear and neediness often leads to unhealthy interpersonal relationships and to low self-esteem, anxious dependency, agitated confusion, and even depression.

As a psychologist, I've worked with many people who sacrifice themselves, appearing good-hearted and humble, in order to gain love and acceptance. Research suggests that approaching relationships in that way undermines our self-esteem and leaves us feeling insecure.

When we suppress our real views and feelings and play a role to gain others' acceptance, we find it particularly painful when we do not succeed. Sacrificing so much of ourselves and still not being accepted makes us feel like failures. Even if we do succeed in gaining someone's approval by playing a role, their praise does not help us feel better about ourselves. Deep down, we feel that they are praising the role we've been playing rather than praising us. Therefore, rather than increasing our self-esteem, such praise makes us feel more insecure and pressured to continue fitting ourselves into a false role.

So, for Westerners in particular, it's important to differentiate between the practice of joyfully losing an argument and the codependent tendency to lose an argument joylessly out of insecurity or fear. Joyfully losing an argument is primarily a process of inner transformation. We do not suppress our real feelings and opinions; instead, we transform or transcend them by means of compassion. One way of checking whether you're practicing compassion or codependence is to see whether you are afraid to confront the other person about things they do that are causing suffering for themselves, for others, or for you and to ask yourself where that fear originates. When compassionate, we energetically confront such behaviors in whatever ways are appropriate to the situation; when codependent, we rationalize not doing so. Another way to differentiate between compassion and codependence is to be aware of how we're feeling when we lose an argument. When we're codependent, we usually feel worried, upset, or anxious. There's also a sense of constriction in our hearts, as though we are making ourselves small so as not to impose on the other person. When we're compassionate, the feeling is very different. Even as we lose an argument, we feel expansive and fully present with the other person. We feel relaxed, joyful, and even extravagant in the process of compassionate self-transcendence.

MADLY, CHILDISHLY AGITATING OTHERS

The differences between losing an argument joyfully and losing it joy-lessly will become even clearer as I describe the underlying psychology of this method.

It's unfortunate but true that when we feel particularly upset, un-happy, agitated, or miserable we often make those around us unhappy as well. Through our words, our sighs, or our gestures we often ex-press our bad feelings in ways that lead others to resonate with our ag-itation. As others get upset they begin expressing this as well, which often leads to an escalation of unpleasant feelings. It is not difficult for misery to find or create company.

Imagine an ordinary man who's had a busy week at work, putting in extra hours. His boss has been demanding, and so he's been stressed and worried. On Thursday night a relative calls late in the evening, and so he goes to bed late. By Friday he's feeling exhausted. Then, in the afternoon, his boss gives him a hard time about the project he's been working on. On the way home he gets stuck in rush-hour traffic and another guy cuts him off. He gets home feeling tired, agitated, and overwhelmed. He sighs, his gestures are gruff, and even his eyes seem to look about uneasily. His tone with his wife is curt, bordering on rude. At first she ignores this, but when she eventually reacts, he blows up at her. At this point she gets upset, and *he feels better.*

Why at this point should he feel better? Why in the world should such misery love company? In reality, he's made things worse. Now he's not only tired and facing a problem at work, he's also facing a problem at home that will make his weekend stressful as well. Psy-choanalysts explain this clearly. As long as we're under the control of narcissism, this is part of the way that our unconscious delusions and sadism express themselves in everyday interactions. This man has been feeling overwhelmed, upset, and out of control. He couldn't control some of the outer events in his life this week, and he also couldn't or didn't control his own emotions. So he projects some or all of his negativity onto his wife, and then he controls her, forcing her to feel some of his misery. It's an infantile and crazy approach to relationships, but nearly all adults do this some of the time. By controlling her in this way, he feels less alone in his unhappiness and also wrongly imagines that he's gotten more in control of himself and his situation.

What ordinarily happens next is that his wife, who's now justifiably upset, begins acting in an agitated way. Overtly, by fighting with him, or covertly through her tone of voice and manner, she expresses her own unhappiness. Why does she do so? Now she, feeling agitated and out of control, is projecting onto him and trying to feel less alone and more in control by forcing him to feel bad. And so conflicts sometimes go madly back and forth, almost endlessly.

If you watch yourself or any other person feeling overwhelmed and upset, it isn't difficult to see efforts to evoke resonant empathy in others—efforts to make others feel upset as well. This is actually a normal part of how young children relate with their parents. They cry and act upset, and their parents have a spontaneous, resonant, empathic response. The parent shares in the child's agitation and therefore responds to the child, striving to remove the source of agitation. The child, feeling understood and cared for by the parent, then begins feeling better.

For an adult, this way of relating is always regressive. And regardless of whether we're feeling anger or some other negative emotion, this is an inherently aggressive way of relating. We are trying to control how another person feels and behaves, forcing that person to feel bad. Even in the midst of very adult conflicts, when we get caught up in agitated emotional states our approach is rooted in a childish part of our mind—the psychology of the baby crying or having a tantrum in its crib. The practice of joyfully losing an argument is a direct way of overcoming our tendency to relate to others in this way.

THE VALUE OF DIFFICULT PEOPLE

Learning to joyfully lose an argument requires growing up emotion-ally. It involves becoming genuinely relaxed, flexible, and self-reliant. His Holiness the Dalai Lama often notes that in order to avert war and bring about disarmament in the world, we must begin by effect-ing an inner disarmament. We must become peaceful ourselves if we wish to create a world in which long-term peace is possible. Each time we practice joyfully losing an argument, we are disarming ourselves, bringing peace to ourselves and to others.

This is a practice, though, that we cannot do on our own. We need other people with whom to practice. Gentle, kindhearted, supportive friends are not useful in this regard. To practice losing an argument, you need someone who will argue with you. You need someone who will be difficult with you, trying to control you and get you upset.

The great Indian Buddhist teacher Atisha transmitted this prac-tice to Tibet. It's said that for many years Atisha traveled around with another monk who was extremely annoying and irascible. Someone eventually asked him why he'd chosen this monk as his attendant, and Atisha explained that one needs difficult people in one's life to practice this sort of method. After he'd been in Tibet for a while, Atisha sent this monk back to the monastery. He said the Tibetans of that time were of such rough character that he no longer needed this difficult fellow for his practice. The character of the Tibetan people as a whole changed over the intervening millennia precisely because they, as a culture, put these teachings into practice. They disarmed their own hearts and then their nation, bringing about centuries of peace.

Most of us don't need to find a difficult traveling companion or travel to a foreign land to locate a person with whom we can practice joyfully losing an argument. Most people I've known who practice this method begin with their spouses, coworkers, parents, and children.

At first, trying to use an argument as an opportunity to develop compassion and find joy seems a bit strange. Someone in your life approaches you in a provocative, agitated, unreasonable, annoying way. You immediately think, *Oh, good, this is my opportunity. Here's an argument starting. Now I can really practice compassion!*

When you're just getting started, you'll be of two minds about the situation. Based on old habits, part of you will want the person to stop being difficult and to act kind and friendly. The part of you that's happy to find this opportunity initially may seem weak or less than genuine. That's all right; it just means that you're not yet accustomed to practicing compassion and inner disarmament. Lama Zopa Rinpoche advises that when you get good at this practice, the thought of enjoying such challenges will arise as naturally and joyfully as the thought of liking ice cream or chocolate. It all depends on what you're accustomed to.

If you're sincerely interested in being a more loving, good-hearted person, then it can be particularly helpful at the beginning to recognize that it's mainly through your practice with difficult people that you will become confident that your inner development is bearing fruit. When we're kind toward people who are consistently kind to us in return, it's difficult to feel confident in the purity of our motives. It's sometimes hard to tell for certain whether we're generous and friendly out of deep compassion or out of a desire to have our kind actions reciprocated. Heartfelt kindness toward someone who has just treated you badly has the clean, pure feeling of a cool creek in the high mountains.

RIDING THE WAVE

As I go through the rest of the inner process of joyfully losing an argument, I'll use another example to help illustrate how it works. John, a Buddhist friend, grew up in a family in which his mother's anger occasionally flared up in ways that made him uncomfortable. He could recall heading off to his room and listening to music when his parents began shouting at each other. So he tended to have a difficult time later on in his life when he and his wife argued about things. His wife had a quick temper. When she got angry at him, he usually became quite anxious and pulled away. On rare occasions, when she pursued him and didn't let him escape, he blew up at her. Then he felt guilty and bad about himself. So he saw any conflict as a catch-22, with every course of action leading to suffering.

When he first began practicing this Buddhist approach to transforming conflicts, it felt very unnatural to him. The thought of seeing his wife's annoyance with him as an opportunity to practice was like a small prayer flag whipped by the strong winds of his aversion and anxiety. However, to his credit, John didn't give up on the process.

Once you've recognized the beginning of a conflict as an opportunity, you have to be careful to avoid focusing too much on the *content* of the conflict. As long as either person is caught up in agitated emotions, even very reasonable solutions won't usually bring resolution. Men in particular often make the mistake of focusing too much on solutions, ignoring the powerful emotions that underlie a conflict. Generally speaking, if one first resolves the emotional issues through empathy and compassion, then finding a solution to the content of an argument is simple.

Though the essence of this method focuses on transforming our own deeply felt emotions, learning to think differently is often helpful in the beginning. When a challenging situation presents itself, we immediately tend to respond as we always have in the past. At that moment, it's useful to stop, be self-aware, and remind yourself of the disadvantages of getting caught up again in negative, afflicted emotional states and childish patterns of reactivity. If you have already used the methods such as the key to happiness or fighting one's inner enemy described in previous chapters, then some of the self-analysis you've already done can be brought to mind in this moment. It's also helpful at this point to remember the great value of cultivating peace and compassion, bringing happiness to yourself and others, decreasing stress and tension, improving your relationships, and improving your health.

In John's case, developing a new way of thinking was simple. When his wife got angry, he easily could identify his own impulses to pull away or react angrily. Based on his experiences, he recalled that following these habitual tendencies led him to his catch-22, to an increase in his own suffering and to tensions in his marriage. He later said, "I knew that following my old patterns always led to trouble for me. I didn't have much to lose trying something new." He also thought about his personal beliefs in the value of patience and compassion, feeling that if he didn't make an effort to put them into practice in moments like this, then his thoughts and prayers for peace and love made in quiet moments of meditation were little more than hollow or even hypocritical words. He said, "How could I pray for peace in the Middle East or in other parts of the world where people were being killed if I couldn't even practice it when faced with small, petty conflicts?"

Next comes the heart of this practice. Ordinarily, when another person expresses overwhelming, agitated emotions through subtle cues, our own nervous system picks up on this through resonant empathy and we become agitated as well. When we realize that we've become upset because of our interaction with the other person, we usually become annoyed with them.

Here instead, allow your natural, resonant, empathic response to occur, but watch the process without reacting, without getting stuck in the negative emotion. Relax into the interaction without holding onto or grasping at anything. Stay open to the other person, and allow your resonant empathy to educate you about the other's suffering. Experientially, it can seem sometimes as though a wave of emotion is coming toward you from the other person, like a churning and powerful wave in the ocean. Fighting against this wave, you wind up in conflict.

Running away closes you off from the other person and from yourself, as you cannot escape from your own inborn capacity for resonant empathy—it's part of your human nervous system.

By allowing this wave of emotion to come into you and allowing your own nervous system to resonate with another's, you gain an intimate experience of the other's suffering. Now compassion becomes the natural response. When you don't allow yourself to fixate on the agitation and don't take the interaction personally by grasping strongly at your own perspective, then your deep understanding of the other person's suffering spontaneously leads to compassion. The more the other expresses agitation, the more energetic fuel you have for your compassion. When you don't grasp at the wave of emotion that comes at you, its very energy becomes a wave of loving kindness that carries you back toward the other person.

Clearly, in this approach, you are not allowing the other person to control you in the aggressive way discussed above. You are not allowing the other to get you agitated. The other person is in a regressive state, but you don't regress. Instead, you remain aware, mature, and cool, which allows you to connect with the other intelligently, offering what help, soothing, kindness, or even humor you can.

An interaction that John and his wife had when he practiced this method illustrates how this can work. She was annoyed with him because he hadn't followed through with some household chores that he'd promised to complete. As she began raising her voice, he found himself feeling defensive and wanting to argue with her. However, he stopped and recognized this as an opportunity to practice compassion. Through his awareness of his own resonant response to his wife, John became aware of how overwhelmed and upset she was feeling. He could see how hard she worked and how her becoming exhausted and frustrated by his lack of follow-through could lead her naturally to become angry at him over what he'd viewed as a minor oversight. While John was caught up in such reflections, his wife noticed that he wasn't responding to her as usual. Not sure if she was getting through to him, feeling alone in her frustration and without control in the situation, she said, "John, why the hell are you just staring at me and smiling? Is something wrong with you? Have you even heard a word I've been saying?"

John practically had to shake himself out of his compassionate reverie. He said, "Oh, yes, I was. I was thinking that you're right. I promised to do those things, and it wasn't right for me to disappoint you by putting them off. I was also thinking about how hard you work and how exhausting it must be sometimes. I was thinking about why you work so hard—because you're so incredibly kind and precious."

John's wife stared at him for a moment, dumbfounded. Then she smiled suspiciously and said, "All right, who are you, and what did you do with my husband?"

He replied, "I want things to be easier on you. Let me do those chores now and then take you out for a drive and some dinner. We could both use a chance to relax and have some fun." She smiled and said, "Okay." As he walked away to do the chores, she called out, "Thanks."

Of course, calming the other person's emotions isn't always achieved so easily. In John's case, there were many other occasions when he didn't do as good a job at joyfully losing an argument or when his wife simply couldn't let go of her frustrations so quickly. However, as he continued practicing, the length and intensity of their arguments consistently decreased.

The essential thing in this method is to use your own nervous system's sympathetic, resonant response to the other person's agitated emotional state—which might otherwise lead you to get upset yourself—as a way of gaining increased understanding of and compassion for him or her.

In terms of how to react to the person, I think that it's best to trust your own intuition. Through repeated, largely unconscious resonant responses, you've gained a good deal of intuitive understanding of the other people in your life. This is something you can rely on to allow your compassion to express itself in natural and spontaneous ways. I think it's also important not to be attached to having your actions be quickly effective in changing how the other person feels. That would turn this method into just another way of striving to control or manipulate others. If the other person remains agitated, then your own task is to continue using this energy to further strengthen your compassion.

According to recent research on the brain, an individual who practices in this way actually can change his or her neurology over time, developing new, more positive habitual responses. As the emotional centers of our brains develop and change through significant relationships with others, changing our approach naturally leads to subtle changes in those around us over time. By practicing "joyfully losing an argument"—by disarming our own minds—any of us can make a real contribution to peace in our own lives and in the world around us.

THIRTEEN

TAKING AND GIVING

O venerable, compassionate Gurus,
We seek your blessings that all karmic debts, obstacles,
and sufferings of mother beings
May without exception ripen upon us right now,
And that we may give our happiness and virtue to others
And, thereby, invest all beings in bliss.

—The First Panchen Lama,
Lozang Chokyi Gyaltsan

The final method presented here develops naturally out of the other methods we have discussed. If you haven't spent time on those other practices, it will be difficult to understand this one correctly. It might be easy to understand intellectually, but it is difficult to understand with your heart. I think this method is the quintessence, the pure, distilled essence, of all other practices for developing compassion.

In India and Tibet, this practice originally was transmitted by a teacher only to close disciples who showed a special aptitude for compassion. Later on Tibetan lamas began teaching it openly. To make good use of this practice, you must understand the nature of narcissism, see how it causes suffering, and have begun abandoning the habit of cherishing superficial self-images.

I present this method as it has been done by Mahayana Buddhists for over a millennium. I use Western psychological ideas to help explain some of the surprising psychological benefits that can arise from doing this practice, but I make no changes to the method itself.

At first this practice may seem a bit strange or uncomfortable. It's important to understand that such discomfort has little to do with the fact that this practice comes from another culture. When Buddhist masters first taught this method, their Indian and Tibetan students found it uncomfortable and foreign as well. This practice directly and radically undermines our narcissism in favor of compassion; therefore it is uncomfortable to our narcissism and foreign to our ego. Our discomfort comes mainly from the extent to which we still cherish and identify with superficial, narcissistic images. As we analyze the psychological principles underlying this method, you'll see that they are not uniquely Buddhist at all. They are the principles of conquering our narcissism in order to achieve a joyful, open heart wholly dedicated to compassion.

In our battle against the inner enemy of self-cherishing, this method is an incredibly powerful weapon. It helps us develop a warrior's spirit of courage in our practices of love and compassion. If we get good at this practice, we'll be able to face all sorts of circumstances in our lives with a remarkable sense of integrity, love, and joy. Particularly when we come upon hard times in life, there's a danger of losing our sense of confidence, feeling lost, and becoming discouraged with our progress in inner development. This practice teaches us to face such circumstances bravely, using them as powerful fuel for developing compassion. If we spend the time necessary to understand and get good at this practice, any of us can reap the reward of an unshakable confidence in our capacity to be wholly present with any experience that may come, conquering the narcissism in our hearts so all that's left is radiant love.

Beyond even that, if we continue making efforts at this practice over a length of time, gradually we can make compassion our natural way of relating to the world. People who engage in this practice regularly find that the impulse to give of themselves and to relate lovingly arises more and more spontaneously. Developing the totally spontaneous instinct for expansive compassion is one of the main benefits of this method described in Buddhist psychology. Eventually this practice can make compassion our primary, instinctual way of relating to the world so that in each moment from morning to night and even in our dreams, compassion and love come as naturally as breathing in and out.

According to the Buddhist tradition, throughout the past millennium practitioners have found also that doing this practice can have positive results for health and well-being. Tibetan lamas often advise doing this practice not only for developing compassion but also to help with healing various psychological and physical ailments. Many meditation and prayer techniques have been shown to be beneficial in mind-body research, and people in Asia and the West who have done this practice well report a wide range of health benefits, so I believe that this is an interesting area for further scientific study. The Buddhist tradition emphasizes, though, that healing mental or physical ailments is only one benefit of this practice; its main functions are to help us develop spontaneous compassion, universal altruism, and an extremely expansive sense of blissful inner peace.

TAKING SORROW

Before engaging in the practice of taking and giving, I think it's important to review some key points from the methods already presented. Begin by spending some time developing a sense of empathy and affection for others. In order to deepen your empathy, recall that everyone is just like you in wanting happiness and not wanting to suffer; in this sense we're all precisely equal. In order to deepen your affection, look at others through eyes of gratitude, recollecting how all of your own happiness comes from the kindness of others. It's also helpful at this point to review the insights from the key to happiness, remembering that each and every suffering we experience comes from a self-centered approach to life, while all happiness for ourselves and others comes from kindness, from the good heart. You may want to recall especially your resolve to overcome the greatest obstacle to compassion—your inner enemy, self-cherishing or narcissism—which has hidden so often in the recesses of your heart, destroying your relationships and ruining your peace. Of course, you need not review every one of these points before engaging in this practice, but they do provide the context that makes it effective and meaningful.

The method itself is called "taking and giving." Taking comes first. Begin by thinking about any of the many sufferings that the countless beings in the universe experience. Actively cultivate empathy and strong compassion as you think about such sufferings. You can begin small, by thinking about the suffering of a headache or stomachache that you may experience some time in the future. As you get better at the practice, you can be bolder in your compassionate vision, thinking of the sufferings of people in the depths of depression, of those dying of cancer, of people who are lonely, mourning, penniless, wounded, paralyzed, losing their minds, imprisoned, physically tortured, oppressed, starving, terrified, suffocated, demented, or filled with hate. You can think also of the sufferings of animals that are overburdened, sick, and alone, hungry, wet, frightened, or are being slaughtered by humans or eaten alive by other animals. Can you train your inner eye of empathy to look upon such agony without blinking, without closing? In brief, you can think compassionately of any suffering conceivable to the human imagination, and given the nature of things, this could include some awfully bleak, nauseating, and hellish visions of pain—sadistic, masochistic, and dizzyingly meaningless pain—that would break open the heart of any sane and decent person. In fact, what such compassion breaks in our hearts is a shell of narcissistic denial, leading to a new capacity for awareness. Only in facing such pain do we develop the brave, open heart of a warrior for compassion.

Next, focusing on whatever portion of this suffering you can hold honestly, compassionately in your mind, imagine that it arises away from those beings, cut away from them as cleanly as hairs cut by a sharp razor, and that it takes on the form of black light, like some surreal clouds of misery pollution sucked up from underworld factories. By the force of your compassion, you draw this dark energy toward yourself. If you feel afraid as you try to draw it toward you, recognize the fear as coming from your narcissism and disidentify from it.

Now, in the center of your own heart, you imagine your inner enemy, your narcissistic self-cherishing. Imagine the entirety of that dark misery cloud absorbing into your inner enemy, destroying it. One great Tibetan practitioner of this method, Kyabje Ribur Rinpoche, says to imagine all that suffering absorbing "right in the center of the demon heart of the self-cherishing thought . . . striking at it very strongly" and obliterating it. Here, your strong compassion becomes a weapon, directly destroying the narcissism in your heart.

You can do this practice of taking again and again. Tibetan teachers advise that it's often best to begin small, focusing on your own future sufferings and on relatively small sufferings of people you already know and for whom you care (for example, your friend's worries or your spouse's backache). Then you expand the practice outward, including greater and greater clouds of misery. Each time you do the practice, begin by developing the strong compassion that takes on responsibility for others' welfare and that would take on their suffering gladly to free them from it. And each time, imagine that the suffering absorbs into your heart, destroying your inner enemy. If you feel particularly fearful or uncomfortable as you try this practice, remember

that those feelings mainly derive from continuing to identify your self
with your self-cherishing. Make efforts to recall why self-cherishing is
your enemy and to recognize how identifying with it always leads you to
suffer. In destroying the narcissism in your heart, you are not destroying
yourself; you are freeing yourself and leading yourself to happiness.

GIVING JOY

Having done the practice of taking, you now proceed to giving. If taking is based primarily on compassion, on the wish to free others from
suffering, then giving is based primarily on love, on the wish to give
others happiness. Enhancing your feelings of empathy and affection
for others, you feel happy at the thought of freeing them from suffering, but you feel that this is insufficient. They also need happiness.
And so you imagine either that light rays stream forth from your body
or that many replicas of your body go out from where you are and become everything that anyone wants or needs to be truly happy. Here
the vision can be as vast and sublime as your loving imagination allows. You can think of manifesting as a dear friend for all who are
lonely, as a builder for those without homes, as a teacher for those
wanting knowledge, as a caring doctor and nurse for those who are ill,
and as a protector for those who are afraid. You can think of manifesting as an ingenious adviser for those who are confused, as a parent for
orphans, as a musician who uplifts others' spirits, and as a spiritual
guide for those seeking one. You need not limit your vision to the
human; you can offer cool breezes, rains of flowers, inspiring ideas, fireworks displays, piles of jewels, cars, boats, parks, palaces, libraries, wonderful feasts, moving works of art, medicines, and anything else that
brings people happiness. You can even imagine giving others positive
inner states such as peace, affection, love, compassion, contentment, joy,
and enlightenment. In doing this contemplation, I sometimes think of
Leonardo da Vinci, who once wrote, "I never weary of being useful. I

do not tire of serving others." Da Vinci conceived of offering the people of the late 1400s flying machines; well-planned cities; beautiful churches and buildings; religious paintings; portraits; statues; huge bridges; canals for travel; new forms of irrigation; new knowledge in fields as diverse as the arts, physiology, philosophy, optics, mathematics, engineering, and hydrodynamics; and human-made garden paradises filled with cool breezes in the hot summer, fountains, baths, small brooks with gentle fish, "orange and citron trees," unending "music from all sorts of instruments," and aviaries so that the natural music of birdsongs could be mixed with the sounds of human music and the scent of lemons. In this practice of giving, you imagine giving everything and anything that brings happiness; you cultivate an expansive and ingenious spirit of generosity.

Of course, da Vinci did not succeed in giving everything he imagined to the world. But what he did give was so beautiful, and the bold expansiveness of his genius was so remarkable that it still inspires others today. This is a good analogy for part of what happens through practicing taking and giving. It's not that one magically causes lonely people to have friends or the hungry to have food simply by visualizing it. What does happen is that your own feelings of love and compassion increase, and you become more willing to do things for others, even to take on hardships yourself in order to accomplish good things for others. And the scope of your thinking and creativity about how to benefit others gradually expands. It's clear that thoughts and ideas, when they have a strong force of motivation behind them, can bring about big results. Ideas fueled by fear and hate have produced world wars; thoughts fueled by greed have produced huge corporations. When people develop thoughts and ideas strongly motivated by compassion, external manifestations (large and small) of these ideas naturally follow as well.

Once you become familiar with each of the two main elements of this practice, you can then engage in each slowly, thinking of many details. If you become strongly interested in this practice, you can do taking and giving along with your breathing. Many people are familiar with simple breath awareness exercises to calm and focus the mind. Here you use the breath as a continuous reminder for cultivating compassion. With each in-breath, you do the practice of taking, imagining the sufferings of others being absorbed into yourself, destroying the "demon heart of the self-cherishing thought." And with each out-breath, you do the practice of giving, imagining light rays going out, bringing happiness to all beings. Once people are familiar with this practice, they often do it with their breathing while interacting with others, using it especially when difficult circumstances arise. This is also the form of the practice often used for healing when people are ill. At such times, they may imagine taking in the suffering of all others who are ill with similar diseases, thereby using their suffering to help them develop expansive empathy and compassion. Many people have described how this brings them peace of mind in the face of illness, and some have reported positive physical effects as well.

TRANSFORMING SUFFERING INTO PURE JOY

When a person seriously engages in this method of taking and giving, certain benefits to others in society are likely. At the very least, that person will become less likely to harm others. When other people are angry or irritated, she will be more likely than before to remain calm and to help others through their difficulties. Even if she doesn't engage in large projects to benefit society, she at least is likely to become gradually more patient, honest, ethical, generous, useful, and kind to those around her. And if many people engage in this method, as occurred in Tibetan society, then some likely will be inspired to do great, even surprising things to relieve the suffering of others and bring them happiness.

At this point, I'd like to focus on some of the surprising psychological benefits that can arise from doing this practice. Earlier I mentioned a venerable teacher and precious friend of mine, Kyabje Ribur Rinpoche, who is a great practitioner of this method. I'd like to share some details from his life story to illustrate the effects that this practice can bring about.

Ribur Rinpoche was born in eastern Tibet in 1923. While he was still a young boy, Ribur Rinpoche was recognized by the previous Dalai Lama (the "Great Thirteenth") as being the reincarnation of a great Buddhist master of the past. From the age of twelve on, he was raised as a monk and was taught Buddhist philosophy, psychology, and meditation at Sera Monastery. He studied closely with many of Tibet's great yogis, including his main teacher, Pabongka Rinpoche, who also was a great practitioner of the taking and giving method. After completing his scholarly training early at the age of twenty-five, Ribur Rinpoche spent a number of years mainly engaged in solitary meditation retreats in the forest. He traveled occasionally to teach others and to continue with his advanced studies, but he spent most of his time in meditation. Always, meditation on compassion was the heart of his practice.

Soon his ability to remain compassionate and peaceful was severely tested. In 1950 the army of the Communist government of China invaded Tibet. By 1959 the situation had escalated, and the Dalai Lama along with roughly a hundred thousand other Tibetans escaped, taking asylum in India and forming a government-in-exile. Ribur Rinpoche did not escape from Tibet at that time. In 1959 he was arrested as a political prisoner by the Chinese government. During the years that followed, the government carried out a genocidal campaign in Tibet that experts estimate resulted in over 1.2 million deaths, the destruction of over 6200 monasteries and nunneries, and the destruction of most of Tibet's libraries, sacred art, and indigenous culture.

For almost twenty years Ribur Rinpoche underwent many hardships as a political prisoner. He says, "I was beaten, forced to do so many things. . . . The things they used to do to us are something you would never witness in your life. If I told you what happened on a daily basis, you would find it hard to believe." In the years that I've known him, I've never heard Rinpoche detail the forms of torture he experienced during his imprisonment, but hundreds of published accounts indicate that standard forms of torture by the Chinese officers included hanging monks from ropes by their wrists or thumbs or ankles and then beating them, beating monks with clubs, shocking them with cattle prods, attacking them with trained guard dogs, refusing them food for days at a time, giving inadequate food, and leaving them throughout the Tibetan winter in rooms with an average temperature below freezing with only a small blanket to be shared by prisoners. Many reports indicate that Chinese officials were particularly hard on reincarnate lamas. In brief, one can assume that Rinpoche underwent the worst kinds of physical abuse and torture during his many years in prison.

Rinpoche notes that he felt bad for many of his fellow Tibetan prisoners, who previously lived normal lives and now "were really devastated, they didn't know what to do or what to think or what was going on." Rinpoche himself did the practice of taking and giving throughout his years of terrible hardship. When a good practitioner of this method meets with difficult circumstances such as illness, loss, and physical pain, he uses them to inspire greater and greater compassion. People who don't practice taking and giving find the experience of intense suffering meaningless, unbearable, and devastating. They may become enraged, confused, and hopeless, feeling that their sense of identity is falling apart and that human life itself is unbearable. For someone who has invested time learning to do the practice of taking and giving, though, even intense sufferings become a reminder of the faults of the "demon heart of the self-cherishing thought" and become a means for powerfully deepening empathy and compassion for the terrible sufferings of others. At any given moment, each of us knows that people with whom we're not acquainted personally are experiencing unbelievable, horrific sufferings. We may care in some vague way, but mainly we feel that their sufferings are not terribly important to us. Our narcissism keeps us from recognizing our interdependence—how injustice or suffering anywhere is a threat to justice and happiness everywhere. Concerned almost exclusively with ourselves and our immediate circle of family and friends, we're often indifferent to the intense sufferings of others. The attitude of those who sincerely practice taking and giving is just the opposite. Developing an expansive sense of compassionate concern for others makes their own suffering less overwhelming and even less important in their eyes. Rather than allowing such suffering to upset their minds, practitioners use the practice to help them empathize with others, transforming suffering into fuel that feeds a great light of loving compassion in their hearts.

People may be tempted to assume that Ribur Rinpoche's unusual ability to face such sufferings with compassion came from his being a Tibetan lama or a monk. Particularly when thinking of the normal, everyday occurrences that get us annoyed, upset, or worried, we may feel that we're inherently different from someone who can transform years of torture and imprisonment into pure joy. I strongly disagree with such interpretations. I assert that, psychologically, anyone who chooses to invest the required time and energy in practices like taking and giving can also reap remarkable results. It all depends on how we choose to train or habituate our minds.

Ribur Rinpoche notes that when a practitioner of this method experiences intense suffering, she "immediately puts it in the practice of taking and giving, by taking all the sufferings of all sentient beings exactly on that." He says that such a practitioner will "actually embrace" the suffering that he's undergoing "in order to practice taking and giving more deeply." When we meet with any kind of suffering in our daily lives, whether it be a headache, a traffic jam, a difficult coworker, relationship problems, or even a serious illness, rather than just getting upset, we can choose to use such situations as a means to open our hearts more deeply to others by doing the practice of taking and giving. Ribur Rinpoche goes on to explain that when a person does so,

> Although that doesn't relieve him or her from that particular sickness or that particular problem or that particular unfavorable circumstance, the immediate result would be that . . . his or her mind would be totally unaffected by the sickness or by the unfavorable circumstances. And this is very true. This practice brings an unbelievable amount of courage and peace of mind as well, right when you need it. . . . This I can tell you for sure from my very own experience.

Rinpoche explains that by training the mind intensively in taking and giving, we can be happy in any circumstances. He explains that through his engaging in such practices, "my experiences in confinement were transformed into nothing but pure joy." If such joy seems too exalted or extravagant to be possible for us, then we should try this practice using the small sufferings that arise in our daily lives in order to begin experiencing for ourselves some of the courage and peace that result. In that way, by gradually making effort over time, we may be surprised by the spontaneously compassionate, loving, brave, and blissful feelings that eventually result.

After being released from prison, totally without anger or resentment, Rinpoche worked with Chinese officials to restore some of the greatest works of art in Tibet that had been damaged, broken, or taken by the Chinese army. Having focused for so long on the practice of taking on the suffering of others, he was now able to focus in his activities on the practice of giving. After leaving Tibet, Rinpoche lived near the Dalai Lama and wrote many historical books and biographies to help preserve his culture for future generations. In recent years, he has traveled all over the world to teach.

I've known Ribur Rinpoche for a number of years now. Often as you get to know someone better, you discover faults that were hidden before. I can say honestly that as I've gotten to know him better, I've been surprised repeatedly by the true extent of his contentment, humility, compassion, and joy. Not so long ago, I visited for a couple of nights at a house where he was doing a meditation retreat. On the first night I was there, he was very kind in staying up late to talk and meditate together. I then went to sleep. I woke up at one point in the middle of the night, surprised to hear in the distance Ribur Rinpoche, wide awake, playing a drum and bell as he happily sang ancient Tibetan songs about enlightened compassion. In the early morning he was still there in the same spot, smiling, laughing, singing, and meditating on compassion. I thought about his body, now old and badly damaged from his years in prison, and I wondered what sort of mind one might develop that would lead to that kind of joy—spontaneous, independent of circumstances, unassailable, and always flowing outward.

COURAGEOUS COMPASSION

With regard to taking and giving, I'd like to address some important psychological points, beginning with the issue of bravery or courage. Ribur Rinpoche says of taking and giving, "This is actually a meditation on great courage." Any attempt to increase our compassion involves some courage, as we are stepping out of familiar, self-centered habits and are also facing the sometimes unpleasant truths about others' suffering. The practice of taking and giving directly brings up the need for courage in letting go of old limitations and opening our hearts to the suffering of others.

Sometimes when I'm with someone who is suffering intensely I become afraid that I won't know what to do to help that person. At such times I do the practice of taking and giving. Our fears that we won't know how to help come from our narcissism—from the self-centered notion that we must have the answers because we are so great, helpful, or kind. By doing this practice, we can use our empathy for the other person's suffering to destroy such narcissistic fantasies. Once they are destroyed, we can be right there, wholly present in the moment with the other person. Without narcissism in our hearts, we will not become overwhelmed by others' suffering; we simply can be compassion manifest for the other person, perhaps doing nothing more than sharing a compassionate presence.

When I discuss this method with others, they often say that when they see that big, dark, billowing pollution cloud of suffering coming toward them, they become very afraid. As one man put it, "I don't want other people's cancer or AIDS." Some people say that they temporarily feel physically upset or sick when imagining taking on others' suffering. Others practically leap up and run out of the room when they imagine a dark mass of misery coming toward them. Another friend said, "At first I couldn't do this practice at all. Now I can do it genuinely for about a minute and a half. So I guess my compassion is increasing slowly."

I think that facing such fears in one's practice of this method is good. It's very honest. Of course we don't want to be sick, imprisoned, and the like. Real courage comes about through facing such fears. It's like that moment in the life of Saint Francis of Assisi when he confronted his fear of being near people with leprosy by approaching them, giving them gifts, and kissing their hands. His fear of being near them reflected his self-centered wish to avoid having to face what they symbolized to him at that time—our terrible, human vulnerability to illness, loss, humiliation, poverty, and death. By opening his heart to those individual lepers, he was opening his heart to everyone, including himself, who is subject to suffering, sickness, and loss. Only by facing our fears can we transcend them.

Narcissism strives desperately to avoid awareness of our vulnerability. At the heart of narcissism is grandiosity, a gross overestimation of our own importance in the universe. Terrified of our true situation as tiny, fragile beings in an infinitely vast universe filled with countless other beings, we grasp strongly at a superficial, idealized image of ourselves. The narcissistic self-image is always false; it is an illusion that we make up to comfort ourselves. Emphasizing appearance over substance, we hold onto our idealized image and simply deny or repress contradictory evidence of our fragility, impermanence, and interdependence. To feed this delusion, we compulsively build up fantasies of unlimited success, beauty, brilliance, or love. Wanting infinite gain or wealth, we deny the inevitability of loss; wanting infinite power and health, we deny the truth of illness and weakness; wanting infinite respect and praise, we deny the truth of our own flaws and failings; and wanting infinite life, we deny the truth of impermanence and death. We distance ourselves psychologically from the sufferings of others, which remind us of the things we wish to deny, so that even as we speak of suffering we don't feel its reality empathically. There is even a serious danger of our using fantasies of unlimited compassion, spiritual virtue, or enlightenment to feed our narcissistic delusions, if we grasp at some image of these things rather than do the hard work of developing them in our lives. The practice of taking and giving works directly against all these aspects of narcissism. It cuts through the illusory security blanket in our hearts and works against our delusions and defenses.

So when we feel afraid as we do the practice of taking, this is because we are identifying strongly with our own narcissism—with our inner enemy. Unable to tell the difference between ourselves and our self-cherishing, we feel that we will be destroyed when it is destroyed. Imaginally taking in the suffering of every person on the planet who has AIDS cannot give you AIDS. (Really, if you could eradicate all of the AIDS on the planet by taking it on yourself, wouldn't that be wonderful?) The point is to bring up your fears as you do the practice; they are signs that you're getting to your inner enemy. A certain amount of fear and psychological discomfort or even temporary disorientation in your practice may be a sign that your narcissistic defenses are beginning to break down. If you don't ever feel afraid when doing taking and giving, then you probably aren't doing the practice deeply. On the other hand, if you give in to your fears by remaining emotionally detached from others' suffering, then you're letting narcissism win, ensuring that you will remain trapped in a claustrophobic and endlessly frustrating world of illusory images. The brave approach at this point is to use your fear or discomfort to further your practice of taking and giving, expanding your empathy to the countless other beings who are afraid and uncomfortable or who, like you, use narcissism to deny and suppress such feelings.

As you do this practice of taking again and again, focusing on various kinds of suffering, if you do it well you are deconstructing your own narcissism. Jung once noted that the "fear of self-sacrifice lurks deep in every ego," and he went on to explain that the ego separates itself from the living, dynamic world out of fear, thereby gaining only a partial and illusory sort of security. The narcissistic ego is never at home in the world. Too afraid to open itself in joy to real experience or to open itself in compassion to other beings, it holds on to petty illusions, rigid expectations, and grandiose fantasies.

Taking and giving is a profound psychological method. It's a subtle but extremely important point psychologically that one is taking all that suffering and smashing it into the "demon heart of the self-cherishing thought." You aren't using it to destroy yourself. This is not a masochistic approach. It's just the opposite of masochism. It is intended to bring you courage, love, and joy. But it's an easy point to misunderstand. To do this method well, you must work continually at disidentifying from your self-cherishing narcissism. Narcissism gets destroyed over and over again.

Who is left when narcissism is destroyed? The open heart, the good heart, the heart that radiates with love. This method is about creating a new sense of identity for the person who practices it. Before, we were essentially narcissistic. That's why the demon of self-cherishing is visualized at our hearts in the practice of taking. The psychology of normal narcissism is one of partial engagement with the world, driven by hope and fear: we connect with others, hoping to get what we want from them, but also keep much of ourselves apart for fear of being hurt; we work in the world to gain wealth and status but escape into fantasies of effortless success, grandiose achievement, or escape and retirement. We love what is pleasurable in ourselves and our worlds but live with projections, denial, and anger to try to block out unpleasant reminders of aging, loss, humiliation, illness, and death. In the practice of taking, we use the compassionate awareness of suffering to destroy this way of being in the world. Again and again, we use awareness to destroy our denial and our projections. We aren't destroying ourselves in the process. It's a very precise attack on our denial, our prejudice, our grandiosity, our delusions, and our terrible selfishness. We are destroying that old, rigid, self-centered, joyless identity.

As the attack on self-cherishing progresses, genuine giving becomes more possible. We become more capable of feeling joy, of accepting life as it is, and of truly loving others. It's not that we ever seek out suffering for ourselves. Without the narcissism that holds us as the center of the universe, though, the suffering that we do experience pales by comparison with the vast suffering of countless others. If we undergo some hardships in the process of trying to be of service to others, that may even appear wonderful. We all undergo hardships, sicknesses, and death anyway. How much more meaningful, tolerable, and even beautiful they are when experienced for the sake of love. Through the practice of giving, we can create a new identity based on openhearted, generous love. Where narcissism was, now love, compassion, and radiant generosity shall be instead.

In terms of developing a new, compassionate identity, I'd also like to address briefly the issue of using your breathing as a means for doing the taking and giving practice. Of course, when you have time it is helpful to do the process slowly, in order to imagine things in detail and go in depth in developing the relevant emotions. However, I think some special benefits ensue from doing the practice along with one's breath. First, both Western and Buddhist psychology note that our breathing is intimately connected with our emotional states. If you are mindful about it, you note that when you have a strong emotional reaction such as fear, anger, sadness, or joy, your breathing changes. Particularly when it comes to our emotional life, our minds and bodies are intimately connected. This is why people who often get overwhelmed by negative emotions like anger are taught to take a number of deep breaths as part of a strategy for gaining control over their emotion; it helps to stop one of the physiological elements of this negative emotion.

By doing the practice of cultivating love and compassion in relation to your out- and in-breaths, you start using this mind-body connection to your advantage. When you get even a little bit accustomed to doing this practice in conjunction with your breath, I think you'll find that your body becomes calmer and your mind more relaxed and open, and your face may even open spontaneously in a sincere smile. This mind-body connection may play a role also in the health benefits many people have reported experiencing from this practice.

By doing this taking and giving practice in conjunction with the breath over a long period of time, we gradually transform our physiological responses to various situations in daily life. In this way, both the mind and the body gradually adjust to a new sense of identity in the world. Along with our thoughts and feelings, our facial expressions, subtle gestures, breathing, and even our blood pressure and heart rate change to suit a new, kinder sense of ourselves in relationships.

Doing this practice with the breath becomes particularly interesting as we go about our days relating with other people. The breath becomes a natural reminder to continue developing compassion. Then people we meet throughout the day naturally become the focus of our practice. We take on their specific sufferings and give them happiness. Particularly if we do the practice in conjunction with our breathing, this changes relationships in subtle but important ways. One of the mechanisms for resonant empathy is that we pick up on other people's breathing. When someone near us is angry or afraid, our breathing subtly shifts in resonance with theirs. Often, if another person is agitated and is striving, consciously or unconsciously, to get us upset, we are able to retain our own calm breathing pattern for a while, trying to reject that person's negativity by keeping up a psychological barrier. This usually only leads the other to try harder to break through our barrier. If the other succeeds and we begin reacting, then our breathing will shift. In this way, the cycle of passing negative emotions back and forth—of agitating each other—continues.

However, if we get even a little bit skillful at doing taking and giving along with our breath, then perhaps we can handle the situation differently. As we imaginally take in the other person's suffering, we stay open to that person. Even if the other escalates in agitation, this only increases our compassion and openness. As the other's breathing becomes shallow and quick, we may start breathing deeply, with our hearts open, taking it in, breathing in all that agitation and suffering, giving it to our self-cherishing. As we breathe out love, the openness in our expression and manner will affect the other unconsciously. In this way, our own breathing never shifts into an agitated pattern, and our emotions also don't shift to annoyance or anger. We remain compassionate and relaxed. Thus we give ourselves peace. At the very least we don't make things worse for the other person. If the other is open to us and relates to us often, positive changes are likely to take place in that person as well, through resonantly responding to us.

DYING WELL

In the Tibetan tradition, this practice of taking and giving is seen not only as a way of living well but also as a way of dying well. Ribur Rinpoche says that among the many practices taught in the Tibetan tradition for the time of death, this is the most effective. He notes that most people die in pain, which may make it difficult to concentrate on other practices at that time. But with taking and giving, one can use the pain to deepen one's practice. Rinpoche says that if you do this practice "while you're going through your life, you will acquire lots of mental happiness and a great deal of courage; I can tell you for sure. And this courage and this happiness will tag along with you when you're dying." It's often when people are facing suffering or death that the extent to which they've developed a capacity to find peace and happiness from within becomes clear.

Just how universal is the value of finding peace in one's heart through compassion was brought home to me through an experience with my own grandmother. Having grown up as an orphan in New York during the Great Depression, she always treasured her family when she became an adult. Years ago, when I'd just graduated from college, my grandfather phoned me and told me to come and see her; she was terminally ill with liver cancer. When I got there, I could see that she was in terrible pain. The only way to ease the pain was to take so much medication that it rendered her unconscious.

To spend time with us, she insisted on taking less medication. It was terrible to see her in such physical pain, but I also treasured the time with her. One day, as she lay in her bed holding her abdomen, she looked me in the eyes and said in a low voice that she prayed that her pain could serve as a ransom for any pain that her family, her friends, and everyone she'd known might ever experience, that it could be taken away into the pain she was feeling. I looked at her, surprised. She'd uttered it as such a pure prayer. A few minutes later, she told me that she was ready for the end of her life. And then she said, "I'd have liked to be able to stay in this life, but God must have someplace else where I can help others more." I stared at her with eyes wide open, as I thought, *So this is what's been there in her heart, unseen, all along.* Knowing her religious background, I thought she might look forward to a heavenly paradise. But I realized that for her, paradise had to involve serving others. Although she knew almost nothing about Buddhism, from her heart she knew the essence of the practice of taking and giving. She deeply wished to take on the sufferings of others and to go wherever she could best give help to others who might need her. She wasn't a saint or even a very religious person. However, through her years of bearing many hardships in life, she'd learned to be humble and to take her refuge in love and compassion—to find her happiness there. And so she was able to turn there at the time of her death.

Regardless of their religious faith, those who have overcome their own narcissism and given themselves over to love and compassion seem to die well regardless of the outer circumstances. There are many examples of this, some rather extreme. From the Jewish tradition, there is Rabbi Akiva, who in his life taught that the essence of the Torah was "Thou shalt love thy neighbor as thyself." Condemned to death by the Roman emperor Hadrian, he shocked the torturer who was killing him because he continued to pray, calmly and happily, until death took him. Saint Francis of Assisi was the first European to manifest the stigmata. In his great devotion to Christ, who took the sins and sufferings of all humanity upon himself when crucified, Saint Francis would weep in sympathy. In the final culmination of Francis's compassion, it seems that he sympathetically took the suffering of the crucified Christ—and thus, by implication, of all humanity—upon himself. Though he was terribly ill before his death, one of his colleagues asked him to sing his songs of joy less loudly, so as not to shock normal people by seeming "overly cheerful."

To call such joy shocking seems something of an understatement. For those of us who live with narcissism in our hearts, the joys of life are always partial as we struggle not to lose them, and death is our final defeat. For those who conquer their self-cherishing, though, it seems that their compassion grants them an unadulterated joy from which they can sing freely in the face of life or death. In the face of our normal, narcissistic, inner poverty, the songs of those who have conquered themselves reflect an almost unimaginable wealth, a dizzyingly wild extravagance of heart. The technique of taking and giving is a direct method to discovering such expansive joy; it suggests that in the very moment when the demon of the self-cherishing in your heart is destroyed by the force of sincere compassion, you find that the priceless source of such extravagance was there all along, hidden inside.

CONCLUSION

VISION AND EMBODIMENT

While reading about and practicing the methods presented in this book, you may have noticed that developing compassion often involves letting go of illusions about ourselves and others. If we sincerely wish to follow a path of compassion, then we must overcome gradually the ego's hopeless project of finding happiness by way of following compulsive desires. We must let go of our projections that idealize or devalue others. And we must focus particularly on abandoning our attachment to superficial, narcissistic images of our existing as solid, permanent, self-sufficient beings whose happiness is somehow more important than and independent of the happiness of others.

As we gradually abandon our illusions, we're left with a realistic view of ourselves as utterly impermanent and inextricably linked with others through vastly complex bonds of mutual responsibility and interdependence. When we view ourselves and others realistically, the natural emotional responses are compassion and joy. Viewing ourselves and others through eyes of compassion, in turn, helps us see things realistically. What we gain by cultivating a realistic, compassionate approach to life is genuine, psychological maturity and, with it, a capacity for freedom, love, creativity, and joy that goes far beyond what's possible when we're still trapped in the limited, narcissistic world of the desire-driven ego.

A core finding of Buddhist psychology is that unhealthy emotions like hatred, craving, and jealousy are always grounded in unrealistic views about ourselves and the world around us, while positive emotions derive from and support accurate perceptions. I think that this leads to a useful and broad view of mental health. In looking at severe forms of mental illness, such as schizophrenia, psychotic depression, or manic grandiosity, Western psychology recognizes the link between unhealthy emotions and unrealistic or deluded views of reality. However, it has not studied extensively the links between realistic views and positive emotions. Only by exploring such links will psychology be able to develop a consistent, meaningful, and useful understanding of mental health as a continuum, something more than the mere absence of pathology. Seeing how our grasping at illusions and getting stuck in negative emotions are linked empowers us to begin freeing ourselves from suffering in practical and systematic ways by letting go of illusions, using reason to analyze experience in order to develop realistic views, overcoming unhealthy emotional habits, and cultivating positive emotions. Individually and culturally, understanding how accurate views about reality and healthy emotions support each other is essential to developing our positive psychology.

HEAVEN AND HELL

How we perceive the world and also what sort of world we create for ourselves and for each other depends largely on the thoughts and emotions to which our minds have become habituated. Working with severely mentally ill patients while also spending time with great meditators has helped me see how incredibly powerful our minds are. The emotions, ideas, aspirations, and thoughts to which our minds become accustomed serve as causes for a wide range of experiences, from incredible love and bliss to horrific hate, fear, and pain.

From a psychological perspective, our projections about heaven and hell are rooted in and provide an interesting window into our positive and negative emotions. If you read the descriptions of hell in Western or Eastern religions, you can see that they are extreme magnifications of the very worst qualities of our human hearts. You can read of beings burning alive in the fires of rage and hate, which cause intense pain, agitation, and breathless agony without allowing for escape into sleep or death. There are also descriptions of beings frozen in an infinite, icy tundra of utter isolation, entirely disconnected from all that lives or loves. Isolation, disconnection, rage, terror, envy, and hate are the feelings that underlie the archetypal, psychological phenomenon of hell. When we get caught up powerfully in such emotions, we are even capable of creating approximations of hell on earth. We know obvious examples of this, such torture, terrorism, and war. On a smaller scale, the same sort of thing happens in families. I recently worked with one family in which the father repeatedly had attacks of rage, cursing, shouting at the top of his lungs, and breaking things. Others in the family reacted to this by pulling away from each other and by struggling with intense feelings of anger, resentment, and fear. His wife said, "We've got this big, beautiful house here in the suburbs, but the atmosphere inside is so toxic. It's hell living like this." The preadolescent son, who often reacted to the family situation with fear and also with rage of his own, eventually shared his personal sketch pad with me. It was filled with drawings of monsters and demons who had scowling faces with fangs and horns, with weapons for hands, who were engulfed in worlds of dropping bombs, whizzing bullets, flames, and screams. I asked him what could create a world of such demons filled with powerful destruction and rage. He replied, "Evil." I asked what created evil. He thought for a while and then said, "Anger and hate. They create the evil that makes that world."

By contrast, the archetypal, psychological idea of paradise or heaven, which has appeared in so many cultures and times, is rooted surely in the best qualities of our hearts—in love, compassion, joy, gratitude, contentment, generosity, and peace. Dante's descriptions of paradise mirror those of many other cultures; he describes a place where voices as beautiful as lyres and lutes speak only true and kind words in an environment filled with jewels and jewel-like flowers. Glowing rivers emit angelic sparks, angels whose very substance is translucent and divine love sing eternally and dance in a divine festival of unimaginable joy, and everything is bathed with a living light whose very nature is pure and limitless love.

When compassion, appreciation, love, and gratitude inspire us to do things like voluntarily setting aside land and resources to create playgrounds, community centers, museums, and local or national parks, we are allowing this natural linking of positive emotions and paradise to express itself in practical ways. Whether we're creating a flower garden in our own yard or a new recreation center for our town, positive emotions move us to create environments that, in turn, will evoke positive emotions in others. I recently visited a new group home, the For Children's Sake Diagnostic Center, designed to provide a safe haven for children who have been severely abused or neglected. It's a beautiful house in the country, not far from Washington, D.C., surrounded by fruit trees and situated beside a horse farm. Mary Leidy, who cofounded the place, took me on a tour, mentioning that people in the local community had donated toys or furniture, given them a van, and volunteered to paint the house and to build a great play room. As I did a psychological evaluation of a young girl whose mother was a heroine addict and whose father was in prison, I thought about the various hellish events and environments to which she'd already been exposed and of the sincere efforts people were making to create a place where they hoped her life might begin taking a new and better direction influenced by the force of compassion.

In our daily lives, we should not underestimate the real power of expressing our love and compassion, whether we do so through a kind look, a meaningful conversation, cleaning the house, helping a neighbor, or giving our time and energy to some project that touches our hearts. If you want to be more content and happy with the world around you or if you want to contribute to the welfare of others, nothing you can do will be more effective than cultivating positive emotions in yourself and then expressing them in as many moments as you can. Research suggests that one of the best ways to teach children and even other adults to be more empathic and kind is to model empathy and kindness yourself. If you want the world to be a more compassionate, positive place, then your best contribution will be setting a beautiful and inspiring example of compassion yourself.

It's also powerful and effective to do things in your home and community that reflect and inspire compassion. Tibetans developed many unique, cultural expressions of this kind. The prayer flags that you see in many photos and video images of Tibet and Nepal are one such cultural expression. Tibetans would print their prayers of love and compassion on pieces of brightly colored cloth so that the breezes lifting the flags would pick up the energy of their good intentions, blessing the animals and people downwind. They viewed their country as a place where even the air reverberated with the relaxed energy of compassion. Stones everywhere were inscribed with the mantra of compassion, which also filled prayer wheels that could be turned by hand or by the power of water and wind. The idea was to have reminders of love and compassion everywhere, to inspire everyone to cultivate what was best in themselves.

Another intention was to create a cultural vision of other beings and of nature as blessed or sacred. As a Tibetan would turn a prayer wheel and recite the mantra of compassion, she would develop a feeling of compassion while also imagining that she herself and the entire environment were filled with enlightened, compassionate energy or awareness. Like Dante in his vision of paradise, she would imagine everything embraced and illuminated by a living light or awareness of limitless love and compassion.

I'm not suggesting here anything like naive utopianism. I am suggesting, rather, that compassion evokes in us a vision of others and of the environment itself as precious and even as sacred. Stepping out of our narrow, self-centered, ultimately illusory view of ourselves as solid, permanent entities inherently separate from others and accurately recognizing our interdependence with others naturally evokes certain deeply human feelings of self-transcendence, expansive sympathy, loving connection, and even awe.

Jung often noted that regardless of our personal affiliations, religious or spiritual feelings are a natural function of the human psyche. Compassion is one means of evoking positive, spiritual experiences, and a positive spirituality can be useful also in developing compassion. Here, I'll briefly address one spiritual practice that appears in many different religious traditions and is an effective means of increasing compassion.

SEEING THINGS AS SACRED

In this method we use our archetypal sense of the connection between positive emotions and paradise as a means for cultivating love and compassion. People from various religious traditions practice seeing others and the environment itself as expressions of the divine, thereby developing powerful feelings of sympathy, awe, transcendence, love, and compassion.

Practitioners from different religious traditions have different views of the divine, the sacred, or the absolute, and my intent is not to deny these differences. What I suggest, though, is that despite these differences, when people from any religious tradition engage in the practice of seeing the environment and other beings as sacred, certain positive psychological results ensue. When you strive to see the divine everywhere, including within yourself, you naturally begin feeling a sense of connection and kinship with others and with the world around you. Cultivating such a vision undercuts self-pity and low self-esteem, and it also works against compulsive desire. To the extent that you see the world in this way, you begin feeling perfectly content with who you are and what you have; you feel a sense of gratitude for anything and everything you've been given and even for the infinite richness of a universe always freely available within and around you. Perhaps paradise is less a place than the experience of relating to any place or experience through positive thoughts and emotions.

In Tibetan history, by viewing the wind, water, earth, and other beings as blessed and sacred, practitioners naturally were restrained from harming the environment or others. Beyond this, a vision of the sacred gave them a sense of connection to the environment and to others as well as a sense of the potential for beauty and goodness that always exists everywhere. When you see the environment as sacred, you become less interested in using it for selfish motives and more interested in preserving it, beautifying it, and relating to it as a means of awakening the best in yourself and others. And when you view yourself and others as sacred, then you naturally see beyond any temporary limitations and negativities to each person's underlying vast potential. This keeps you from giving up on yourself or others. If you are not sustained by a vision of people's sacred potential for goodness—their sometimes deeply obscured genius—then seeing their (or your own) pettiness, selfishness, and even cruelty can be discouraging. When you have a sense of everyone's sacred potential, then even the worst negativities can just be seen as simply a challenge to be overcome. Tibetans sometimes liken people's hidden, sacred potential to a flawless, precious diamond hidden inside a pile of smelly filth. You'd have to be crazy not to reach through some rotten filth if you saw the Hope Diamond sticking out from it. Similarly, Tibetan practitioners who see others' hidden, sacred potential view it as mad to reject anyone wholly, refusing to reach out with compassion to find the precious diamond within.

The Zen master Dogen gave some teachings that were quite similar to the Tibetan view on this practice. He sometimes quoted an ancient Buddhist verse that included the lines,

> The entire universe is the gate of liberation. The entire universe is the eye of Vairochana. The entire universe is the dharma body of the self.

Vairochana is the name of a Buddha. So this verse asserts that the entire universe can be identified with the vision or the awareness of the Buddha. In commenting on this verse, Dogen refers to the thousand eyes of Avalokitesvara, the Buddha of Compassion. He says, "A Buddha may have one thousand eyes. . . . It is not mistaken to say that this eye [of Vairochana] is one of the many eyes of a Buddha, just as it is not mistaken to understand that a Buddha has only one eye." Seeing the divine—in this case the Buddha—everywhere becomes inseparable from seeing the universe through eyes of compassion. Dogen also taught that by practicing Zen well, one essentially could bless the world or transform the environment so that even the "voices and figures of streams and the sounds and shapes of mountains" would join with you in teaching the path to enlightenment to all beings. As compassion is the Buddha's nature, seeing the divine everywhere and in everything naturally means that you're also seeing and experiencing compassion everywhere. If you practice seeing the divine in yourself and everywhere else, then you become inseparable from divine, enlightened, compassionate awareness. Thus the sound of the Buddha's compassionate voice is not experienced as different from your own voice or the voice of the rivers and mountains.

Scholars such as William James, C. G. Jung, and Joseph Campbell have noted that experiences of the sacred and transcendent appear in an incredibly wide range of times and cultures. Some Western psychological thinkers have held that these experiences are somehow regressive—harking back to the symbiosis of infancy. This is totally incorrect. In the symbiotic experiences of infancy there is a positive experience of affectionate love. However, developmental psychologists have found that a primary factor in infantile symbiosis is the child's focusing almost exclusively on pleasurable, physical sensations. Focusing on pleasurable sensations in this way is driven by desire, and in this state the child strives to block out awareness of anything unpleasant. Symbiosis naturally involves a denial of differences, individuality, and suffering. Denying the existence of others, a person in a symbiotic state cannot give rise to conceptual empathy. Denying suffering, he cannot give rise to compassion.

The transcendent experience I'm discussing here is very different. Although the feeling of affection is also present, the practitioner is driven by compassion rather than desire. She does not focus on specific, pleasurable sensations, closing off from the rest of reality; instead, she remains open to all that is around her. She doesn't deny differences; instead, she sees the deep, interdependent connections that provide the context for differences. She does not block out the unpleasant; instead, she keeps the unpleasant in her awareness, which further enhances her compassion. Immature people want to find pleasure without any pain. By contrast, those with a mature sense of the sacred face pain and suffering directly, embracing it in loving, compassionate awareness.

Seeing the sacred in everything also has been practiced with positive effects by many from the Jewish and Christian traditions. For example, some Hasidic Jewish rabbis found powerful inspiration by striving to see God's presence in everything. They took up the practice of joyful song and dance as a form of prayer because their experience of the divine in the here and now could evoke an ecstatic rapture, which it seemed only natural to express in dance. Rabbi Nahman of Bratslav taught that God made the world by way of love just as he gave the ten commandments and the Torah out of love. So Nahman asserted that the Torah—the essential and loving word of God—could be found or read "in every word and every deed" and even in all of creation. Because the truth of divine love was hidden to our normal perceptions, though, Hasidic rabbis like Nahman felt an absolute responsibility to find or reveal the truth, and a primary way to do so was through good acts inspired by love and faith. Some of these rabbis felt that acts of prayer and compassionate service to others would further reveal the omnipresent divine. Being good and loving could reveal God's hidden goodness and love all around them. This is an important point from a psychological perspective. Even if their outer lives involved many hardships, by practicing seeing divine love and wisdom in everything, these Jewish practitioners developed internal feelings of gratitude, fullness, and wealth. Sometimes they felt full to the point of overflowing, which led to ecstatic, prayerful song and dance. Their fullness at seeing the sacred led to a sense of compassionate commitment or responsibility. To the extent that you saw God's love, you were bound absolutely to embody that love in your words and deeds. This was true in all the different traditions where this practice was done sincerely. Seeing the sacred that others may not see leads to a feeling of absolute responsibility for revealing love or wisdom to others through your own compassionate example. What is emphasized among such practitioners is not teaching some rigid doctrine but rather embodying the essence of the sacred, which is pure love.

This raises an important issue. Over the centuries, many violent deeds have been done in the name of religion. People often wonder how this can be. From a psychological perspective, it seems clear that it occurs when religion exists as a set of doctrines, ideas, rituals, and experiences divorced from any deep and expansive sense of empathy or compassion. Without empathy, people's religious ideas become yet another means of seeing others as "different" and of distancing oneself psychologically from them. Feeling disconnected in this way, people devalue others, leading to intolerance and the tendency to inflict their views on others. When this happens, even the most beautiful and inspiring religious doctrines become like poison, serving as causes for prejudice, anger, oppression, and even violence. By contrast, when religious ideas are conjoined with a deep sense of empathy and compassion, they can serve as a bridge, allowing people from different backgrounds to connect and to share the best of themselves. When we have empathy and compassion for others, we can honestly respect each other's differences. And from a feeling of compassionate responsibility, we can share the best of ourselves with others and encourage others to find and share the best of themselves as well.

The life and writings of Mother Teresa show that seeing the divine in others was her primary practice for developing compassion. When young, she was inspired by the passage attributed to Jesus that says, "I was hungry and you gave me to eat, I was naked and you clothed me, I was sick and you visited me. Whatever you did to the least of my brethren, you did it to me." Serving others became a form of worship or prayer for her. She once wrote, "I see God in the eyes of every child." She also said, "O beloved sick people, you are doubly dear to me because you personify Christ, and it is indeed a privilege for me to be able to care for you."

This raises one more important point about compassion. When we do something for others, we may think that they are privileged to receive our care and that they should feel grateful. In fact, when someone gives us an opportunity to feel and embody compassion, we ourselves are the primary beneficiaries. Genuine compassion may or may not succeed in benefiting the other person, but it certainly benefits us. When our compassion is not yet deep or genuine, we may find it difficult to develop the joy and contentment to which compassion eventually gives rise. Therefore, we imagine that our compassion mainly benefits others. Such thoughts are just a sign that we need to deepen our practice. As we begin discovering the joy, fullness, and sense of meaning that compassion brings, we begin developing gratitude for those who give us the chance to practice compassion. Compassion then leads to gratitude, which leads to affectionate love, which leads to more compassion. In this way, an ongoing and escalating cycle of love, happiness, and compassion is set in motion. Only when people develop such positive feedback cycles can they sustain compassionate service to others, as Mother Teresa did. Only when we learn through our own experience that giving leads to fullness and to wealth will we want to give of ourselves continually.

Those with strong religious feelings may find it useful to strive to see the sacred as they understand it in themselves, in all others around them, in nature, and in everything. More generally, we all can come away from the discussion of this practice with certain insights that are essential to the deep psychology of compassion. One such insight is that when we view others through eyes of compassion, then no one—no matter how dirty, difficult, angry, or annoying he or she may be—is beyond deserving our compassion. Psychologically speaking, the impulse to totally close ourselves off to someone is rooted in the infantile desire to escape from suffering through denial and symbiotic fantasy. Of course there will be people we cannot help directly, but when we cut off our empathy and compassion to anyone, then we are choosing denial over truth and, ultimately, blocking off a part of ourselves. Even when there is nothing we can do to help someone else, keeping our heart open to compassion for that person allows us to maintain a sense of wholeness and integrity within ourselves and leaves open the possibility of some positive interaction with that person in the future.

This discussion also can serve as a reminder of how powerfully our emotions determine the sort of world we experience and create together. Emotions color how we see the world around us, they affect how we are in any given moment and how we behave, and ultimately they serve as the motivating forces for how we humans transform the world around us. If we spend time dwelling on our desire, we gradually cocreate a world driven by greed, advertising, and compulsive consumerism. When we dwell in anger and fear, we cocreate a world filled with weapons, conflicts, and wars. To the extent that we dwell in love and compassion, we cocreate a world characterized by peace, mercy, safety, and inspiring beauty. We need not believe in paradise to see how compassion makes our homes, our towns, and our world better places in which to live.

To achieve our own welfare and to benefit others, it is incredibly important to practice regularly the methods presented in this book. Cultivating compassion and joy is not a linear process; it's organic, like growing flowers. If you work regularly at decreasing your compulsive desires and narcissism while also striving to develop compassion, it is like weeding and then planting, fertilizing, and watering seeds in your garden. Big results do not come immediately. However, if you choose a few of these methods and practice them each day or each week for a while, gradually you will see beautiful results. There is nothing more marvelous than the flowering of compassion in our hearts and relationships.

As you engage in these methods, you are working not just with your conscious mind but also with the unconscious. You're transforming the deep sources of your moods, emotions, dreams, and projections. By working at these methods in a flexible, playful, patient, and consistent way, you essentially are remaking yourself. The Tibetan tradition of mind training is designed to help us retain and develop our best qualities while abandoning our craving, fear, anger, and narcissistic illusions. Once we understand how to work with our emotions, our happiness and suffering are in our own hands. The Buddha always emphasized that each individual's liberation from suffering was her own responsibility. Whatever we think and do determines the sort of person we become and whether or not we find happiness, so it's essential to find time in our daily lives for practicing the art of compassion.

Finally, I think we can come away also with a recognition that regardless of our theoretical or doctrinal beliefs, on a basic, human level powerful feelings of love and compassion do lead to experiences that are sacred, transformative, or self-transcending. Whether you think of Tibetan lamas' visions of a pure and blissful universe of ever-flowing blessings, of Dogen's description of mountains and rivers ringing with the sounds of compassionate wisdom teachings, of Hasidic Jews' ecstatic dance expressing divine love, or of Mother Teresa's overflowing love, it's clear that compassion is an essential part of people's most positive and spiritual experiences. Even a little bit of genuine compassion can carry us beyond the somewhat claustrophobic world of the desire-driven ego, and the more we learn to give ourselves over to embodying compassion, the more we open ourselves up to the most positive sorts of human experience—to gratitude, inspiration, and love as well as to awe, joy, and even ecstasy. This is not particularly mystical. It's the nature of how emotions work. Just as our most negative emotions derive largely from suffering and lead to more extreme suffering, so also do our most positive emotions develop out of peaceful, positive states of mind and lead to greater peace and happiness. As we open ourselves up to such positive experiences, they can energize our practices further for developing compassion, leading to ever increasing positive emotions, experiences, and actions. It's the best use we can make of our human lives.

SUMMARY OF COMPASSION PRACTICES

FROM CHAPTER 4: CULTIVATING COMPASSION FOR YOURSELF

1. *Introspection:* Begin by relaxing and becoming aware of the ongoing flow of thoughts, feelings, and images related to desire that are passing continually through the mind. Just watch what is happening in your mind. If you become distracted, bring your awareness back to the task of being introspective. Spend time just being aware of exactly what you're thinking and how you're feeling.

2. *Self-Analysis:* Now take a look at the thoughts and feelings you've been observing in your mind and ask *why* you have been thinking those things. Take note especially of the role that desire plays in your mind. Notice how many of your thoughts and feelings relate to seeking happiness through wanting something. Take note of how you view objects, how you feel, and what you think when you are craving for something. Notice what happens when you don't get what you want. Also notice what happens when you do get what you want.

3. *Analyzing a Specific Desire:* Next you can deepen your self-analysis by choosing a specific desire on which to focus. It's best to start with something that you desire often and toward which you feel a fairly deep, almost involuntary, compulsive craving. Typical desires of this type might be for money, praise, attention, sex, alcohol, drugs, or any number of unhealthful foods. You may have many such desires,

but it's useful to begin by focusing on just one. Spend time regularly observing how your desire for this object functions. Take notes on what you discover. Does your desire come up most strongly when you are stressed or when you are upset about something? Is it strongest in the morning, during the day, or late at night? Is it typically associated with certain other feelings such as loneliness, insecurity, or feeling tired? Specifically take note of what happens when you do and when you don't succeed in obtaining the object of your desires.

4. *Letting Go of Desire:* Once you have gone through the process of deeply analyzing a specific desire, spend some time focusing on the various sorts of suffering that this desire causes. Contemplate the suffering of wanting, of not getting what you want, of being bored and dissatisfied when you do get what you want, and also of losing what you have. Next try to practice letting go of your desire for that object. Remember here that you're focusing not on the object of desire but on the feeling of desire itself, and just letting go of that. Don't repress the desire. See it there in your own mind with your full awareness; recognize through your previous analysis how it only causes you suffering, and with your eyes wide open just let it go. When you let go, notice yourself right there in the present moment, without tension or stress, feeling complete, satisfied, and open to the reality of your life.

FROM CHAPTER 5: MOURNING THE LIVING

1. *Mourning Yourself:* Imagine yourself at some point in the future—later today, later this year, or some years down the line. Imagine what you'll be doing then. Next imagine yourself dying at that time. Go into as much detail as you can. Imagine what is killing you. Imagine your final contacts with other people in your life. Think about having to say good-bye to everyone and everything you've ever known—your home, your possessions, your loved ones, and even your own name, body, and face. Imagine how you feel in your final moments. Ask yourself, from that perspective, what is really important in your life.

2. *Seconds Flowing By:* Place a watch or clock with a second hand in front of you on a table. Choose in advance a certain length of time to devote to the exercise. Watch the second hand as it clicks along. Recall that it is absolutely, positively certain that with each click of that second hand, you are moving closer to your death. You have a limited number of moments left, and they are pouring away like water seeping out from your cupped fingers. With each ticking of that second hand, recall that your life is unalterably heading for its end, and repeatedly ask yourself what matters. Sit with the question of what matters, allowing the question to sink more and more deeply into your psyche with each passing second. If your mind drifts away to some other topic, just bring it back to watching the second hand, noticing your life slipping away, and asking what matters. When the predetermined length of time is finished, resolve to spend wisely the rest of the incredibly precious seconds that remain to you.

3. *You May Die Today:* Upon waking up, think as follows: *How wonderful that I am still alive; my life is so fragile, and I definitely could have died last night, so it's really wonderful that I woke up and am still here.* Recall the fact that other people in the world did die last night, but you managed to stay alive up to now. Also recall that many different factors can cause your death easily and quickly. A car wreck, a heart attack, a stroke, a murder, or an accident could take your life easily today. For a few moments, viscerally imagine yourself dying later on today. Think as follows: *It's absolutely true that I may die today, and there's nothing at all that I can do about that fact; therefore, I'm going to live this day as though it may be my last.* Recognizing that today literally may be the last day of your life, decide how you are going to spend this day. Think about what is important to do, about how you want to go about the activities of your life today, and about how you want to relate to the other people you see. End the exercise by strongly resolving to spend your day wisely.

4. *Mourning the Dead:* Spend some time thinking about people you have known, cared about, or loved who have died. Try hard to be

honest with yourself about how you feel about those people now. Are there feelings with which you have avoided dealing? Consider talking with other people you trust about your feelings. Think about the roles that those people played in your life. How is it not to have them available any longer to play those roles? How do you get those desires met now? Finally, try to connect deeply with your empathy and love for those who have passed away. Try to feel a sense of cherishing for the people they were.

5. *Mourning the Living:* Recall the simple truth that you have absolutely no idea how long any of the people in your life will live. Remember that some people die young and others die old. Not only people who are ill but also healthy people often die suddenly. Briefly recall some of the many means by which people are suddenly taken from this life: heart attacks, strokes, accidents, murders, and the like. Now think of one person to whom you're close. Think about how this person could die any time; she or he could even die today. Try to imagine how you would feel if this person died. What would you miss? What might you regret having done or not done? Cultivate a sense of cherishing this person—of seeing this person's preciousness.

FROM CHAPTER 6: SEEING THROUGH PROJECTIONS

The following methods can be done on your own in a quiet place or, once you are familiar with them, in the context of your relationships.

1. *Friend, Enemy, and Stranger:* Begin this exercise by thinking of three different people and imagining them in front of you. The first should be someone who upsets or annoys you (an enemy); the second should be someone you like being around and to whom you feel attached (a friend), and the third person should be someone you don't know well and toward whom you feel indifferent (a stranger). Start out by just noticing your current, genuine feelings about each of these three people. Then, thinking of each of those people in turn, contemplate the following questions in as much detail as you can. *How did*

you come to see the person in this way? Did you always see the person in this way? Does everyone see the person as you do? Do other people see qualities in this person that you don't? If you got to know the other person by empathizing with his or her perspective on the situation, would your view change? Is this person like every other human being in wanting to be happy and wanting to be free from suffering? Be sure to spend time focusing especially on this last question, developing a feeling for how this person also wants to be happy and free from suffering.

2. *Watching the Mind Project:* Think about a particular object or person in your life. Spend some time analyzing how your mind has created various projections about that object or person. Notice your internal image, and ask yourself in what sense this image corresponds with outer reality. Notice the various thoughts, judgments, labels, and emotions that you associate with that object or person. When you are actually relating to the person or thing in your daily life, try to be mindful of how your projections affect what you experience and how you behave.

3. *Integrating Projected Aspects of the Psyche:* Choose a specific relationship to look at, assessing whether you are projecting an aspect of yourself. Begin by asking yourself the following questions about that relationship: *Do I often feel conflicted or ambivalent regarding my relationship with this person? Do I repeatedly have the same kind of discussion or interaction with this person without finding a satisfactory solution? Do I experience strong feelings about the person that I can't quite explain? Do I often feel excited, inflated, upset, anxious, angry, or obsessed about our relationship?* If you answer yes to any of these questions, it's likely you are projecting unconsciously some significant, disowned aspect of yourself in that relationship. An easy way of getting at what you're projecting is to ask yourself very specifically what you feel strongly about in the other person. Be sure to define this quality clearly, for that is the very quality you're most likely projecting. Once you have identified the quality, it is important to try to catch yourself when you start

projecting it onto that person again. In working on your projections, it can be useful to take particular note also of ways in which you may manipulate the other person to play the role you're projecting onto them. If you find yourself doing such things, try sincerely to stop because inevitably it is hurting you and the other person. Finally, make an effort to deal consciously with whatever you have been projecting. Do this by recognizing that what you were projecting is really an emotion or capacity of your own mind that you have not been dealing with effectively. That's the hardest part—really admitting to yourself that it is you. Then you must spend some time making conscious, reasoned decisions about how you want to deal with or express that part of yourself in your life.

FROM CHAPTER 7: PRACTICING EMPATHIC, LOVING COMMUNICATION

You can practice empathic, loving communication in any moment, during any interaction with another person. Here I briefly review some key elements of this method, emphasizing how you might apply it with someone close to you.

1. *Being Honest:* Spend some time analyzing your own thoughts and feelings about this other person. Ask yourself the following questions regarding your relationship: *Are there things about the relationship that I've been feeling or thinking but haven't admitted to myself or addressed with the other person? Are there things that get in the way of my being closer with this person that I'm not doing anything about? What sorts of projections based in attachment, aversion, or indifference do I have about this person? Are there ways in which I've been overtly dishonest with this person by lying or been covertly dishonest by not being genuine in the relationship?* Resolve to be more deeply honest and genuine with them in line with your answers to these questions.

2. *Cultivating Empathy:* Practice actively empathizing with this person. During your conversations with this person, look at them with

your full attention. Listen carefully to what they say, also attending to tone of voice, facial expressions, and gestures. Specifically practice conceptual empathy by thinking about what you have seen and heard. Relate what this person communicates to what you have experienced, heard about, or read about in the past. Actively imagine yourself experiencing the world from inside this person's perspective. Also practice resonant empathy during your conversations. Take note of your feelings and emotions as the other interacts with you. Contemplate the source of those feelings and emotions, analyzing whether they likely derive from projections or from a resonant, empathic response to the other person.

3. *The Power of Love:* As your empathic understanding of this person increases, also specifically cultivate a feeling of connection. Notice the roles that this person plays in your life and the ways in which your well-being and theirs are interdependent. As you develop your resonant empathy, focus on the deep sense of connection out of which such empathy arises. From your empathy, develop as much feeling of connection, caring, and love as you can. Then, while dwelling in that feeling of love, ask yourself what you can communicate that will be most beneficial to everyone involved. Then, from your heart, strive to communicate it with the power of your love and empathy present in your words and gestures.

FROM CHAPTER 8: CULTIVATING THE RADIANT HEART

1. *Limitless Love and Compassion:* Begin by sitting down, getting comfortable, and focusing on your breath for a few moments to calm your mind. Next, start giving rise to the feeling of compassion or of love toward yourself. Begin thinking *May I be free from suffering.* Focus on yourself for a while, and keep thinking *May I be free from suffering.* Recall times when you were suffering in some particular way, or bring to mind the image of yourself as someone vulnerable to all sorts of potential suffering, as you continue thinking *May I be free*

from suffering. Next, start thinking about people or animals to whom you feel close. Think *May they be free from suffering.* While you think that, also start imagining compassion radiating out from your heart, reaching out to those beings and washing away their suffering. Focus on the specific sorts of suffering they experience in their lives. Imagine compassionate awareness reaching out from your heart to them, gently touching them, soothing them, and removing their suffering. Then begin doing the same practice focusing on strangers. You can think of specific strangers who are suffering in various ways, or just generally think of all the people you don't know in your town, state, nation, and so on. Develop the wish *May they be free from suffering.* Imagine compassion radiating out from your heart, freeing all those beings from suffering. After having focused on strangers, next focus on enemies or people you're ordinarily averse to, developing compassion for them as well. Again, think *May they be free from suffering,* and imagine compassion radiating out from your heart, washing away their suffering and problems. Finally, think *May all beings be free from suffering,* and imagine compassion reaching out from your heart to embrace the entire planet and then radiating out to the whole universe. Really try to feel that your compassion is vast and limitless.

2. *Radiant Roadways:* Try putting the above method into practice while you are walking or driving around. Specifically, as you see people or animals, practice thinking *May they be happy and free from suffering* while also imagining compassion radiating out from your heart and benefiting them.

3. *Universal Responsibility:* Once you have practiced the methods just described for a while, add in the thought *I myself will lead them to happiness and freedom from suffering.* Spend some time thinking about how wonderful it would be if you could help them, and cultivate the thought that the very purpose of your life is to free yourself and others from suffering.

4. *Compassionate Actions:* Once you're able to develop feelings of

love and compassion, practice joyfully putting those feelings into action. Specifically, focus your empathy on those around you in your daily life. After you cultivate a feeling of love or compassion for them, think about something specific that you can do for them. As you do the action, go out of your way to really enjoy the process. Once you've done it, take time to rejoice in your own development of compassion, in your doing a positive action, and in any beneficial effects you have brought about for the other person.

FROM CHAPTER 9: CULTIVATING GRATITUDE AND INNER WEALTH

In developing gratitude, you can use any one of the following approaches, or, even better, you can combine them. Depending on your individual history, you need not do them in order. Particularly if you have a difficult history with your parents, then you may wish to focus primarily on the first few approaches. The main goal is to develop a deep feeling of gratitude and affection, leading to the wish to repay or pass on kindness.

1. *Being Thankful for What You Have:* List some of the good things you have in your life. Begin with the physical things you're able to use and enjoy. Recall that many other people don't have what you do and that you may not always have these things. Really rejoice in your good fortune. Then take time to appreciate the less tangible things you enjoy, such as your relationships, health, capacity for positive emotions, freedom, intelligence, knowledge, and so forth. Also spend time rejoicing in the opportunities you have for doing positive things such as letting go of desire, learning new things, and helping or being loving with others. Really strive to develop a sense of thankfulness and appreciation for each of the good things in your life.

2. *Asking for, Accepting, and Appreciating Kindness:* In relation to the people close to you, think about specific support or help they could give that would be meaningful to you. Facing any feelings of unworthiness

or mistrust that you may have, decide on some things for which you would feel safe enough to ask them. To whatever extent you can tolerate, open up to these people in your life and ask them for what you want. Even if their response is not perfect, practice accepting their kindness. Spend time focusing on the kindness and love they do show you. Let their kindness or compliments sink in, developing as much appreciation, gratitude, and affection in response as you can. Dwell in these positive feelings for as long as you can.

3. *Remembering the Kindness That Others Showed You in the Past:* Spend time thinking about the many people who were kind to you in the past. Remember as many specific incidents of kindness as possible, focusing particularly on those that move you emotionally. Think about grandparents, aunts and uncles, and other relatives and friends who were supportive, generous, and kind to you when you were young. Think as well about teachers and mentors—those who taught you to read and write, who taught you all that you know, and who inspired you. Think of those who taught you right from wrong and of those who helped you gain the knowledge and skills you need to earn a living. Finally, cultivate a wish to repay and to pass on this great kindness.

4. *Remembering and Imagining the Kindness of Parents:* Even if we cannot remember our first few years of life, it is not difficult to imagine what others did for us when we were infants and toddlers. So spend time imagining the kindness that your parents showed you, beginning when you were in your mother's womb and from the time you were born. Think about the hardships they must have gone through, getting up in the middle of the night to feed and change you. Think about how they held you, kept you safe, bought you toys, talked with you, and taught you so many things. Think of the many hardships they underwent on your behalf. Imagine as many details as you can from the period before you can really remember, and then recall as many examples as possible of things they did for you and the

love they shared with you during your childhood years. Again, to whatever extent you can, focus on and dwell in feelings of warm affection, love, and gratitude.

5. *Expanding Gratitude:* Once you have engaged in these first four methods, try using your imagination to expand your feelings of kinship, loving affection, and gratitude as vastly as you can. Do so by imagining how all of the love and kindness you've received in your life depended on similar sorts of kindness being shown in previous generations. Try to imagine all of this vast kindness reaching back over millennia, and strive to feel how you are now the living manifestation of all that love. If you like, you can also strive to imagine having received limitless loving kindness from infinite mother-beings over countless previous lifetimes. In either case, strive to expand your deep feelings of gratitude, cultivating an expansive sense of inner wealth and love.

FROM CHAPTER 10: USING THE KEY TO HAPPINESS

Begin by choosing one specific problematic issue in your life, working on it until you see some improvement—until you approach that issue in a more compassionate way and you feel more joyful and contented in that area of your life. Then you may want to move on, using the method with another issue, and another after that.

I suggest getting started with paper and pen, writing out your thoughts. It's useful to work on this a little at a time, writing out some thoughts and then coming back to it later in the day or the week to add more.

1. *Contemplating an Issue:* Start out by giving the problematic issue a name. Examples would be "feeling lonely," "problems with men," "anger at my father," or "anxiety at work." Then spend some time thinking and writing about four different things: your history with this issue, how the issue is affecting your life now, how you imagine this issue will affect your future if you don't change, and how this issue has affected the lives of other people you know.

2. *Seeing the Issue Through Eyes of Compassion:* Begin by asking the following questions: *What is the image of myself I'm grasping onto in these situations? Am I really empathizing with and feeling compassion for others? What possible solutions am I just not seeing? How might my efforts at protecting myself or gaining happiness for myself be causing me instead more suffering?* Take some time and be honest with yourself about this. Next, make a list of all the difficulties that arise from following this self-centered approach. Use what you wrote in the first part of the exercise, and add to it by creating a list of the disadvantages of your current approach. Then make a different list, describing the possible advantages to you and others of taking a more open, loving, compassionate approach to the problem.

3. *Walking Through the Door:* Now make a plan for experimenting with a new, more compassionate approach to this issue. Be sure that your plan includes ways of working with your thoughts, feelings, and behaviors. Focus initially on working with your thoughts and feelings. You can use some of the methods from earlier in the book to help. List thoughts, images, and memories that may be useful in evoking positive feelings on this issue. Really strive to develop a sense of curiosity, playfulness, and enthusiasm for checking out a new approach. Remember that the purpose of this exercise is to help you be happier in this area of your life. Set some small behavioral goals to start with. Be sure to monitor how you're doing, checking up on whether your plan is actually helping you become more openhearted in this area of your life and whether you are feeling more contented and joyful.

FROM CHAPTER 11: BATTLING YOUR INNER ENEMY

As you set out to battle your inner enemy—your own narcissism—be sure to start with a goal that's realistic. Trying to battle at one time every self-centered habit you have probably will lead only to feeling exhausted and giving up. Start gradually with those tendencies that cause you and others the most suffering. Then with each victory you can use your new confidence to take on additional enemies until you've conquered narcissism itself.

1. *Identify an Enemy:* Begin by identifying a few of your own narcissistic patterns that cause suffering for yourself and others. Take note of situations in which you cherish your self-image, comfort, possessions, and status more than you cherish other people. Make a list of some small things you do in your daily routine that express narcissism, such as leaving unpleasant tasks for others, striving to be the center of attention, disregarding those you see as lower than yourself, getting on other people's nerves, complaining when doing so won't help change things, saying things that hurt others' feelings without a deep reason, or getting angry when others don't do what you want. Spend some time observing such narcissistic tendencies in yourself, getting to know the enemy that causes suffering for yourself and others.

2. *Personify the Enemy:* Once you've chosen one or a few of your narcissistic habits to battle, personify those habits. Create an imaginary figure, or choose one from literature or from your dreams, who embodies the narcissistic qualities you're going to strive to conquer in yourself. Spend a little time imagining how this character thinks and behaves. The main goal in this step is to disidentify from your own narcissistic habits. If you think that your narcissism is you, then battling it will degenerate into a form of self-hatred. As we often grossly exaggerate the positive qualities of our narcissism, it's best to choose a clearly negative figure to counter this unhealthy tendency. Tibetan practitioners often think of evil dictators, thieves, or demons. Be creative in coming up with your own personification. And once you've done so, strongly remind yourself that he or she is not you!

3. *Create and Implement a Battle Plan:* Now create a practical plan to battle this inner enemy. Your plan should include actively doing things that will harm your narcissistic tendencies. The plan should include new ways of thinking and feeling so that when you catch

yourself starting to follow an old pattern you can stop and replace old habits with new ones. It is particularly important that you actually do the things that your narcissism wants you to avoid. If your narcissism usually leads you to avoid mopping the floors, spending time with someone who's ill, or giving up some sleep to work for others, then practice doing just those things. If your narcissism usually leads you to criticize other people, speak harshly to coworkers, or sigh when you wait in lines, then practice avoiding just those things. You may wish to create some rules for yourself to follow for a set period of time, designing them so that they keep you from engaging in the specific, narcissistic habits you identified in step 1. When you act against your narcissism, it will feel uncomfortable. This is a good sign that the battle has begun. Don't be afraid of bearing some hardships as you continue the struggle until you have succeeded in conquering the narcissistic tendency you set out to fight. You'll know you have won when you can empathize with and feel compassion for others in situations in which previously you did not. Another sign of victory is being able to sincerely enjoy doing things your narcissism used to prevent you from doing.

FROM CHAPTER 12: JOYFULLY LOSING ARGUMENTS IN DAILY LIFE

It's relatively easy to understand intellectually how we can put into practice the art of joyfully losing an argument. However, reversing old emotional habits requires considerable effort in the beginning. Here I review the steps involved so that you can try them out in your own relationships.

1. *Valuing Difficult People:* Identify one or more people in your daily life who sometimes give you a difficult time. Make a decision to try to practice this method in your relationships with them.

2. *Recognizing an Opportunity:* Then, when one of those people is agitated for some reason and starts giving you a hard time, pause for a

moment and remember that this is your chance to practice this method.

3. *A Cognitive Intervention:* To help keep yourself from falling into old, reactive patterns, remember some of the disadvantages of reacting to the person in an agitated way. Also remember some of the advantages of peace, patience, and compassion.

4. *Riding the Wave:* Now relax and remain open to the other person. Allow the person's wave of agitated emotion to come toward you and to evoke a natural, resonant, empathic response. Use your own deep awareness of this person's suffering and the energy of the emotion being expressed as ways of connecting with this person and increasing your compassion.

5. *Lose the Argument:* Now go ahead and lose the argument. Trust your own intuition as you express your compassion for the other person. Remember that the point isn't to control how the other feels. The point is to be genuinely kind, open, patient, and compassionate. Trust in and enjoy the process.

FROM CHAPTER 13: PRACTICING TAKING AND GIVING

1. *A Preliminary:* Before beginning this method, it's important to prepare your mind by remembering the faults of narcissistic self-cherishing. Recall the various reasons that narcissism is your inner enemy, causing you and others so much suffering. Make an effort to disidentify yourself from your self-cherishing; remember that the various superficial images you sometimes cherish are not you. Also spend a few minutes actively cultivating a sense of even-mindedness, empathy, and affection for others.

2. *Taking Sorrow:* Think about some of the sufferings that the countless beings in the universe experience. Actively cultivate empathy and strong compassion as you think about such sufferings. Begin small, by thinking about the suffering of a headache or stomachache that you may experience some time in the future. Gradually become bolder in

your compassionate vision, thinking of the more intense sufferings that people and animals experience, including illness, relationship problems, wars, famines, and the like. Focusing on whatever portion of this suffering you honestly and compassionately can hold in your mind, imagine that it arises away from those beings, cut away from them as cleanly as hairs cut by a sharp razor, and that it takes on the form of black light, like some surreal cloud of misery pollution sucked up from underworld factories. By the force of your compassion, you draw this dark energy toward yourself. Now, in the center of your own heart, imagine your inner enemy, your narcissistic self-cherishing in the form of a black seed. Imagine that entire black misery cloud absorbing into your inner enemy, totally destroying it.

3. *Giving Joy:* Having done the practice of taking, you now proceed to giving. First, strive to develop a sense of affection and love for others, wishing them happiness. Next, imagine either that light rays stream forth from your body or that many replicas of your body go out from where you are and become everything that anyone wants or needs to be truly happy. Be creative, cultivating as vast and sublime a loving vision as you can. You can think of manifesting as a dear friend for all who are lonely, as a builder for those without homes, as a teacher for those wanting knowledge, as a caring doctor and nurse for those who are ill, and as a protector for those who are afraid. You can think of manifesting as an ingenious adviser for those who are confused, as a parent for orphans, as a musician who uplifts others' spirits, and as a spiritual guide for those seeking one. You need not limit your vision to the human; you can offer cool breezes, rains of flowers, inspiring ideas, fireworks displays, piles of jewels, cars, boats, parks, palaces, libraries, wonderful feasts, moving works of art, medicines, and anything else that brings people happiness. Ultimately, imagine that you give everyone everywhere every sort of bliss, happiness, peace, and joy.

4. *Practicing with Your Breathing:* Finally, once you've done the practice slowly for some time, try doing it in conjunction with your breathing. As you breathe in, imagine compassionately taking in the dark cloud of others' suffering. As you breathe out, imagine lovingly giving all beings every possible happiness.

RESOURCES

In this book I have integrated ideas and methods from the Tibetan Buddhist tradition with Western psychology to provide readers with practical means for cultivating compassion in daily life. Should you feel inspired to learn more about the Buddhist practices as they were traditionally done in Tibet, the following list offers books by Tibetan Buddhist masters on training the mind.

BOOKS BY TIBETAN LAMAS
FOR WESTERN AUDIENCES

The Dalai Lama. *Kindness, Clarity, and Insight.* Ithaca, NY: Snow Lion, 1984.

The Dalai Lama. *A Flash of Lightning in the Dark of Night.* Boston: Shambhala, 1994.

The Dalai Lama. *Transforming the Mind: Teachings on Generating Compassion.* London: Thorson's, 2000.

The Dalai Lama. *An Open Heart: Practicing Compassion in Everyday Life.* New York: Little, Brown, 2001.

Deshung Rinpoche. *The Three Levels of Spiritual Perception.* Boston: Wisdom Publications, 1995.

Dilgo Khyentse. *The Heart Treasure of the Enlightened Ones.* Boston: Shambhala, 1992.

Rimpoche Nawang Gehlek. *Good Life, Good Death: Tibetan Wisdom on Reincarnation.* New York: Riverhead Books, 2001.

Geshe Rabten and Geshe Dhargyey. *Advice from a Spiritual Friend.* New Delhi: Publications for Wisdom Culture, 1977.

Geshe Lhundub Sopa. *Peacock in the Poison Grove.* Boston: Wisdom Publications, 2001.

Chogyam Trungpa. *Cutting Through Spiritual Materialism.* Berkeley: Shambhala, 1973.

Khensur Lobsang Tharchin. *Achieving Bodhichitta.* Howell, NJ: Mahayana Sutra and Tantra Press, 1999.

Lama Yeshe. *Becoming Your Own Therapist.* Boston: Lama Yeshe Wisdom Archive, www.lamayeshe.com, 1998.

Lama Yeshe. *Introduction to Tantra: A Vision of Totality.* Boston: Wisdom Publications, 1987.

Lama Zopa Rinpoche. *The Door to Satisfaction.* Boston: Wisdom Publications, 1994.

Lama Zopa Rinpoche. *Transforming Problems into Happiness.* Boston: Wisdom Publications, 2001.

TRADITIONAL BUDDHIST SOURCES IN TRANSLATION

Gampopa. *The Jewel Ornament of Liberation.* Berkeley: Shambhala, 1986.

Glen Mullin. *Selected Works of the Dalai Lama I.* Ithaca, NY: Snow Lion, 1981.

Pabongka Rinpoche. *Liberation in the Palm of Your Hand.* Boston: Wisdom Publications, 1991.

Patrul Rinpoche. *The Words of My Perfect Teacher.* San Francisco: HarperSanFrancisco, 1994.

Sakya Pandita. *Illuminations: A Guide to Essential Buddhist Practices.* Novato, CA: Lotsawa, 1988.

Santideva. *A Guide to the Bodhisattva Way of Life*. Ithaca, NY: Snow Lion, 1997.

Robert Thurman. *Essential Tibetan Buddhism*. San Francisco: HarperSanFrancisco, 1995.

Tsong-Kha-Pa. *The Great Treatise on the Stages of the Path to Enlightenment*. Vols. 1–3. Ithaca, NY: Snow Lion, 2000.

Geshe Wangyal. *The Door of Liberation*. Boston: Wisdom Publications, 1995.

BIBLIOGRAPHY

Bentley, Jr., G. E., *Stranger from Paradise: A Biography of William Blake* (Yale University Press, 2001).

Bion, W., *Seven Servants: Four Works by Wilfred R. Bion* (Jason Aronson, Inc., 1977).

Bowlby, J., *Attachment* (BasicBooks, 1969).

Dalton, D., *Mahatma Ghandi: Nonviolent Power in Action* (Columbia University Press, 1993).

Davis, M. H., *Empathy: A Social Psychological Approach* (Westview Press, 1994).

Deshung Rinpoche, (Trans. Jared Rhoton), *The Three Levels of Spiritual Perception* (Wisdom Publications, 1995).

Dharmaraksita, (Trans. Geshe N. Dhargyey, S. Tulku, K. Tulku, A. Berzin, and J. Landaw), *The Wheel of Sharp Weapons* (Library of Tibetan Works & Archives, 1981).

Dillard, A., *Pilgrim at Tinker Creek* (Harper & Row, 1974).

Dillard, A., *For the Time Being* (Vintage Books, New York, 1999).

Dogen, (Ed. Kazuaki Tanahashi), *Moon in a Dewdrop* (North Point Press, 1985).

Elliot, T. S., "The Lovesong of J. Alfred Prufrock," in *The Norton Anthology of Poetry* (W. W. Norton & Co., 1983).

Emerson, R. W., *Essays—Second Series* (Houghton Mifflin Co., 1929).

Freud, S., *The Standard Edition of the Complete Psychological Works of Sigmund Freud* (Hogarth Press, 1958).

Freud, S., *Beyond the Pleasure Principle* (W. W. Norton & Co., 1961).

Gampopa, (Trans. H. Guenther), *Jewel Ornament of Liberation* (Shambhala, 1986).

Gorree, G. and J. Barbier, *Love Without Boundaries* (Our Sunday Visitor, Inc., 1974).

Green, A., *Tormented Master: A Life of Rabbi Nahman of Bratslav* (Schocken Books, 1979).

Gyalstan, Panchen Lozang Chokyi, The First Panchen Lama, *The Guru Puja* (Library of Tibetan Works and Archives, 1984).

Gyatso, Tenzin, His Holiness the Dalai Lama, *Kindness, Clarity, and Insight* (Snow Lion, 1984).

Gyatso, Tenzin, His Holiness the Dalai Lama, *The World of Tibetan Buddhism* (Wisdom Publications, Boston, 1995).

Gyatso, Tenzin, His Holiness the Dalai Lama, *Transforming the Mind: Teachings on Generating Compassion* (Thorsons, London, 2000).

Gyatso, Tenzin, His Holiness the Dalai Lama, *The Compassionate Life* (Wisdom Publications, 2001).

Gyeltsen, Geshe T., *Keys to Great Enlightenment* (Thubten Dhargye Ling, Los Angeles, 1989).

Hamilton, N. G., *Self & Others* (Jason Aronson, 1990).

Hillman, J., *Re-Visioning Psychology* (HarperPerennial, New York, 1975).

House, A., *Francis of Assisi: A Revolutionary Life* (HiddenSpring Books, Mahwah, New Jersey, 2001).

Jones, E., *The Life and Works of Sigmund Freud* (Anchor Books, 1963).

Jung, C. G., (Trans. Richard & Clara Winston), *Memories, Dreams, and Reflections* (Vintage, 1965).

Jung, C. G., (Trans. R.F.C. Hull), *Psychology and the East* (Princeton University Press, Princeton, 1978).

Jung, C. G., (Trans. R.F.C. Hull), *Psychology and Alchemy* (Princeton University Press, 1980).

Jung, C. G., quoted in Marie-Louse von Franz, *Projection and Re-Collection in Jungian Psychology* (Open Court, London, 1980).

Kerouac, J., *Desolation Angels* (Perigee Books, 1960).

Kim, H., *Dogen Kigen: Mystical Realist* (University of Arizona Press, 1975).

King, Jr., M. L., (Ed. Clayborne Carson), *The Autobiography of Martin Luther King, Jr.* (Warner Books, 1998).

Klein, M., *Envy and Gratitude and Other Works 1946–1963* (The Free Press, 1975).

Kohut, H. *The Restoration of the Self* (International Universities Press, 1977).

Lear, J., *Love and Its Place in Nature* (Farrar, Straus & Giroux, 1990).

Lewin, R., *Compassion: The Core Value that Animates Psychotherapy* (Jason Aronson, 1996).

Lowen, A., *Narcissism: Denial of the True Self* (Touchstone Books, 1985).

Marguilies, A., *The Empathic Imagination* (W. W. Norton & Co., New York, 1989).

McNally, D. *Desolate Angel* (Delta, 1979).

Milarepa, *The Hundred Thousand Songs of Milarepa* (University Books, New York, 1962).

Mogenson, G., *Greeting the Angels: An Imaginal View of the Mourning Process* (Baywood Publishing, Amityville, New York, 1992).

Mother Teresa, *Meditations from a Simple Path* (Ballantine Books, 1996).

Mullin, G., *The Fourteen Dalai Lamas* (Clear Light Publishers, 2001).

Nagarjuna, (Trans. J. Dunne and S. McClintock), *The Precious Garland* (Wisdom Publications, 1997).

Nanamoli, Bikkhu, and Bikkhu Bodhi, *The Middle Length Discourses of the Buddha* (Wisdom Publications, 1995).

Pabongka Rinpoche, (Trans. Michael Richards), *Liberation in the Palm of Your Hand* (Wisdom Publications, 1991).

Rabten, Geshe, and Geshe Dhargyey, *Advice from a Spiritual Friend* (Wisdom Publications, 1977).

Rabten, Geshe, *Mind and its Functions* (Editions Rabten Choeling, 1992).

Ribur Rinpoche, (Trans. Fabrizio Pallotti), transcribed from a discourse given on June 9, 2002, Wastonville, CA (available in audio format at www.lamrim.com).

Ribur Rinpoche, (Trans. Fabrizio Pallotti), "Transforming Suffering into Pure Joy," *Mandala Magazine* (Taos, NM, March/April 1997).

Rosenberg, E., and P. Ekman, et al., "Linkages Between Facial Expressions of Anger and Transient Myocardial Ischemia in Men With Coronary Artery Disease," in *Emotion* (June, 2001, Vol. 1:2).

Segal, H., *Introduction to the Work of Melanie Klein* (BasicBooks, 1974).

Seligman, M., and M. Csikszentmihalyi, "Positive Psychology: An Introduction," in *American Psychologist* (Jan. 2000).

Shantideva, *A Guide to the Bodhisattva's Way of Life* (Library of Tibetan Works and Archives, Dharamsala, India, 1979).

Snyder, G., *Turtle Island* (New Directions Books, 1969).

Thoreau, H. D., *Walden or, Life in the Woods & On the Duty of Civil Disobedience* (New American Library, New York, 1960).

Tustin, F., *Autistic States in Children* (Routledge & Kegan Paul, 1992).

Twain, Mark, *Personal Recollections of Joan of Arc* (The Stowe-Day Foundation, 1980).

Wangyal, Geshe, *Door of Liberation* (Wisdom Publications, 1995).

Winnicott, D. W., *Playing and Reality* (Routledge, London, 1971).

Winnicott, D. W., *Home is Where We Start From: Essays by a Psychoanalyst* (W. W. Norton & Company, New York, 1986).

Yeshe, Lama Thubten, *Becoming Your Own Therapist* (Lama Yeshe Wisdom Archive, 1998); (available at www.lamayeshe.com).

Zopa Rinpoche, Lama Thubten, *The Door to Satisfaction* (Wisdom Publications, 1994).

Zubov, V. P., (Trans. David Kraus), *Leonardo da Vinci* (Harvard University Press, Cambridge, MA, 1968).

ACKNOWLEDGMENTS

I cannot find words to truly acknowledge the contribution that Kyabje Lama Zopa Rinpoche has made to my understanding of compassion. From the first time I met Rinpoche he seemed like a masterful jazz musician of enlightenment, joyfully and spontaneously improvising within the ancient rhythms of Buddhist compassionate wisdom, creating an entrancing and blissful music to inspire and educate the heart. His input and encouragement have been invaluable to me personally and to this book's development.

I'd also like to thank Kyabje Ribur Rinpoche for his permission to share some of his story here and also for his pure teachings on bodhichitta. Not only his words but also his presence and gestures profoundly elucidate the meaning of compassion.

I offer sincere thanks to all of my teachers for their kind patience. I apologize to them and to the readers for instances of my own petty, narcissistic preoccupations getting in the way of what's real and valuable.

I would like to thank the patients I've seen over the years who've shared their stories and their deep struggles through suffering toward happiness and who've taught me so much.

For his permission to share his story here and for his example of brave compassion, thanks to Venerable Roger Kunsang. Thanks as well to George Farley for telling the details of a wonderful story and to Venerable Lhundrup Nyingje for sharing some insights from her years of retreat. For his guidance and support, thanks to Patrick Mahaffey, Ph.D. For his teachings on object relations and on how to help patients by skillfully facing the darker aspects of the psyche, thanks are due to Avedis Panajian, Ph.D.; I offer thanks as well to Marc Nemiroff, Ph.D., for his skill and guidance in helping me to become a more useful psychotherapist. I'd also like to acknowledge Robert Thurman, Ph.D., for his encouragement, feedback, and expansive, bold example. For their practical assistance and support at various points in the process of writing, I'd like to acknowledge Alex Campbell, Ph.D; Wilson Hurley, LCSW; Eric Propst, Psy.D.; and Jeff Woodard. The timely, practical assistance of Nick Ribush, M.D., was also invaluable. For helpful comments in response to an early draft and for his contributions to the field, thanks as well to Mark Epstein, M.D.

For her practical assistance and her faith in this project, thanks to my agent, Eileen Cope. Acknowledgment is particularly due to Anne Connolly, editor at HarperSanFrancisco, not only for her very hard work over many months in guiding this book toward completion but also for her incisive wisdom that sees through to what is most essential. I'd also like to thank everyone else at HarperSanFrancisco for the genuine care and energy they put into this book.

Working with this material also often brought back memories of the great kindness shown to me by my parents and grandparents when I was young. I hope that these efforts serve to begin repaying their kindness, and I dedicate any merits I may have generated to their welfare. And, finally I offer thanks to my wife, Terry, for her great forbearance during my months of work on this project and for her beautifully generous and loving spirit.